Men, Myself, & I:
Revelations of an Opened Marriage

(A Memoir and How Not To)

by Minda Lane

Author's Note

This is a true story, reconstructed from the memory of my experience. All the names and many identifying characteristics have been changed to preserve the anonymity of the people I have written about. In a few cases, I have modified or compressed the chronology of events for the sake of narrative flow.

Copyright © 2023 by Minda Lane
www.mindalane.com

Published in the United States by Tender Human.

All rights reserved. No portion of this book may be stored or reproduced—mechanically, electronically, or by any other means, including photocopying—without written permission of the author and publisher.

LCCN: *(pending)*
ISBN 979-8-9891285-1-8 (paperback)
ISBN 979-8-9891285-5-6 (ebook)
ISBN 979-8-9891285-0-1 (audiobook)

Cover art by Gianna Spangler.

This book is dedicated to the woman who embraces her own becoming, and especially to the woman who cannot.

Table of Contents

1. *Unthought Known*	*9*
2. *Love Story*	*14*
3. *Drive*	*24*
4. *Living for the City*	*29*
5. *Wonderful Tonight*	*36*
6. *If This is It*	*40*
7. *Tiny Dancer*	*47*
8. *I Think That I Would Die*	*55*
9. *Everlong*	*57*
10. *Into the Mystic*	*64*
11. *Ob-la-di, Ob-la-da*	*67*
12. *Alive*	*71*
13. *Little Lies*	*82*
14. *Graceland*	*83*
15. *Time After Time*	*91*
16. *Risk It*	*92*
17. *Don't Wanna Fight*	*103*
18. *Dirty Work*	*104*
19. *bad guy*	*112*
20. *Into the Great Wide Open*	*117*
21. *Situation*	*124*
22. *Don't Think Twice, It's Alright*	*130*
23. *Stuck in a Moment You Can't Get Out Of*	*136*
24. *Take Me to Church*	*140*
25. *Panorama*	*149*

26. Come Back	*151*
27. I Just Want the Girl in the Blue Dress to Keep On Dancing	*157*
28. WAP	*166*
29. The Greatest Love of All	*178*
30. Trouble	*179*
31. New Rules	*186*
32. Believer	*189*
33. Bitter Sweet Symphony	*190*
34. Little Boxes	*198*
35. Backlash Blues	*208*
36. Mess is Mine	*211*
37. The System Only Dreams in Total Darkness	*220*
38. Somebody to Love	*222*
39. Last Kiss	*227*
40. I'm Goin' Down	*234*
41. Ramble On	*240*
42. Coming in From the Cold	*247*
43. Reckoner	*249*
44. Defibrillation	*256*
45. Anything, Anything	*263*
46. Someone Great	*264*
47. Sun Comes Up, It's Tuesday Morning	*270*
48. The Peace of Wild Things	*273*
49. The Beginning Is the End Is the Beginning (Epilogue)	*279*
Acknowledgment	*285*

it was when i stopped searching for home within others
and lifted the foundations of home within myself
i found there were no roots more intimate
than those between a mind and body
that have decided to be whole
—rupi kaur

1. Unthought Known

I had no idea what I was getting myself into when I suggested to my husband that we open our marriage. There is so much I didn't know.

For starters, I didn't know the first thing about consensual nonmonogamy, apart from its most obvious definition—sex with other people that your spouse or partner agrees to. I didn't know the difference between swinging and polyamory, or what relationship anarchy was, or what it meant to be "solo poly." I had never heard the term metamour and had no idea the word "nonhierarchical" could refer to relationships, or how. I didn't know that there are as many expressions of nonmonogamy as there are monogamy.

Neither did I know how to go about opening our marriage. If monogamy meant only having sex with one person, and nonmonogamy meant having sex with more than one person, then I guessed that was the basic gist of what a person needed to do to open their marriage: start having sex with other people. On this point, especially, I didn't know how much I didn't know.

Before we opened our marriage, I didn't know that dating is different when you don't have an end game—marriage, family—in mind. I didn't understand that there are varying degrees of "open," nor the relevance of context when meeting someone new.

I didn't know that I was not the only partner in my marriage with desires outside of it.

I didn't know I would meet someone who would change my life.

I didn't know how I would beg for him to dominate me or why, nor how my affection for him would devastate my husband.

I didn't know there was an addict in me, lying in wait, or how the cumulative effects of childhood trauma were influencing my choices.

I didn't know Jack and I wouldn't make it.

The one thing I did know by the time I obliquely suggested that we open our marriage was that I was unhappy, which I only realized after hearing myself insist several times that the opposite was true.

"Everything is perfect," I told my sister Mari over lunch.

We were dining on the patio of a restaurant in downtown Seattle, near her office, on a warm spring afternoon. I was referring to the pleasantness of the day, but also my life in general—not everyone could take off for two hours in the middle of a Wednesday to enjoy a long lunch. But I was only seeing three or four clients a week at my reiki practice, so I had lots of flexibility.

When I wasn't with a client, I wrote blogs or planned and organized the yoga retreats I hosted a few times a year. Some days I stayed home to spend time with our son, Asher, or went to coffee with a fellow yogi after class, or left the office early to meet a friend for a walk. In other words, I basically did what I wanted.

Not that I took it for granted. On the contrary—I knew how good I had it. That my husband, Jack, supported my pursuits wholeheartedly was yet another reason I kept telling myself my life was perfect.

A few days after the conversation with my sister I heard myself tell my mom on the phone one evening, "I have such an easy life. You know?"

I felt guilty as soon as I said it, because I knew she didn't know; her life had never been easy. At age 18 she'd moved from living with her parents—an unavailable, alcoholic father and a harsh, overly critical mother—to living with the man who would become my dad.

The reason was: she was pregnant. She was supposed to leave for college the day after she found out. Instead, she gave up that dream and moved to Syracuse, where my dad was already in college on a football scholarship. Over the years that followed he became an alcoholic, just like my mom's dad, just like his own. Not only did my mom have to give up her dreams, but in the sixteen years they were married, her life became a waking nightmare—he was a serial cheater, domineering, and physically abusive.

My mom left my dad once, but he begged her back with sweet nothings and loaded promises that he'd sober up. The night she returned home he held her by the throat and told her if she ever took his kids across the state line again, he'd "fucking kill her."

Afraid for her own life and the lives of her four children, she finally mustered her courage to leave him for good when I was 18 months old. She called my dad's brothers to help. Two of them drove with us from Georgia, where we lived, to Ohio, where my mom had family and a modicum of support. Another of his brothers stayed behind to keep my dad from following us and trying to stop her.

The pivotal moment of my realization that I wasn't as happy as I'd been professing to be—the moment that started this whole thing—came a short time after my lunch with Mari and the phone call with my mom. I was sitting in my therapist, Dianne's, office. I don't remember the context, but I said it again: "I'm so happy!"

Dianne looked at me and said nothing, but I heard her words: "Me thinks she doth protest too much."

Her mouth didn't move but I heard her say it. Or, I thought I did.

Or was it my own voice that I heard?

I sat with her silence for a moment before realizing it was me. It was my own internal voice: *Me thinks she doth protest too much.* I wasn't happy.

But how could I be unhappy? I had a very nice husband who was warm, witty, and loving. He was handsome, successful, and affectionate. I felt his love every single day in the way he seemed so content with our life, so comfortable. I felt it when he took pictures of me, often when he didn't know I sensed him. I felt his love in his commitments to me and our five-year-old son, Asher—the way he got up at dawn every morning for his job in radio and never complained, did the dishes regardless of the mess I made cooking, took out the garbage without being asked.

He never nagged me about money, didn't pressure me for sex, indulged my family's frequent presence, and he was an engaged, doting dad. We got along easily, we laughed together frequently, and we never fought—a few tense words on a couple occasions were the extent of our marital strife.

What is there to be unhappy about? I asked myself. I had a privileged life. I was in great health, got to do work I loved, set my own schedule, had lots of friends, enjoyed relative financial security, and, in addition to a wonderful husband, had a healthy, energetic son who I adored.

A part of me was afraid to jinx my good fortune and I thought I should stay quiet and be grateful. But in the same way that a reminder of "starving children in Africa" did nothing to compel me to finish my dinner when I was a kid in the 80's, telling myself to stay quiet and be grateful did nothing to quell the truth of my unhappiness. It only fed my self loathing and created more shame.

If you asked me at the time why I was so unhappy, I would have said I didn't know.

But in fact, I did know. The reason was an unthought known.

An unthought known is, as psychoanalyst Christopher Bollas describes it, something we know with certainty but cannot allow ourselves to think. It's a notion that our psyches will protect us from entertaining because it is too threatening, too scary, too risky, or too awful to contemplate, even though we know it way deep down.

Which is to say: I knew there was a problem. But I wouldn't—couldn't—let myself think it. I refused to acknowledge it. I never journaled about it, confided in a girlfriend about it, I never even told Dianne. I didn't breathe a word of it. And yet, it remained.

The reason I refused to think, much less talk about the unthought known, was that I didn't want it to be true. Also, I was afraid. I was afraid of hurting my husband. I was afraid it would lead to our undoing. And I was afraid what would happen if I had to face life again on my own. So for eight years, I said nothing. I said nothing, but I knew. And that knowing had begun to make me restless.

The process of coming to terms with the unthought known, and bringing it to the surface for evaluation, was long. But now that I'm on the other side of it, now that I've admitted it to myself, and to my husband, I can tell you what it was. Even though it's still hard for me to say. Even though I still don't want it to be true.

My unthought known was, essentially, sexual chemistry. Or rather, a lack of it. As much as Jack and I loved each other (so much), as much as I liked him (tons), I never felt that certain spark between us that made me want to tear his clothes off. We had intellectual and companionable chemistry, even romantic, but we lacked the ineffable urge. And the parts of me that are nurtured by my sexuality—my passion for life, my creativity and pleasure, my personal expression—were withering in the absence of that fuel. Instead, I felt stuck, depressed, and restless.

For my whole life I had observed long-term couples with wonder. How did they do it? Were they happy together? What sacrifices had they made for the sake of their relationship? I noticed how often it seemed the sacrifice had been largely hers: *her* fulfillment, *her* expression, the realization of *her* biggest and brightest dreams. Family friends, clients I worked with, mothers of my friends…I had observed so many women who arrived at a particular stage of life—after kids, before retirement—who seemed to be asking themselves the same questions. They'd done everything they were "supposed to": gone to a good school, married a nice guy, bought a cute house, had a couple kids. But somewhere in the hustle they lost contact with their sense of self, with their stream of vitality, with the power of their choices and the force that animated them.

I didn't want that for myself. I knew I had to do something. So, I cheated.

2. Love Story

The week I met Jack began unremarkably. I woke up in my one-bedroom apartment on Monday morning and snoozed for half an hour—longer than it took for me to get ready for work. I didn't bother with any beauty regimen beyond cleaning my teeth, brushing the tangles out of my long hair, and throwing on some mascara because there was no one at work I needed to impress, no tenable prospects. At the time, that's how I perceived virtually every attractive, available man I encountered: as a prospect. But the guys I worked with—mostly software developers—were more interested in getting their work done than flirting with the company's Community Manager. I wiggled into a pair of skinny jeans and pulled on a short sleeve printed blouse that set off the tan of my olive complexion. I added a pair of open-toed Mary Jane heels and headed out the door into the midsummer light.

As soon as I got to the office, I made myself a cup of tea and sat down to check email, beginning with my personal inbox. The first message was from my favorite radio station announcing a contest to win tickets to an intimate performance with my favorite band later that week. For the next half an hour I buckled down—not on the white paper I was supposed to be writing for a prospective customer, but entering the contest over and over again, until it finally occurred to me to email the station directly and ask if I could come.

Jack in the Morning was the one to reply. My stomach fluttered at the inbox brush with celebrity: Jack was a deejay I'd listened to every weekday for close to ten years. Suddenly there he was in my inbox, responding to my request.

"Let me see what I can do," he wrote.

A few minutes later I got the confirmation. "All good; you're in!"

Beside myself with anticipation, I took that Friday, the day of the concert, off work, still hardly believing I was going to get to see them up close. *For years* I had loved that band. The first time I saw them perform I was so affected by their music and the spectacle of it all that I stood in the crowd crying happy, I'm-so-glad-I'm-alive-to-experience-this tears and repeating prayers of gratitude. *Thank you for singing my heart.* From that point on I would be unable to talk about this band without completely losing my cool. I had no chill, only effusive superlatives spoken a little too loud.

The morning of the show I sat front and center during the performance and cried more tears of joy through every song. It was my dream come true. If the sincerity of my admiration made me look like a lovesick teenybopper, I didn't care. I couldn't think of anything in the whole wide world that would mean more to me than an experience like this.

After the performance, standing in line to meet the lead singer, I noticed Jack in the Morning standing nearby. With beautiful blue eyes behind artsy glasses, bleached white hair that stood up like David Byrne's, and a John Slattery cool, he was unmistakable. I'd seen his photo a couple years before when I had looked him up on the station's website. I noted several things about his profile at the time: he liked to road bike and do Pilates. He played the piano, loved dogs, and enjoyed a weekly martini. Also, he looked older than me—(25 years, to be precise)—and he was married. I let the thought go.

Standing there in the studio with him, I decided to introduce myself. I thanked him for the opportunity. We exchanged a few words until I realized I was holding up the line. I said a quick goodbye to Jack and stepped forward to meet the musician, the closest thing I'd ever had to a hero.

It wasn't just that I loved his songs, or what he stood for, or his skill as a songwriter and musician, or the way he looked and carried himself, or the power he conveyed. The Musician inspired me to a better version of myself. He appeared to be so fully realized that I felt empowered to express myself similarly.

I wanted to know that feeling of self-possession and mastery in my own life.

I handed him my journal to sign. He asked why I wasn't at work. I told him I had taken the day off to be there.

"You should come hang out," he said.

"I was planning to go to a yoga class this afternoon," I stammered.

"Why don't we go together?"

A little scared but utterly giddy and trying to play it cool, I suggested a yoga studio near the venue where they were playing. I gave him my number and could hardly believe when he texted me an hour later to coordinate. I floated through the rest of the day, most of which I spent sorting out my yoga outfit and what I would wear for the show itself.

After yoga, I followed him to the venue, where he took me straight to his bedroom at the back of his tour bus. I don't remember what we talked about, just that there was nowhere to sit but on his bed, and that within a few minutes, without warning, he stripped off his yoga clothes and pulled on his outfit for the show. I definitely don't remember what we talked about after that.

I do remember that he stepped away at some point so I could change, and that when he returned, he invited me to ride with him on the bus overnight to Portland.

My excitement bubbled up and I burst out, "I packed a bag!"

A part of me thought it was wishful thinking when I threw an extra outfit and a pair of pretty underwear into a backpack in my car *just in case*, but another part of me must have sensed the opportunity.

I was already planning to go to the Portland show the next night. I just never dared to dream that I'd get to go as The Musician's guest, nor that I would get a ride there on his tour bus.

I felt so fancy milling around backstage during the show, though I watched most of it from the audience so I could see him and be a part of it all. My whole body felt filled with helium.

After the show he led me to the after-party, then back to the tour bus for the after-after party where we danced in the aisle between the bunks of his bandmates and he sang their new record quietly in my ear. It was the absolute most spectacular turn of events that I could ever have imagined.

When we finally got in his bed, he seemed fully in command of the experience he wanted to have, beginning with a suggestion to straddle his lap. He pulled my shirt over my head, so I moved to take off my bra. He stopped me.

"I like a slow reveal," he said.

I felt silly for plunging forward too quickly. He must have noticed my energy flag because he added, "I just want to appreciate every moment of this." Which, naturally, made me feel like the Queen of the Universe because I thought he meant he wanted to savor *me*. It did not occur to me that he was manipulating the circumstances for his own gratification, or that it mattered less who I was than what I looked like and how I regarded him. The night continued like this—him subtly asserting control, me complying and eating it up.

The next morning we were cuddled up together when he said something about when we would be able to be together again.

"That we pass this way only once is what makes life so sweet," I replied, feeling very clever that I had any capacity whatsoever to recall Emily Dickinson.

He asked me to repeat what I said, so I did.

"Don't say that!"

His tone surprised me. I thought it was obvious to us both that this would be a one-night stand, but he actually seemed to want to see me again.

I knew better. There was no way he'd bother to keep in touch. Why would he? We occupied different worlds. He could have any woman he wanted. Also, I didn't think seeing him again could possibly top the night we'd had. I figured I should quit while I was ahead. We left it unresolved, him insisting he wanted to see me, me not believing it for a second.

I'd planned to spend the day in Portland with my mom, who lived nearby. It was a little awkward explaining to her how I'd gotten to Portland, and that I needed her to come and pick me up, but she went with it. I borrowed her car to get back for the show that night.

The Musician seemed standoffish when I arrived, which felt like emotional whiplash after our morning of sweet nothings. Within a few minutes, he disappeared to take a call, leaving me with some of his instrument techs. Intuitively, I knew he was on the phone with a woman. He had told me the night before he was in something "kind of complicated."

When he reappeared he was moderately more welcoming. I didn't ask him what was wrong or why he acted so cold, because I didn't want to bother him. At show time, he pulled me into their prayer before they went on stage, which ended with everyone smiling and jumping up and down. It felt so good to be included in the circle that I forgot all about him ignoring me.

He had to leave right after their set because they were driving to Central California overnight. We said a long goodbye and he told me he'd see me soon.

I stayed with my mom that night and took a Greyhound bus home to Seattle the next morning. When Mari picked me up from the bus station, I insisted, "I'm taking you to lunch."

Ostensibly it was to thank her for picking me up, but mostly I just needed someone to debrief the weekend. I was absolutely beside myself. I still couldn't believe I had met The Musician, let alone spent the night with him, and he said he wanted to keep in touch. I could hardly fathom it.

After lunch Mari and I were standing outside the restaurant about to part ways. I was still rattling on about the weekend when a man approached, walking his dog. As he passed, I realized who it was—Jack in the Morning. I couldn't believe the coincidence.

"Jack! Hi!" I called to his back.

He glanced back and gave a half wave.

The very next night I was sitting in a restaurant among friends when Jack in the Morning walked in with a companion and sat down at a table ten feet away. I was, again, struck by the serendipity.

Two weeks later when I saw him yet again outside yet another restaurant, I forgot myself for a second and gave him a hug, then explained how I kept seeing him.

"That was me that said hi to you on the street the other day. And then I saw you out to dinner. It's the craziest thing…" He was smiling, so I continued, "We should have lunch or something."

My motives were innocent—I wasn't suggesting a date. It just seemed like it had to mean something that I kept running into him. I followed up with an email and we planned to meet for lunch the following week. Clearly something between us was meant to be; at least that's the meaning I made of it.

When the day finally rolled around, I was more nervous than I expected I would be, so I sat in my car outside the restaurant and practiced a breathing technique I had learned in my yoga teacher training the weekend before. Several notches calmer, I glided into the restaurant with as much confidence as I could muster. He was, after all, a local celebrity. I'd been listening to him on the radio for almost a decade. I couldn't believe I was about to meet him for lunch.

Jack had already gotten a table and stood to greet me. Immediately I blurted out that I was just woo-woo breathing in the car because I was nervous. He laughed and waved it off.

"Nah," he said. "I'm sure I'm even more nervous than you."

We settled in quickly, talking until the last possible minute, when he had to race to a meeting. Before we parted, he invited me to dinner the following week.

We picked up right where we'd left off. He told me more about growing up in Detroit with his ad exec dad and journalist mom, who had been happily married until his dad died earlier that year. He told me how they would summer on Lake Michigan and described fishing, boating, and sleeping outside with his brother and sister.

He joked about being a troubled loner in high school and described how he preferred to hole up each Friday night with his headphones and the latest record he'd purchased rather than going out with his friends. Music, it was evident, was always in his blood.

I didn't say much about my personal life since I thought it would pale in comparison. I hadn't accomplished much professionally—more or less bouncing between roles in marketing and project management—and our family lore featured more horror stories than it did bucolic tales of good times in the great outdoors. There was no way I was going to admit the reality of my childhood to him on our first date.

My mom was supposed to leave for DePauw University with her best friend the day after she found out she was pregnant with my oldest sister, Ellen. Instead, she and my dad had a shotgun wedding two months later and started their life together in New York.

After my mom left my dad when I was 18 months old, I didn't see him again until I was five. My mom had remarried, and my stepdad got a new job in Washington State.

Before we moved from Ohio to Washington, my mom allowed my dad to take Mari and me to stay with him in Georgia for a week. In violation of their agreement, he kept us for three.

I didn't know it then, but I wouldn't see my dad again until I was twelve, so my early childhood memories of my dad are all from that one visit.

The memories are hazy.

Like, I can't remember if he called my name one particular evening. He must have. Why else would I have left my dolls or coloring book and walked to the bathroom door?

Did he ask me to come closer? I think he must have, because why else would I have walked past the threshold of the bathroom door while my dad was in there, naked, sitting in six inches of bath water.

Did he ask me to touch it? I guess he must have. Because I never would have walked into the bathroom on my own accord and asked, "Daddy, can I touch your penis?"

I never would have done that.

The memory is only a snapshot, like a Polaroid. The beginning and end are the same moment, an instant. In the frame I see my little hand, reaching forward. And there is his penis in his right hand, probably the first one I'd ever seen. Yet I knew well enough—knew all too well, in fact—that what I was seeing wasn't meant for little girls. This was not supposed to be happening. *I was wrong to be there.*

In addition to the Polaroid moment, I remember feeling tiny there in his trailer, and anonymous, like a little black dot that could be blotted out with one swipe of the pink part of a pencil. How would anyone know where I'd gone? How would I ever find myself again?

The only good things that happened in my dad's trailer on that visit were Slush Puppies, sugar cereals, and Mari, with whom I had safety in numbers. Except one time, when there was no safety at all. We got in a fight over a coloring book. Specifically, who got to color the grapes and who had to color the orange. Grapes were more fun to color than an orange, and I knew she was trying to dupe me out of some happiness, as if I wouldn't notice the orange was just a big circle instead of a dozen small ones. One circle was a dumb planet. Several small ones were a whole universe.

We took the argument to our stepmom, who was washing dishes at the sink. We wanted her to do something. Help us. She must have called for backup, or my dad heard the commotion, because he came roaring in. The bickering escalated, with my stepmom yelling at him for yelling at us. Pandemonium ensued. I slipped in some water on the floor. No sooner had I smacked the ground than he picked me up, swatted me on the butt, and threw me onto the banana bed in the corner of the living room. He heaved Mari onto the other one, the blueberry bed. You can guess the color of the worn polyester blankets that covered each.

In another circumstance this would have been fun. "Throw me, Daddy! Throw me!"

But this wasn't fun, it was terrifying. He could destroy me.

He made us sit there so long I believed we'd been forgotten. But the worst part of it all was being almost the entire width of the trailer away from my sister, my only safety. I needed to be next to her again, to feel the anchor of our mother in her bones.

Nearly every day of that childhood-defining visit, my dad worked on the house he was building behind his mobile home. I often stole sips of his beer. I wanted to know: what was this prized elixir? It was obviously important to him because I saw him drink it all the time.

One day I drank the whole thing, giggling as I did it, curious how he would react. He smirked when he noticed, which made me proud. Then he yelled at my stepmom through the open window to bring him another one.

Another day on the jobsite I struck out on my own, walking far away up the dirt hill next to the driveway, which led to the gravel road that would eventually take us out of there and back to our Motherland in Ohio.

That day I turned and sat down on the hillside, looking toward where my dad worked and Mari sat on the cinderblock steps looking at her books. I felt a psychological complexity well beyond my years. I stared at the ground around me and wondered why it was so bare. There was no grass, just ugly dirt and rocks. I saw a cigarette butt. I picked it up and pretended to smoke.

The chasm in our backgrounds did nothing to divide us. Though Jack and I had vastly different childhoods, we had plenty in common and our conversation flowed easily over dinner. We didn't look up from one another until the food was gone, the drinks were drunk, the check was paid, and the restaurant was quiet. A small cluster of staff was eyeing us from the corner in their black aprons, waiting. As soon as we realized it, we apologized for keeping them and made haste, grinning at how we'd lost ourselves in the reverie of the evening.

Jack offered to walk me to my car and put his hand gently against my back. I was wobbly with wine and anticipation because I knew we both knew what came next.

When he opened my door for me, I mumbled something about my car—a gold sedan I was a little embarrassed about. He told me I made it look good—the first time he'd been directly flirtatious. I can't tell you what I said in reply because I was too nervous and distracted by what I guessed was coming.

I looked up.
He leaned in.
Our lips met.

I felt nothing.

I adjusted my mouth and we kissed again.
Again, I felt nothing—no wave of desire, no hunger in my skin.
This did not reconcile with my attraction to him. Jack had so many appealing qualities—he was bright, well mannered, and made me laugh easily. I felt so comfortable and welcome in his presence. We'd had two incredible dates and clicked in so many ways. And yet I still didn't get that stirring, polarized, can't-keep-my-hands-off-you feeling.

We hugged once more and said goodnight. I drove away, buzzing with the energy of our conversation, amused by the circumstances, and completely baffled. *Nothing?*

3. Drive

Jack called a couple days after our first official date and reiterated what a great time he'd had.

"I'd like to take you out this weekend, if you're free?" he asked. "There's a place called Silence Heart Nest. I was thinking we could get brunch and then walk through the Fremont Market."

To say I was flattered by his thoughtfulness would be an understatement. Silence Heart Nest was a restaurant "owned and operated by students of the spiritual master Sri Chinmoy." In other words, it was a little…unusual. Monks in robes with shaved heads—men and women—waited the tables. The whole place had an air of preserved calm. Plus, it was vegetarian. All this and a walk around a craft market? It sounded too good to be true. I was so touched he thought of me.

When we met that morning, it even felt too good to be true. Sitting at brunch, laughing and sharing our food, I felt like we'd shared lifetimes. I told him this as we walked to the car to head home.

"Do you think we might have known each other in a past life?"

"Maybe—" he smiled as our eyes met.

His car was in the shop, so I had driven that morning, but he opened my door for me, anyway. Before I got in, I wrapped my arms around him in a full body hug and relished the fated feeling of our friendship. I gave him one last squeeze, then got in the driver's seat.

And thus began our bi-weekly ritual: dining out, drinking a lot, laughing more, and ending the night with a more-abrupt-than-he'd-like kiss. Occasionally he hinted at coming inside when he dropped me off, or he would invite me back to his place, but I always declined.

There were several reasons I was averse to escalating our relationship. The first was that we were in very different places in our lives. Four months before Jack and I met, his wife of more than twenty years had died after contracting some kind of germ, which had caused an infection in the lining of her heart. The infection led to a stroke, which caused extraordinary brain damage, and she died two weeks later.

Jack was undoubtedly still very tender. I was mindful of his vulnerability and felt ill-equipped to hold him in a kind of grief I could barely comprehend.

As for me, I was in the midst of rearranging my life. Months away from turning thirty, I had decided I was ready for a change. I had a great job and lots of friends, but I didn't feel fulfilled the way I wanted to. I'd recently begun a yoga teacher training, and I was thinking about moving cities. Since a trip to San Francisco two years earlier, I'd been dreaming of moving there, and with every day that passed I felt more energized by the idea. I wasn't sure yet how I'd pull it off, but I was nearly certain I was going to do it. It was a bad time to be starting a relationship in Seattle.

I wasn't sure I was even available for a relationship because, much to my surprise, I was still corresponding with The Musician. The night on the bus turned out to be the beginning of an on-off affair that consumed me. I knew better than to believe we'd ever be together in any real way, but that didn't stop me from making him larger than life in my heart and mind, dreaming of possibilities, and wondering when I'd hear from him again, generally two or three times a week. Otherwise, he was on the road, or recording, or somehow preoccupied…there were any number of excuses he could have used. I didn't want to need too much from him in terms of reassurance or frequency of contact because I didn't want to turn him off by seeming needy, so I settled for what he offered. I never challenged him at all.

When he did get in touch, it was usually a text asking when I'd be available to Skype—a platform I hadn't heard of until he asked me to download it. Next, he asked me to buy a webcam. I was flattered because I thought he wanted to see my face. Instead, he gradually began to instruct me on other parts he wanted to see. He invited me to remove my clothing and touch myself. Soon our Skype "dates" were Skype "sex," mutual masturbation in front of our cameras.

Before I met The Musician, I had never even had phone sex, and certainly not Skype sex, but I loved the attention and realized I was good at it. It felt like an embodiment of creativity and power.

I still couldn't believe that a man I admired so much had taken an interest in me. I began to feel different in my skin—more comfortable, more feral, more free.

Another reason I was concerned about trying to forge a romantic relationship with Jack was that I was concerned we might ruin our friendship. I was beginning to experience my sexuality as something more expansive than I had ever known. I felt the embodiment of my wildness for the first time, which did not reconcile with our wholesome friendship. What if we had sex and it didn't go well? I wasn't about to risk ruining the unique and special bond we shared.

And then there was our age difference. I'd always been attracted to older men, but Jack was the oldest man I'd ever gone out with—even platonically—by a considerable margin, and I was sensitive to what other people would think.

I realize now his age is part of what attracted me to him. Growing up as I did, with a single mom, absent dad, somewhat fending for myself, I didn't have much of a sense of security. But Jack was mature. He'd been in the same job for nearly two decades. He owned a home. He knew who he was. I wasn't conscious of it at the time, but I think a part of me was drawn to his stability. He was a shelter in the storm, and a known quantity. Dating a man my own age seemed risky—who knew how he would turn out? By comparison, dating Jack seemed safe. But safe wasn't sexy. Maybe our lack of chemistry started there.

We talked about the reasons for my apprehension—not in much depth, but enough to make it clear that while I had an attraction to and deep affection for him, I didn't want to have sex—and he was okay with that. He was actively grieving his wife's passing, which took up a fair amount of his time and energy. And he knew I was beginning to plan for my move. We didn't need our friendship to be anything other than what it was.

Instead, we savored what we had, stretching every night out together to accommodate one more funny story, one more thoughtful question, one more belly laugh.

We were just friends, but he had felt like a best friend since our first lunch together. We were just friends, but I knew I loved him, and that he loved me.

It happened on my thirtieth birthday, right before I moved to San Francisco. I saved the evening to spend with Jack, who made reservations for us at a new restaurant in the center of the city. Outside, busses roared by among commuters shuffling home. Inside, the evening was pristine. Jack and I gazed into each other's eyes, narrowly avoiding the elegant stemware and myriad forks with our intertwined fingers. The glow between us mirrored the crackling fire nearby. We must have looked like lovers. It was the most romantic date of my entire life.

After dinner we went to Jack's house to open gifts, an excuse to make the night last a little longer. As we settled in, Jack told me he needed to grab something. He disappeared upstairs.

When he returned he stood directly before me. Without saying a word, he handed me a card he had made. The front featured notable words from memorable conversations we'd had; he had turned them into graphic art. Inside he wrote a beautiful, heartfelt message.

I had long envied women who dated or married men who did things like this for them, but so far had largely gone without that kind of personalized attention. I could barely admit it was something I longed for, that I wanted to be the woman a man thought of when he acted selflessly. I wanted to be worthy of his selflessness, *just for being me*. The thought of a man loving me authentically—not because of my body and sex, but because he actually, really loved *me*—that just seemed like a fantasy. But I wanted it more than anything, especially from someone important like Jack, who was publicly esteemed, or The Musician.

The night of my thirtieth birthday, hanging out with Jack at his house with his sweet black and white dog, Zoe, and the cozy fire nearby, I felt safe. I felt nourished in a way I never had. The fact that Jack and I had never slept together led me to an essential conclusion about the authenticity of his love: I knew it was true.

Feeling Jack's love that night, I had a sense of healing, as if his love had initiated a repair within me. I didn't know any more than that, just that I felt deeply nurtured. His abiding affection and confidence in me buoyed my belief in myself, and it changed me. But it didn't change our relationship status. A week later, I moved to San Francisco as planned.

4. Living for the City

Shortly before moving to San Francisco, I was telling a girlfriend about my plans. She insisted I was moving to be closer to The Musician, but I swore up and down that wasn't it. We weren't in a relationship—I knew that. Nonetheless, I hoped he would be excited when I told him I was moving nearby. Instead, he got distant, which, for the most part, he remained.

The reason I gave for moving to San Francisco was that I was turning thirty, I loved the City, and I wanted to change my life. Seattle felt too passive and repressed for me. I wanted to live someplace stylish and sprawling, on the ocean, with diversity and culture and verve. Perhaps I also wanted some distance from the life I had made for myself in Seattle, which was more consistent with my security-seeking than my freedom-loving self.

I thought I'd come up with the perfect plan, which was to teach yoga and try and scale the hobby jewelry business I'd started years before into something that could sustain me. In the meantime, I needed a paycheck, so I found a position as a family assistant in Pacific Heights. The dad was a hedge fund manager with an MBA from Harvard who drank Diet 7-Up compulsively, forbade his children to touch his BMW 7 series, and seemed to harbor a phobia of avocados…I think it was the fat. The mom, also a Harvard MBA, stayed at home with the kids, volunteered on auction committees, ran long distances, and lived on dry roasted almonds, red wine, and little stashes of M&Ms she shoved in random places like a squirrel.

It didn't occur to me that based on our respective positions, and dispositions, this was not a good match, because I was too excited about the new life I was making. Desperation does a good job of obscuring a bad fit.

I'd been there ten weeks when the mom came to the door of my apartment one day and told me her husband didn't "get" me.

"The yoga, the tattoos, the organic food," she explained. "I think he just misses our last assistant. She coddled him."

"I'm sorry—what?"

"He just doesn't get you," she repeated. "I guess I didn't realize you were so crunchy; I should have known that wouldn't work for him."

"Crunchy?" I asked, gradually realizing the implication: I was being fired.

"Yeah..." she said, like I was in on the joke. "You know, like granola. Hippie."

"But we have a contract," I said, realizing we had agreed to a year via email but never signed anything.

I looked out the window and watched as two spectacularly thin women walked by on the sidewalk in virtually matching outfits—tidy tennis skirts and stark white shoes. I recognized one of them from the dinner party my employers hosted the week before, which I had catered and served for them. It had been a peek into the world of the 1%. All night they spoke as if I wasn't there. No one made eye contact or said thank you. My employers acted like they'd never seen me before, unless they wanted something. I'd resolved that night not to work there a day longer than I had committed to.

She was still talking. I hadn't heard a word.

"...not a fit. I'm sorry."

"So what am I supposed to do?" I asked.

"Well, you don't have to move out right away. Maybe by the end of the month?"

It was 2009, the peak of the Recession, and I had gotten rid of nearly everything I owned when I moved. Now I had two weeks to find another job, a bed to sleep on, and a place to put it.

It was a stretch, but somehow things fell into place. Since I had been fired, I qualified for unemployment. And when I told my friend Alyssa what had happened, she asked if I wanted to get a place together—I didn't know she had been thinking of moving to the Bay Area, too.

We found a two bedroom in Berkeley and moved in the following month. I got a mattress from IKEA that I pushed into the corner on the floor of my room, then added a bankers box that I called a bedside table. I was home.

No one was more riveted by the turn of events than Jack. We kept in close touch, sending one another long, involved emails that read more like creative nonfiction—or love letters—than basic greetings.

I always had lots of updates for him. In spite of my job not working out, I was thrilled. Life in the Bay Area was—as I had hoped—ecstatic and expansive, and I felt closer to my authentic, fearless self than I ever had. I was living a life by my own design, albeit on unemployment.

Nonetheless, I had a distinct, somewhat unsettling sense that I was breaking a rule about what I was supposed to be doing with my life. All of my girlfriends in Seattle were working good jobs, marrying nice men, and buying their first homes, the same things I had always imagined and somewhat expected for my own life. Yet I had never been further from every one of these things. I was jobless, single, and broke.

But I was beginning to realize contentment was possible on the other side of social norms, and happily skipped off with new friends to festivals where I went braless, danced in broad daylight, and wore clothes that felt like an expression of myself that my mom would have thought "looked weird." I ignored the Monday to Friday schedule and occasionally stayed up all hours of the night working on jewelry or journaling or engaged in some project I thought might change the world. I started writing a vegan cookbook called *Eat Like a Yogi*. I was full of energy and wanted to try everything. Without my family nearby to remind me of the past, and without my very nice group of friends to remind me who I should be (at least, if I wanted to be like them), I felt a sense of freedom to explore who I was and try on who I wanted to become. I started to push my own boundaries. Especially, my sexuality.

It's worth acknowledging that since approximately second grade I have always had a love interest. This was the potency of my need.

Regardless the environment—school, summer camp, work—I would always find someone, and I would train myself on him, no matter how well suited he was or wasn't for me. It didn't matter how small the sample size, I would pick out the most appealing, the most viable, and—eventually, as I got older—the most fuckable candidate. Since I was around eight. My criteria changed over time, but the compulsion—the addiction, you might even say—did not.

Naturally, it didn't take me long after moving to the Bay Area to find someone to vie for, pine for, and create drama with. The Musician had made himself unavailable—a painful rejection even though I knew he was problematic—so I opted for the next best thing: his Tour Manager, who I'd met at a show a couple months before.

I doubt I would have gotten to know him if it weren't for my ulterior motives—to maintain access to The Musician—but once we started spending time together, we became fast friends. He was unlike anyone I'd ever dated. He wore dark glasses and long dreads piled into a gigantic knot on top of his head. He grew weed and quoted Rastafarians. He was fun to be around and easy to laugh with and I quickly grew to love him. It was not a complete love, and it was fraught with complications. But it was *a* love.

Like, I loved the way he fucked me—dirty and hard and without any eye contact, usually from behind, sometimes in the ass.

I loved how he handled himself when he was working, and the strangeness of his world, which made my own seem more interesting.

Also, I loved how he would blast reggae at full volume in the afternoons while I cooked him Persian food from his mom's old cookbook, and how at night we'd watch movies and eat Ben & Jerry's until our stomachs hurt, stoned out of our minds.

The Tour Manager wasn't the only one. For the first time in my life I resisted the urge to assume monogamy with the man I was sleeping with. We were both determined—and reiterated frequently—that we were not in a relationship; we just liked fucking each other.

This seemed like progress, somehow, a measure of agency I'd begun to claim for myself.

One afternoon, sitting in a Peet's near the Berkeley campus, looking for a job to replace the one I'd lost, I noticed a tall blonde guy at the next table. He looked like a surfer—well muscled with long, sun bleached hair. I found a reason to talk to him and we left together to walk around campus. He told me he was "poly"—the first time I'd ever heard of polyamory in any relevant context. After we had sex for the first time he asked if I'd be willing to meet his girlfriend. I agreed with a shrug. My interests in him were specific, and limited, but if it made them more comfortable, that was fine. "Poly" seemed sort of novel, and the sex was great. But it seemed like it would be complicated having to deal with his girlfriend. The possibility of new friendships and expanded community never occurred to me, because I didn't want to become a part of their lives. Instead, I guessed they must both just love drama and let it go after about a month.

There was another man I met during this period. Alyssa and I had gone to Harbin Hot Springs—a retreat center near Napa Valley—for the day, which we occasionally did when we got our unemployment checks and felt flush.

As we were approaching the registration booth to check in, I locked eyes with him in line ahead of us. He was bald and wore a long white tunic with loose white pants underneath, like a monk. He had the most piercing aquamarine eyes I had ever seen. He appeared older, but how old? I couldn't tell. His body exuded life but his skin was weathered enough I figured he was at least a couple decades older than me. The current between us was so strong it was hard to take my eyes off him. He seemed to feel the same.

I was intrigued by his age. What was his body like? Were all bodies of a certain age the same? I was wondering, because it remained one of my fears about sleeping with Jack, which I'd been thinking more about lately. Would his body be different? Would it change the way I thought of him?

It seems like such a shallow thing to get hung up on, but it was very real to me at the time. I didn't want anything to change our friendship.

When I looked up from completing my registration, The Monk was gone. I tried to forget about it. Alyssa and I made our way to the silent, co-ed soaking pools, mentally preparing to be naked among strangers...the hot springs were clothing optional. We undressed and stashed our things in the lockers. I tried to act as natural as possible as I made my way, naked, to the main pool. As I looked up to take the handrail, there he was, The Monk, watching me.

I pretended I couldn't feel him holding my bareness in his sight as I lowered myself into the water. There was nowhere to go but toward him. I took my place next to him against the wall and closed my eyes as if preparing to meditate, my heart pounding. He was inches away.

After several minutes he leaned in.

Whispering, he said, "My name is —."

His voice was heavily accented; I couldn't understand. But I didn't want to say it—"Whaaat?"—because I thought it would sound too crass, too American.

So I adapted myself; it was a reflex. I whispered back as delicately as I could, "Pardon me?"

He repeated himself in my ear. I nodded.

"Where are you from?"

"Poland," he whispered.

Again, I nodded. I whispered my name.

We rested in silence next to one another for twenty minutes or so. My eyes were closed when I heard, "It was nice to meet you, Meenda."

I smiled and waved and watched as he went.

Alyssa and I eventually got out and had dinner in the café, then took a restorative yoga class in the center's Temple. Afterwards we decided to go back to the pools to soak awhile longer before departing for home.

The main pool was half as crowded and even quieter than it had been in the daylight. I felt less inhibited and used the shower next to the pool this time, in plain view of the other bathers. I felt him watching me before I saw him in the corner, at the far end. When I stepped into the water, I walked straight to him and wrapped my arms around his neck. I had never done anything like this, but it felt like the most natural thing in the world. I pressed my breasts against his chest, my cheek against his neck. The rest of the pool was quiet—the other four or six people were resting or meditating, paying us no mind.

The Monk ran his fingertips down my spine to my hips to my upper thighs, which he lifted and spread. In seconds he was inside me. It was an idiotic risk, but thrilling. I wrapped my legs around his back and we stayed like that, mostly underwater, breathing together and holding each other, until Alyssa gave me a silent wave from the other end of the pool and pointed to the parking lot. I whispered my email address in his ear as clearly as I could, three times, and hoped he would remember it.

This is how the Monk helped me know: sex with an older man is like sex with any man. There are always differences. That's part of the fun.

5. Wonderful Tonight

Although I'd moved a thousand miles away, Jack and I managed to see each other at least every couple months. In late May, home for my nephew's third birthday, I made sure to leave time for a night out with Jack. His birthday was the following week.

Jack picked me up from my girlfriend's house where I was staying, and we drove to dinner at a restaurant next to Pike Place Market. He put his arm around me as we walked behind the hostess and pulled out my chair for me when we got to the table. I'd always appreciated his chivalry, and especially now. Whatever refinement I'd known in my previous life was all but absent from the way I'd been living.

The hostess quickly returned with a glass of champagne for each of us because we were celebrating.

"Cheers!" she said as she walked away. We clinked glasses and settled in.

Conversation always came easily between us. I was amused by Jack's snark and he laughed at my jokes. I don't think of myself as a particularly funny person but seeing myself through his eyes, I felt like it. With him I felt dynamic and insightful, like my very best self.

Because of his job as a radio personality, he had to be up on everything that was happening in the world, so he always had interesting things to talk about. It was his job to be entertaining, and I was charmed. I loved how happy he looked sitting across from me. It had been a year since his wife died and his dating life was taking off. I welcomed his stories. When our martinis arrived, we shared another toast.

"Happy birthday to the best friend I never saw coming," I told him. "I feel so lucky the Universe put us together. I love you."

My eyes welled with tears of affection. I had told him I loved him in the emails we exchanged, but never out loud.

"Awww."

He put his hand over his heart the way I'd seen him do when he was touched by something.

"Thank you. I love you, too. But really, I'm the lucky one. You gave me hope in the future when I couldn't see a way forward."

We stood up from the table to give each other a hug. When we sat back down, we both had to wipe away tears.

Halfway through my entrée, full of martini and wine, I told him something I hadn't yet. "Did I ever tell you I went and saw a psychic shortly after we met?"

"No," he said, smiling. "This oughtta be good."

"Well, right after I met you, I kept having this feeling about a baby. I found myself thinking about it all the time, almost like I was already a mom. I thought it was my biological clock ticking."

"Uh, okaaay…"

I knew his biological clock had never ticked. Jack didn't have kids and never planned to.

"So you went to a psychic?"

"Yes. And before I even had the chance to ask her about it she got very serious and said, 'There is a spirit waiting to come to you. If you don't want to be pregnant soon you need to be very careful in the physical reality. He's drawn to the music.' Isn't that so crazy?"

It didn't take Jack long to get it.

"Oh! So you're going to have a baby with The Musician?" he asked.

I feigned indignance, but Jack knew me better than that, and he was right. I had wondered if that's what it meant.

Or did it mean I was going to have a baby with Jack, who I'd listened to on the radio every day for years? We'd been to several shows together already, we liked the same music…it was the whole reason we met. I was still musing about the psychic when Jack spoke up.

"You know, if you want to have a baby, I would do that for you."

I might have choked on my dinner. Just like that, out of the blue, he offered to make a baby with me. In the most general terms of things I wanted, becoming a mother was at the top of the list. It was a ridiculous idea given my circumstances, but the thought made me excited.

"We could do it however you wanted to," Jack continued. "I mean, you could tell it I'm its dad, or I could just be a family friend or something. If that's what you wanted."

As I recounted our night to a girlfriend later that weekend she said, "You always have such a great time with him!"

She asked why we couldn't date, which was becoming harder for me to answer convincingly. Around the same time, another friend mentioned a friend of hers was dating Patrick Stewart, despite a thirty-five-year age difference. She said about them, simply, "They're really happy."

A few months later when Alyssa and I decided at the last minute to drive home to Seattle for Thanksgiving weekend, I made sure to fit in some time with Jack. I asked if I could stay with him Friday night, which might have suggested more than I meant for it to. I wasn't ready to go all the way yet, but I'd been thinking about it since The Monk.

We went to dinner, then back to Jack's. Zoe greeted us at the door. I called to him as he let her out.

"Should we go upstairs?"

"Sure!"

I found a eucalyptus-scented candle on the bedside table that I lit with matches I found in the top drawer. I turned the bathroom light on so it wouldn't be too dark, or too bright. I sat on the bed and waited.

Zoe came in first and hopped up next to me, then Jack emerged with a small glass of wine for each of us.

He crawled toward me on the bed and kissed me. It was an awkward angle because I was sitting up, leaning against the headboard, so I slid down on my back, and he laid down next to me. One-by-one, articles of clothing were removed until we got to our underwear. If those came off, I knew we'd have sex, and I wasn't ready for that yet.

Our groping was sweet but awkward. Without a swell of passion and pheromones to take me out of my head, I felt somewhat like I was ticking boxes: touch here, kiss there, suck this, lick that. Nonetheless I plundered forward, fueled by intention and alcohol.

It's bound to be a little awkward the first time, I thought. We had been non-sexual for over a year. Now we were attempting to change the shape of our relationship using willfulness as our chisel where raw chemistry had failed. We were carving something new through the inertia of friendship. It seemed a given that our fondling would be a little awkward. We didn't yet have the language of lovers that says when I go here you go there, and a moan like this means yes-please-more, and a moan like that means I'm nearing my edge.

In time, I began to relax. I'd been so worried that we'd ruin our friendship, but it was fun. We laughed and smiled and talked. I figured it could only get better. Maybe when we actually had sex. Yes, I reasoned. I had had sex without love. This was the first time in my life that I had love without sex. Yes, I reasoned. When we started having sex our love would surely grow. Lust would emerge. Isn't that how it works?

6. If This is It

When I flew home for Christmas a month later, Jack picked me up from the airport. We retreated immediately to his bed. I had imagined that we would wait until Christmas Eve, when I would be wearing stockings, a push-up bra, and a fancy dress. But now that it was a foregone conclusion, neither of us could wait that long. We weren't rushing intentionally, and we didn't mean for it to be over so soon, but we were both all in and one thing led briskly to another.

Afterward we were casual and comfortable with one another. It felt good to have removed that psychic barrier. Things flowed much easier without feeling like we had to avoid contact between certain parts. I was not overwhelmed with lusty desire for him, as I vaguely hoped I would be, but I told myself that was okay. We had the future ahead of us to enjoy one another in all the ways couples do. It would come with time, and maybe it was better this way. The sex may have been merely adequate, but our love was abiding and true, as authentic a love as I had ever known.

It did not occur to me that it was possible to have both the security of abiding love and the eroticism of passionate sex, because I had never had that before. I had learned to equate passion with risk and companionship with love. I thought I had to pick one. So, much like I did the first time I got married, I chose safety.

I met my first husband, Ethan, at a Christian camp when I was 15. We reconnected when I was 18 and married when I was 20. He was 24. We went to church every week at his insistence. He taught Sunday school and was emotionally abusive, though I didn't know at the time that's what it was. I thought he was just better than me, that he wanted me to be better, and chastising me was his way of helping.

And I tried. When he called me a slut because the brand-new Costco sweater I'd splurged $20 of birthday money on showed a crack of skin when I lifted my arms, I took it off and never wore it again.

When he told me I was vain and didn't care about the environment because I was "wasting" electricity by drying my hair with a blow dryer, I limited myself to three minutes of drying time no more than twice a week…in the dark.

When he said I didn't care about my family (him and the dog) because I was going to the gym after work instead of coming home right away, I started getting up at 4:30AM and going before work.

When he accused me of cheating on him with someone at the gym—why else would I be so committed?—I stopped going. I served on the Board of Deacons at our First Presbyterian Church. I volunteered at the hospital. And I did everything I could to avoid pissing him off.

Our wedding was the summer after my second year of college. At my bridal shower, my sisters gave me a very pretty silk nightgown. It was a rich cream, as decadent to the eyes as it was to the skin. I meant to wear it on our honeymoon—a modest weekend in the mountains—but never did. It sat in my dresser drawer for over a year before I was inspired to wear it for him, because there was so rarely peace between us. There was appeasement. There was waiting for the other shoe to drop. There were nights of making up (the only times the relationship made any sense). There was rarely peace.

I don't remember if this particular night was one of the rare times, or if it was an effort at appeasement, but I decided after my shower that I would wear my beautiful gown for him, if only to cover myself. He had told me a few days before that I looked like I was gaining weight.

"I'd say about five pounds." He poked my stomach when he said it.

I slipped the gown on in the bathroom and left my clothes on the floor. I brushed out my hair and tousled it a little so it didn't look like I was trying too hard. I put on a colored lip gloss I bought at the drug store with money he didn't know I had.

When I walked into our bedroom, I tried to delay getting in bed for a moment so he would see me from his pillow. He didn't look up.

I grabbed a sweater from the top of the dresser and folded it, then walked across the room to set it in the top of my closet, glancing at him through the corner of my eye as I reached, willing my body to his attention. I went back to the dresser, humming quietly, and got a shirt to hang up. I wanted him to notice my gown on his own. I was imagining he would ask me to stop for a moment so he could behold me. I had a lot of fantasies then.

"Wait," he would say. "I want to remember how radiant you are in this moment."

I wanted him to use words like this: radiant, bride.

The fantasy didn't end there. I imagined Ethan would ask me to turn a circle, or even get up off the full-size futon that was our bed and come over to me. He would put his hands on my hips and gaze into my eyes. He would kiss me gently, lovingly. He would run his rough roofer's hands up my sides and over my breasts and tell me that the only thing that felt better than the silk I was wearing was the silk of my skin. He would kiss my shoulder, removing the thin strap as he did. He would take my hand and lead me to bed.

This was the kind of thing I had fantasized and hoped for since I used to play with Barbies as a young girl, the exact type of scenario I would act out between Barbie and Ken before I made them lie down on top of each other, which was how they made their little plastic baby. I could get lost for *hours* in the sagas of my Barbie dolls, all of which mirrored the daytime soaps I watched in the summers while my mom and stepdad were at work.

Ethan said nothing. He did not get out of bed. He did not appear to notice my beautiful gown. After I gave up and got in bed next to him and it was clear we were going to have sex, he asked me if I could take "this thing" off.

"I'm wearing it for you," I said, hoping he might take a second look.

"You know I don't care about that stuff," he said.

I took it off, flattened. I don't remember the sex we had that night, or any night.

Another time I tried to bring up sex toys. I asked if there was anything he was curious about.

"You know I don't like that stuff," he said. "Sex should be between a man and a woman and you don't need any funny stuff."

Ethan and I had vanilla sex, though I wouldn't have called it that at the time because I didn't know any other flavor. But I knew enough to suspect there was more to it. I hinted that we might watch porn to create a mood. I don't even like porn, but I thought maybe it would spark something, or we would see something that looked like fun that we could try for ourselves. Unsurprisingly, he said no. Porn was the work of the devil.

Shortly before Ethan and I divorced, I was looking for a hammer in our storage shed when I found a wide, flat box against a wall behind his toolbox—a substantial stash of raunchy porn. He smiled awkwardly when I confronted him with it.

"You're a fucking liar," I seethed.

Weeks later, our marriage was over.

The morning after our first time together I wiggled under Jack's arm to lie on his chest. We nestled and nuzzled and smiled at being together. We kissed, and he slid inside me. There was rhythm and movement followed by my orgasm, then his. It was simple and pleasant and left plenty of time for the remainder of the day.

It was the week between Christmas and New Year's and Jack had taken off work. We spent every perfect day together taking walks, playing Scrabble, watching movies, and dining out. By the end of the week, I was certain this must be what it was supposed to feel like with the person you're supposed to be with. Jack and I were so happy doing the simplest things. It was, I concluded, because we were meant to be. Clearly—look how many times the Universe threw us together after we first met. And how much we'd enjoyed one another ever since.

But before I could fly back to the Bay, where I would be starting a new job the following week as the Community Manager for a social networking startup, Jack and I needed to have some Real Communication about Hard Things. If I was going to be his girlfriend, which I assumed I was since we were in love and sleeping together, then I was going to have to address my concerns: kids, and marriage. Or, well...the boundaries of marriage.

Okay, sex. It was really about sex. But I didn't see that yet because I couldn't. I couldn't because I didn't want to.

We were finishing lunch and due at the airport when I approached the not-exactly-chitchat subjects.

"So, um...what if you decide you don't want kids?" I asked.

Clearly taken aback by my sudden launch into a serious conversation, Jack hedged, "Well, why don't we cross that bridge when we come to it?"

"Well, I feel like we're probably going to be together for a very long time," I said, clueless to my gracelessness, "and I know I want to have kids."

"Me too, but we don't have to decide now. It's going to take me awhile to get my head around it."

"Yes, okay, that makes sense," I replied emptily. I felt taunted by his unwillingness to give me a guarantee.

Jack almost certainly didn't realize that my very specific goal for the conversation I had initiated was to eliminate risk. Before I could let myself fully commit to our relationship, I needed to know that everything was going to work out. The way I wanted it to. I wanted assurances.

Sensing my anxiety, he put his hands over mine.

"Baby...let's just be together and see what happens. We'll take it as it comes. I'm already going to be an old dad and you have plenty of time. What's another year? Let's see how things go."

I started to fidget. I picked up a pen and reached for an edge of that morning's newspaper, doodling idly. The clock was ticking. We needed to leave for the airport and I still hadn't packed.

But since we were having Real Communication about Hard Things, there was one more thing I needed to say. A thing that might have suggested nonmonogamy was baked into our relationship from the very beginning.

I drew my favorite doodle—a three-dimensional box—attempting to get the angle of each line just right so it looked real. I was thinking about what I wanted to say. I was trying to achieve that perfect 3D illusion I learned when I was young.

"There is one more thing I'm worried about," I began.

He looked a little exasperated. "Okay baby, what is it?"

This felt like the realest communication I'd ever done because it felt so risky. If our partnership was for life, then I needed a contingency. What if our sex life didn't get better? What if wild chemistry didn't grow out of our abiding love? What if I built myself a box I couldn't get out of? I needed an escape hatch, but it was a risk. What if he said no?

I summoned my courage, and my resolve. I knew this was vital.

"I'm afraid…" I began, "…that because of our age difference…I'm afraid that someday you won't be able to have sex."

I spoke quickly to expedite my discomfort and drew another box. I retraced each line over and over, tearing the paper slightly.

"Or that someday you might not want to anymore," I went on, avoiding the fact of the unthought known with a hypothetical. "And if that happens it will mean I can't have sex, either."

The subject felt so loaded. Getting the words out of my mouth felt like a huge accomplishment. I exhaled slowly, avoiding Jack's gaze, staring at my little boxes.

He didn't say anything, so I glanced up. The look on his face suggested he wasn't that comfortable with the notion, either.

"Well I guess if that happens, we'll cross that bridge when we come to it, too."

"Okay," I said. But I wasn't sure he fully caught my drift, so I continued, "I just want to be sure you'd be okay with me potentially having an outside relationship…"

—THERE! Finally, I said what I meant—

"...if you are like, 80, and can't anymore. I'll only be 55." I was trying to sound lighthearted but my throat was tight, my words constricted.

Jack remained even: "Like I said, we're not going to solve this today. And if we don't leave soon, you're going to miss your flight."

I could never have admitted it because it wasn't entirely conscious, but as I hustled upstairs to pack my things, I was relieved. I had planted a flag in the potential of sleeping with other people. This was how I reconciled my choice of a safe, companionate relationship when I knew it lacked the passion I wanted—needed, even—but didn't believe could exist in tandem with security.

That night, back in my apartment in Berkeley, I was writing in my journal when Jack called. It was 11:11, wish minute. He knew I always paused to make a wish or send a prayer when I noticed it on the clock.

"It's 11:11," Jack said. "I wanted to call you now to ask you officially to move in with me."

A month later we drove away from my Berkeley apartment in a 15-foot U-Haul. We arrived back in Seattle two days later, a year to the day that I left.

7. Tiny Dancer

Two months after Jack and I became a couple, less than a month after I moved in with him, we found out we were expecting. We hadn't been trying. Clearly, we hadn't done enough to prevent it, either. As soon as I noticed my period was late, I told Jack my suspicions and bought a test.

The directions said to take the test in the morning. The 18 hours between the realization I could be pregnant and the moment I peed on the stick were long and loaded. We moved suspended in uncertainty. Every moment—every question, every decision, every action, every silence—was loaded with *what if?*

The next morning my bladder was full of the hormone-rich pee we'd been waiting for. I woke early, too uneasy to go back to sleep, and trudged to the toilet, where I'd left the unwrapped test the night before.

While I waited for the test results, I looked long at myself in the mirror and wondered with reluctant hope—was there life inside me? Was it happening already? I was excited by the thought, but I didn't want to make Jack a dad if he didn't want to be. When I couldn't stand to wait another second, I looked at the test.

"Oh *shit*!"

"WHAT?!" Jack was by my side in seconds.

Together we stared bird-eyed at the test, and that tiny blue plus that meant our lives would never be the same. My hands flew to my lower abdomen, where cells were already dividing. Systems were differentiating. Every moment felt suddenly critical. My body was making a human that very second, as Jack and I gasped and stuttered with awe (me) and dismay (him).

This was not what I had anticipated all the many years I'd yearned to be a mom. We were a new couple, unmarried, and Jack wasn't even sure if he wanted to be a dad. But I couldn't help but be excited, too. I was stunned by the miracle of it. I poked at my belly to see if anything was different. I couldn't believe I was going to get to have a baby. I repeated it to myself over and over: I was pregnant.

Jack was not so enthusiastic. The plan we'd settled on was to spend a year together and see how things went. If things were great between us and he'd come around to the idea, we'd think about having a baby. If not, we'd go back to being friends. But we'd taken a chance. We'd left open a window of opportunity and that's all it took. We were pregnant.

Jack's reaction was concerning, but also: it was too late. I was not going to terminate the pregnancy. Maybe he wouldn't want to raise the baby together—I'd move out and he could be a remote dad like he'd suggested nearly a year before. Or maybe he'd come around and we would be a family. Either way, I knew I was going to have the baby.

A few emotional days after we stood staring at the blue plus, Jack found me sitting at the kitchen table before he left for work. He pulled me into a hug.

"It's going to be okay."

"You really think so?" I asked.

"I know so," he said.

"Really? I know you didn't want this. Or didn't know if you did. This wasn't our plan…"

"Baby, it's okay. It's not what we expected, but I'm in. I want to do this with you. We're going to be parents!"

Overwhelmed with relief, I didn't stop to ask him how or why he'd come around. His acceptance gave me permission to be excited with my whole self for the life growing in me. My heart was in my throat and tears were in my eyes as I hugged and kissed him goodbye.

Once the way was clear for me to savor my pregnancy, I cherished it all. Apart from teaching three yoga classes a week, I wasn't working, which meant I had a lot of time to think about all things Baby. I went on daily walks in the arboretum, read about childbirth, went to prenatal yoga, spent time with one of my three girlfriends who were also expecting, wrote lists of baby names, and completed a prenatal yoga teacher training.

I researched the best baby gear, anticipated the ultrasound where we'd find out if the baby was a boy or girl (a boy!), and transformed our extra bedroom into a cozy haven of soft colors, fuzzy animals, and ABCs. Also, I relished my time with Jack. I knew our time as a twosome was limited.

I had a big round basketball belly just like I hoped. Nothing made me happier than holding it and feeling him move, especially when Jack could feel it too, which he did for the first time on Father's Day. We were reading in bed. I felt the baby shift and looked at my belly. A little round bulge moved under my skin like a shooting star.

"Honey, give me your hand," I told Jack.

I put his hand over the spot where I'd seen the baby move. Immediately he stirred again. Jack looked stunned. A smile gradually made its way across his face until he was beaming. For several minutes we delighted in our baby's movements and cried happy tears.

Health-wise, my pregnancy was great, though I couldn't help but worry. A few things I worried about:
1. Did I mess up the baby by drinking alcohol before I knew I was pregnant?
2. How much weight will I gain?
3. Will I be able to lose it all?
4. Will my vagina become cavernous?
5. Will I get stretch marks?
6. What if I get morning sickness?
7. Will I develop gestational diabetes?
8. How many maple bars is too many maple bars?
9. Does Jack mean it when he says he's happy we're pregnant?
10. Is it normal to be so out of breath?
11. Is it normal to be this insanely tired?
12. Is it normal to be repulsed by the smell of everything? (Everything!)
13. Is it okay that all I want to eat is saltine crackers…and maple bars?
14. Is the baby okay if I forgot my prenatal vitamins two days in a row?
15. What happened to my sex drive?

16. Will it ever come back?
17. What if I miscarry?
18. What if my baby gets colic?
19. How will the baby impact my relationship with Jack?
20. Why am I so emotional?
21. Am I getting enough exercise?
22. Did my heart rate just go above 140 beats per minute?
23. Am I remembering the beats per minute rule correctly?
24. Should we do genetic testing?
25. Did I just have an orgasm *in my sleep?!*
26. Why does my _____ hurt?
27. Will I be able to manage the pain of a natural birth?
28. Will I have enough breast milk?
29. What if I get mastitis?
30. Will my baby be able to latch properly?
31. Will the dog like the baby?
32. Will the baby like the dog?
33. When do we need to start saving for college?
34. What if I get placenta previa or preeclampsia or some other badness I haven't heard of yet?
35. How am I going to handle sleepless nights?
36. What if I am positive for Strep B?
37. Should we have them put the gooey stuff in his eyes after he's born?
38. Was Jack's sperm healthy enough?
39. What if the baby has disabilities?
40. Did we get the right car seat?
41. SIDS. (I can't even.)
42. Is it okay that his clothes are not made of organic, non-GMO, sustainably raised, handpicked cotton dyed with vegetable juice?
43. Is Earth going to eject me for using disposable diapers?
44. Will he take a pacifier?
45. What if he won't take a bottle?
46. Which carrier is best for his hips?
47. Should he face out or face in?

48. When should we start solids?
49. Video monitor or just sound?
50. Butt Paste or calendula cream?
51. Should we have a second baby?
52. When do I need to get him on the preschool waiting list?
53. Why are my breasts already leaking?
54. What if I have to have a C-section?
55. Am I stressing the baby by worrying too much?

One thing that never occurred to me: what if our baby is stillborn?

But that's exactly what happened in my 36th week of pregnancy: I woke up one morning, and my baby did not.

When I sensed he wasn't moving, I changed positions in bed. When that didn't work, I ate a banana, then a spoonful of honey, believing the spike in my blood sugar would cause him to stir. But he was still.

We called the midwife and met her at her office so she could find his heartbeat and tell me everything was okay. *Ba bump, ba bump, ba bump*—there!

The wave of relief was fleeting as she matched the rhythm to my pulse and we both realized the heartbeat was mine, not his.

"You're going to need to go to the hospital," the midwife said.

I looked at her as I walked through the door to leave. I saw her heart in her eyes then. Her sorrow and her love. Her eyes told me what was true—there is only one reason an experienced midwife can't find a baby's heartbeat.

Jack drove while I alternated between hysterical denial and stunned silence. He dropped me off while he found a place to park, as if my promptness would make any difference. I wandered inside and boarded an elevator. When the doors opened to the third floor, there were two attendants waiting for me—our midwife had called ahead on my behalf. One of them put her arm around me. No one said anything as they led me back, my face crumpled and contorted by tears.

Just like I had at the midwife's office, I laid back on the bed, pushed down my pants, and pulled up my shirt to reveal the taut skin of my proud dome. The nurse tucked a paper sheet into my waistband and set a bottle of gel next to the ultrasound equipment. My mouth was dry and my eyes were hot as I watched what was happening around us, my baby and me.

"A bit of warm gel."

The doctor squirted a puddle of clear goo on my low belly. I watched her for a sign of hope as she moved the transducer over my skin, but the look in her eyes mirrored the way my midwife had looked at me not 30 minutes earlier. Without knowing, I knew. A moment later she announced his death.

No, I thought. *These people can't know what they're doing.*

I remembered the Imaging department downstairs, where we had the ultrasound months earlier that revealed our baby was a boy. It was such a joyful day. *Surely, they can help me.*

Oblivious to my denial, I asked the tender-eyed doctor if I could go for a more sophisticated test. She agreed in the gentlest terms. As she spoke she turned the screen she had been looking at so that I could see it, too. There he was, our baby. I could see the outline of his perfect little body, just like every black and white ultrasound picture I've ever seen. Exactly like a baby should look. There was his gorgeous round head, arms tucked into legs, the tiny stacked bones of his spine. I couldn't wait to meet him. For a moment I felt expectant and adoring.

And then the doctor put one hand on my knee. She waited for me to look at her before she pointed with her other hand to a cavern on the screen. There was no force in her voice as she said, "This is his heart."

It wasn't moving.

"It isn't moving."

He was dead.

"This is a clear indication that your baby has died."

She looked at me, both of us, defenseless.

"I'm so sorry."

I stared at the monitor, an unbreathing mass of flesh and bone as a current of tears dripped steadily from my chin.

"I am so, so sorry."

The weekend that followed was a hellish, devastating blur. I floated elsewhere, untethered. I needed instructions to do basic things. I was ruined.

When our baby was born two days after we found out he had died, we could easily see there were two strictures in his umbilical cord. It was crimped. They call this a "cord accident."

How could anything about our glorious boy be an accident?

He was impossibly perfect.

I loved him more than living.

We named him Vox Dawson.

8. I Think That I Would Die

Losing Vox is how I learned what a risk it is to love.

9. Everlong

To say that life resumed would be inaccurate, because of course it never stopped—a painful reality for someone in profound grief.

Every morning the sun rose.

Every morning I woke up enduring what felt like an emotional flu.

Every morning I would observe some new way I felt stranger to myself, less known than the day before.

A sweatshirt I used to love I suddenly hated because it reminded me of being pregnant with Vox and the naïve hope I had carried nearly to term. I couldn't cook because I couldn't track linearly. I couldn't take the trash to the curb, let alone go anywhere in public, because I couldn't stand the thought of being seen. I had no interest in reading a newspaper, or anything else, for that matter, because I didn't care what was happening outside my own four walls. Even the slightest emotional intensity—anything that elicited even a mildly sympathetic response—would trigger a meltdown. I was afraid to watch TV because I feared a Pampers commercial, or Children's Tylenol, or Disney Vacations. I couldn't visit with friends because no one understood. I had no idea who I was. I had no baby. I had no purpose. I had nothing.

It didn't take long, however, before I began to feel the pressure of the shoulds: I should get up at a reasonable hour, I should eat breakfast, I should take a shower. These seemed like basic things I should be able to accomplish.

I was relieved to get out of bed, because I had already begun to associate it with nightmares and sleepless terror. But that was the only easy thing. I hated doing anything because it reminded me life was moving on and I hated doing nothing because I felt useless, bored, and could only wallow.

I especially hated bathing, because it forced me to be with what remained of my body, which felt heavy, stretched, and used. The warm water on my breasts would cause my milk to let down, an unfamiliar sensation I quickly began to recognize for the tyranny it signaled: moments later milk would be spraying from my nipples.

During my pregnancy I had worried I wouldn't have enough milk, but I had too much, a creamy horror that reminded me constantly of all I had lost. I wrapped my breasts in cabbage leaves and drank a sage tincture that was supposed to help make the milk go away, and I hated these things, too. The smell of cruciferous vegetables followed me everywhere and the tincture caused a stabbing pain in my stomach. I stopped taking it after a week or so and relied instead on passive prayers I begged in silence:

"Please make this end."

"Please give me my baby back."

"Why?"

I felt a physical void from my shoulders to my hips. Gutted is the word that comes to mind, but my guts were intact. It was a psychic evisceration—nothing more, and nothing less. He was in me, and he wasn't. I couldn't get away from it. He was never there.

I no longer felt like a collaborator or co-creator of life, participating with a benevolent force, as I did when I met Jack, and The Musician, when I was doing my yoga teacher training and moving to San Francisco and life felt full of possibility and magic and miracles. I had learned in an instant that life cannot be trusted. I was at the mercy of chance. Vox's death was the most urgent, powerful reminder I'd ever received of how little control I have over most things, the consequence of which would be crippling anxiety for the first time in my life.

Inside my mind I railed against the injustice. *Why me?* I couldn't stand to see pregnant women, or women with babies. The sight of a stroller made me enraged, then disassociated. There was nothing I'd ever cared about more than my baby, and I felt like I had failed him. The loss of him was my world.

I started seeing a therapist who said the first six to eight weeks were typically the hardest. I held to that like a raft in a storm, telling myself I just had to survive that long.

But after eight weeks, when things seemed to be getting worse instead of better, I started to think more seriously about how I would do it. Exhaust, I thought, would be peaceful. I didn't want to make a mess or cause a stir. I just wanted life to go on without me, as if I had never existed. I just wanted to sleep, finally, without nightmares. I wanted to know where he went. I wanted to follow him there.

In mid-December I found myself home alone at night for the first time in months—I don't remember where Jack was. An hour after sunset I was the most frantic I had ever felt, and, I feared, the closest to ending my life.

For the first time, I wasn't certain I wouldn't do it, a notion that both relieved and terrified me. I called my sister's husband, whose brother had died a year before of colon cancer. He was the only person I imagined could relate to my grief.

It would seem logical that I would have turned to Jack, whose wife had died just over two years earlier, but for some reason that didn't help. I knew intellectually that Jack knew grief, but I didn't see the severity of my pain reflected in his eyes. He didn't seem as affected by it—how could he not be ruined the same way I was? Was it possible he felt the loss as deeply, but had a different way of grieving? I didn't know and, given my state of mind, I could hardly be bothered to ask.

I went to the porch while I was talking to my brother-in-law, probably so I could smoke a cigarette. There I sat on the phone, wrapped tightly in a knit blanket, bawling incoherently.

"I don't want to live," I choked out. It was the first time I had ever said it out loud. I was relieved to find a sentiment that approached the depth of my despair, to admit what I'd been thinking, and to be witnessed in my sorrow.

He told me it would get easier and agreed that it's the most awful thing he had ever endured. I loved him for saying it was awful, without softening it in any way.

I needed to hear that. I needed to let the word sit in the open, exposed, revealing the fullness of my reality. I was living a waking nightmare.

Jack had alluded to waiting to get pregnant again. I was afraid I would kill myself if I didn't get pregnant as soon as possible. We talked about it generally but never reached a conclusion. There wasn't much time to mull it over; I got pregnant on my second cycle.

I knew when it happened…Jack and I had made love in the middle of a Saturday afternoon. Afterwards I was resting on his chest and noticed a prism of light on the dresser across from the bed, a rainbow. I didn't know then that a baby born after loss is called a rainbow baby; it just seemed like a sign. A few weeks later, three months after Vox was born, I took a pregnancy test that confirmed it: I was pregnant again.

When I told Jack, he asked if I was happy. My voice was flat with tense affirmation: "I am." What I meant was: I am happy. Also: I am pregnant. I am here. I am willing. I am scared. I am alive.

I had no idea how lost I was and would remain to grief, only that another pregnancy was the lone reason I could think of to keep living.

Yet my second pregnancy carried with it a threat I didn't anticipate. *If my baby dies again*, I thought, *I am done for*. My pregnancy began to feel like a potential death sentence for me, because I knew there was no way I would force myself to live through the loss of two babies. A cord accident is no more likely to happen a second time than it is a first time, but a grief-addled brain doesn't track with logic. I was tormented for the duration by the fear this baby would also die.

Days passed the same way they had continued to after Vox died. I willed them on, too many days to pray meekly through:

"Please let this one live."

I proceeded like this, in my animal mind, surviving, trying to smile, grateful to be pregnant, daring to hope for the life in me, but petrified.

In mid-summer I found myself on the same porch that cradled me through the phone call with my brother-in-law. It was Sunday afternoon and warm. I had to sit with my knees apart to accommodate my full belly, so I tucked my skirt between my legs in case a neighbor happened by.

Look at all those weeds, I thought, anticipating the work they would require to remove. How was it possible they grew, untended? I didn't plant them, or feed them, or care about them at all, yet they flourished. Life prevailed.

Vox's brother Asher was born at home a few months later on the anniversary of the day Jack and I met for the first time. His birth was exactly what I had hoped for—calm and candlelit. After an exceedingly traumatic labor with Vox, it meant everything to me to have the birth I wanted and to do it on my own terms.

Two hours after Asher was born, the midwives and their assistants went home. All of a sudden it was just the three of us, plus our dogs, Zoe and Gizmo, a small terrier-mix we adopted after Vox died to give me something—someone—to hold.

Around 3AM I set Asher in the co-sleeper next to our bed. I felt a gasp of anxiety as I set his body apart from my own for the first time. Quietly, carefully, disbelieving, I turned out the light and laid down, blinking through a rainbow of emotion.

Minutes later, I whispered to Jack, "Are you awake?"

"Yup." I could hear his smile in his voice.

"Um…there's a baby next to us. And it's ours." I was smiling, too.

I switched on the light and we laughed, semi-delirious. I picked Asher up and cradled him again to my chest. Once I'd soaked up as much of him as I could, I laid him gently back in his co-sleeper and turned off the light again.

A few minutes later, Jack asked, "Are you still awake?"

"Yup!"

Over the next hour we went through this routine several times—turn the light off, startle at our new reality, turn the light back on, retrieve our baby and stare, awed.

I suspect Jack finally fell asleep before I did that night. In spite of the effort of labor, I was wired. I laid there staring at the ceiling, hardly believing my dream had come true. I finally got to be a mom.

I fell asleep with the peace of a longing that had finally been met, and a tentative, fragile-as-a-butterfly-wing hope that maybe I'd be able to create for my son the family I never had.

Nine months later we were in Paris when Jack proposed. He said it spontaneously one evening while we were waiting for Asher to wake up from a late nap.

"Let's get married," he said.

Quickly, he rephrased it. He asked.

"Okay. Yes!"

We had talked about it, but I still couldn't believe it.

The next day we ran through a thunderstorm to find a ring for me, because I was so happy and insisted. There was a shop down the street from where we were staying where I found a thick tungsten band with an infinite line cut into it. It was a men's ring, but I didn't care. I liked the symbolism of the line, which reminded me of a verse in a song we sang when I was a kid at summer camp: *A circle's round, it has no end, that's how long I want to be your friend.*

Once the ring was securely on my finger, we ran through the storm to a street café across from the Louvre, racing the thin black wheels of Asher's crisp red umbrella stroller over the ancient brick streets. We drank red wine and ate frites and other rich things underneath an awning and I asked when he wanted to get married.

"What's the rush?" he asked.

"Well, if we're getting married, don't you think we should decide when?"

It was June when he proposed. Three months later we were attending a friend's wedding and still hadn't set a date. At the rehearsal dinner, I introduced him to someone as my partner.

"You can call me your fiancé," Jack muttered as we walked away.

"I will call you my fiancé when we have a wedding date set," I smiled, pleased with myself for thinking on my feet.

By the end of that weekend we had set the date: December 21, the Winter Solstice.

So it was that, a little more than a year after Asher was born, we made our vows to one another on the day the light begins its return. Among the things he told me, "All that I have I share with you. All that I am I give to you."

I finished mine with, "I choose you."

Both of us, incidentally, included a joke about Scrabble.

We toasted with martinis after the ceremony and sank into a beautiful night with our friends and families that was all about our love. We didn't take much of a honeymoon because Asher was too little to leave for very long, but I didn't mind. I was far more interested in a good night's sleep than honeymoon sex and romance.

We asked the guests not to bring gifts but received many beautiful sentiments in wedding toasts and greeting cards. I never forgot one in particular from my brother, Alex. He wrote, "Congratulations on your wedding, and on your first year of parenthood! The days are long, but the years are short."

I didn't know how right he was—how quickly we would settle into family life, or how the time would fly.

10. Into the Mystic

Shortly after Jack and I got married I began a two-year study of energy medicine with a woman named Clara who was a medical intuitive. Clara could look at a person's energy field and tell whether or not they had cancer, among other things. She could also tell whether or not their prescribed treatment would work. During my course of study with her, I booked a session so I could learn more about how she worked with her clients, because I was planning to open a practice of my own.

The day of my appointment I arrived early and was met by her assistant. She handed me a simple intake form. It was the same type of paperwork you might complete for physical therapy or acupuncture. I was glad to have a few minutes to focus my thoughts because I was nervous, afraid she was going to tell me I had cancer or, more likely, that I had what constituted a drinking problem. Ever since she said she didn't drink when she was seeing clients the next day—that, in fact, she barely drank at all—I had felt unbearably self-conscious any time the subject of alcohol came up in our classes. I'd noticed lately that I couldn't seem to go very long without it. I never blacked out, or even got drunk (most of the time), but it seemed like I shouldn't be so well organized around when and where I'd have my next drink. Like maybe it had become a preoccupation, which made it a thing. If it was a thing, I could no longer believe (in the place where I might admit such things), that it wasn't a thing. That it was no thing, or nothing. Which seemed to make it something.

Clara invited me into her office, which was just inside the front door of her home, at one minute before the hour. It was a nice room that reminded me of springtime. After we exchanged pleasantries, she asked me to lie on the massage table on my back.

I rested with my eyes closed while she worked, moving her hands over and around my body. As she did this, she told me her perceptions. When she felt a block, she made a discordant sound in the back of her throat that she said helped to move the energy and restore optimal flow.

Clara worked off the premise that our injuries—physical, emotional, traumatic, psychological—were all encoded with energy that could get stuck in our body if we weren't practicing good energetic hygiene. This, she said, was the source—or at least *a* source—of illness and disease.

When she started working, she told me almost immediately—out of the blue—that Jack and I were not sexually compatible. I was embarrassed it was so obvious to her, and shocked she somehow pulled the information out of thin air. It wasn't news to me, of course, but I'd never acknowledged it to anyone.

Hearing Clara say it out loud validated the unthought known, but the truth of it was challenging. Was our lack of compatibility an immutable fact? Her revelation begged the question...if—, then—?

I opened my eyes and asked her if it meant we would get a divorce.

"Not necessarily," she said. "You always have free will."

This satisfied me in the moment because I didn't think it all the way through.

Clara told me it was evident that I was skilled in the sexual arts. I felt embarrassed about this, too...what did that mean about me? On the other hand, I kind of knew what she meant.

Clara went on, elaborating. She said that in a past life I was a concubine in 14th Century China. This meant absolutely nothing to me—how could I ever confirm or deny it? Past life?

If she picked up on my doubt, she didn't show it. She continued as if she was stating a fact.

"You were the courtesan of a very wealthy man who had a wife and children. You liked being provided for but hated being sequestered, locked away from the rest of the world...."

I continued to listen, curious. I didn't believe her, but I didn't not believe her, either.

"Oh, this is so interesting!" she said to the movie in her mind.

She was so enthusiastic I hardly batted an eye when she told me: one night he arrived at my home extremely drunk and attacked me. In self-defense, I killed him. Given my lowly rank in society, I knew I would be put to death for the crime; no one would believe my story. I spent the rest of my life on the run—ostracized, hiding, and impoverished.

I didn't think much about Clara's revelation of my lack of compatibility with Jack because I was already well aware. Instead, the session left me wondering whether my supposed past life had anything to do with my present one, specifically my need for acceptance. In one of our recent classes Clara had led us through a meditation that addressed our deepest fears. Mine was unambiguous: I was afraid to be rejected. I was afraid to be alone.

11. Ob-la-di, Ob-la-da

Our life together looked very much like that of many families with young children. Jack worked and I was—apart from teaching yoga and studying energy medicine—a stay-at-home mom. Asher and I did a weekly mommy and me playgroup, and, observing his affinity for all things round and kickable, I signed him up for toddler soccer. My days were a rhythm of play time, nap time, mealtime, story time, and lots and lots of walks.

Although it took a while before I felt comfortable taking Asher on walks by myself. There were too many variables to keep track of—the stroller, the traffic, the dogs. For many months after Vox died it felt like a daily effort to avoid the undertow of paranoia that threatened to pull me from reality in any moment. I knew how quickly, and how badly, life could turn. Every time we stopped walking, I would check and recheck that the stroller brakes were on. I looped my hand through the safety strap and clung to it. I carried bear spray in case we encountered any aggressive dogs or bad guys. Inevitably, despite my caution and care, some horrific scene would occur to me: Asher, strapped into a runaway stroller, careening down a hill and over a ravine or into oncoming traffic. The scenes were like waking nightmares and I never knew when they would come. Every time they happened, I felt flooded with adrenaline, ready to vanquish any threat. But it was all in my head.

"Ma-ma, want to get out." Asher's voice would bring me back to reality. I was charmed by the way he enunciated his words so crisply. He fiddled with the seatbelt buckle with chubby fingers so adorable it made me ache.

One Saturday morning when Asher was around three, we were in the kitchen making plans for the day when Jack's phone rang. It was his sister in Florida. Jack's mom, who also lived in Florida, had been admitted to the hospital overnight. She'd fallen, likely due to a stroke.

We agreed he needed to go. Jack flew out the next morning and went straight from the airport to the hospital, where he received the latest update on her condition. He called me with the news.

"They're moving her to Hospice." He sounded tired and resigned.

"Okay," I said, choking up. I had known this day would come, but I loved my mother-in-law and hoped for more time with her. "When should we come?" I was ready to get on the next plane to Tampa.

"You don't have to do that, honey," Jack replied. "It's okay. She's resting comfortably."

"But I want to see her before she dies. And I think Asher should see his grandma. We should say goodbye."

"You really don't have to do that," he said.

"I know I don't. I want to!"

I couldn't believe he didn't realize how much I wanted to be there with her, and with him. I was not especially close to his mom because we had never lived in proximity to one another, but we had shared a mutual fondness since we'd met, and I thought very highly of her. She was elegant, sharp, funny, loving—many of the same qualities I admired in her son.

"Of course I want to be there with her," I repeated. His resistance was confounding.

"Well, I don't think we should put Asher through that. And it's a lot for you to bring him all the way here by yourself. What would you do with the dogs?"

He must be in grief, I thought. *He's not thinking straight.*

"I can figure it out, honey. Let's talk again tomorrow."

We said goodnight. When we spoke the next day, I told him I'd worked out where the dogs could go. I wanted to bring Asher.

"No," he said. There was no room for compromise in his tone. "It's only immediate family. I don't think you should come."

The first time I admitted the unthought known out loud I was walking around Green Lake—a popular, three-mile loop in central Seattle—with a friend. We were talking about our lives and marriages. Somehow, in the course of our confiding, something loosened in me. I confessed.

"I don't know if Jack and I are sexually compatible." My voice was hushed, yet still sounded too loud to my ears.

"What do you mean?" she asked. "You're so frisky!"

"I know, I think that's part of the problem…"

I trailed off and we strode in silence for a long moment as I prepared to acknowledge aloud what I felt was true.

I began again. "I mean, he's good in bed, it's not that. But I feel like something is missing. With other partners I have felt like the sex we had was bigger than the two of us. And with Jack I feel like it's just the two of us, enjoying each other, but it's not the same."

I was warming up.

"It doesn't feel creative to me, or even like much of an expression. It feels more like scratching an itch. Like, if we don't have sex for a couple weeks, which sometimes happens, we start to get a little snippy. Then we have sex and the tension is gone and we go back to being friendly. But it's not like we're closer or more bonded for the experience."

"Well do you like having sex with him?" she asked.

"I do. I can get myself off, and he always comes. But it's not like we're touching souls, you know? I want *that* feeling. *I want to know him intimately.*"

Four days after he left for Florida, Jack was on his way home. I had already put Asher to bed and was puttering around the house, waiting for Jack's text telling me his plane had landed. I put away some laundry, partially loaded the dishwasher. Unmotivated, I retired to the couch downstairs to watch a show.

Our family couch was old. Not aged, but worn. The once perky pillows sagged. Two of the cushions were torn. Dog hair had woven itself into the upholstery and the fabric bore dozens of (mostly) invisible stains—tears, wine, mashed banana, dog barf, breast milk, spit up, who knew what else. You don't think about these things in the mood lit showroom when you're picking out the one you want.

I was still trying to decide what to watch when I got Jack's text. *"Just landed! See you soon."*

"Okay babes. Glad you're back. xo"

I was glad he was coming home—I missed him—but my stomach was turning. I wanted to be loving and sensitive to Jack's needs when he arrived…his mom was dying. But I was deeply hurt, not to mention confused, about not being given the chance to say goodbye to his mom. Wasn't I part of the family?

Also, didn't Jack want me close to him when he faced such a significant loss? Didn't he *need* me to be there for him?

It was the first time it ever occurred to me that Jack might not want or need the same things from me that I needed from him, that in fact I had no idea what his expectations were of our marriage. That maybe companionship, good food, regular sex, and a great mom for his son were all he wanted. Maybe he didn't want to touch souls. And maybe he didn't want to be known.

12. Alive

Jack and I talked about what it meant that he didn't want me to come to Florida, and that he didn't turn to me for emotional support after his mom passed away. He insisted it was different for him. His mom was 91 and he hadn't lived near her in decades. He said it wasn't the same as if I lost my mom, who I saw regularly and was only 70. But the incident made me realize how I had taken—maybe mistaken—Jack's general warmth and affection for emotional intimacy; these were not the same thing. In one discussion on the topic, I asked if I was his beard. He surprised me with the intensity of his response.

"What? No! What are you talking about?"

"I don't mean that you're gay. It just makes me feel like our marriage is some kind of sham. If we aren't relating as more than friends—if you aren't sharing your inner world with me—what are we even doing together?"

He was still mad.

"Honey, again, I didn't mean you're gay. I meant that the fact that you didn't need me there when your mom died makes me feel like I'm just a pretty young placeholder standing next to you through life, but you don't want anything more than that. And I want to be close with you in all the ways."

I was starting to connect a lot of dots. I always thought the fact that we didn't fight meant we were a perfect couple, an idyllic match. It didn't occur to me it might be that we never fought because we were avoiding issues between us, or that it might have indicated a lack of passion. We didn't fight, no, but we also didn't fuck. Fighting and fucking, I was beginning to realize, were two sides of the same coin.

It was around this time that I began to question how I could feel such a piercing sense of discontent alongside my supposedly happy, easy life. I repeated it again and again, "I'm so happy."

I had said it to my sister, my mom, my therapist...but there was no one I tried to convince more than myself.

A few weeks after the realization in my therapist's office that I wasn't as happy as I'd been professing to be, I noticed the summer concert lineup at one of the local venues. My stomach stirred with excitement when I saw that The Musician and his band were coming. I hadn't seen him in more than five years, since Jack and I found out we were pregnant with Vox. Once I'd sealed up that future, it felt disloyal to nurture any relationship from my past. But all of a sudden, when I heard they were coming, I felt the old familiar pull to go.

I didn't want to buy tickets—that would mean nothing. Instead, I needed to get on the guest list, which meant backstage passes, sometimes all access. All access meant royalty. But securing the keys to the kingdom meant I would have to do the delicate dance of dysfunction. I had learned long ago not to approach The Musician directly for anything—he always referred me to his tour manager. Which meant I would have to ask his tour manager—*The* Tour Manager—for access. I was unsure how my request would be received; it had been a long time.

It might seem like I would have realized The Musician was not really my friend if I couldn't count on him for something as simple as tickets to his show. But I figured tolerating his idiosyncrasies was the price of entry. In exchange, I would get the excitement of backstage and a potential hit of validation. I might get to feel again like I mattered to him.

Another thing on my mind was whether The Musician had a girlfriend. I wanted him to know I would be at the concert in case he was available for some form of connection, but if he was not available, I also needed him to know that I would respect his space. But none of these things could be named directly—better to let things ride and hope for the best than try to nail him down and risk rejection. Plus, by leaving things unnamed, whatever happened could be called happenstance.

I emailed The Tour Manager who responded sweetly and said he'd put me on the guest list. Once I knew I was on the list, I emailed The Musician and told him I'd be at the show, which was still a couple months away. Just like the first time we met, he suggested we could do a yoga practice together.

I was excited to revisit their world, a galaxy away from my staid domestic life, but unsettled by the prospect of seeing him, because there was no ground between us. The one defining quality of our relationship, apart from our mutual preoccupation with sex, had always been uncertainty. It helped that he suggested an activity, but I knew it was just as likely that yoga wouldn't happen as it was that it would.

Next, I mentioned it to Jack.

"Just come home after the show," he joked. "I don't want to wake up to a text from you announcing you're on a tour bus heading south on I-5."

I was glad he didn't ask why I wanted to go, and I avoided digging any deeper into what his comment suggested—that perhaps Jack harbored doubt about my allegiance or fidelity. If he had asked why I wanted to go, I'm not even sure I would have, or could have, revealed the truth. I didn't want to self-reflect, and I didn't want to explain. I was not seeking insight. All I wanted was a distraction, and an escape, even if only for one night.

When the day of the concert finally rolled around, I said goodbye to Jack with a pit in my stomach and drove away. Perhaps it was the strangeness of revisiting a life I'd left behind, or the attachment I still felt to The Musician, or maybe I sensed I was inviting trouble. Whatever the reason, I was jumpy and preoccupied the whole drive there. When I saw him across a field as I was parking, I nearly retreated home. It had been so long since I'd seen him. We were different people than we had been. What was I doing there?

I let the car idle while I played out each scenario in my mind— stay for the concert or leave now—and decided I had to stay. If I left, I knew I would always wonder what I'd missed.

73

I made my way to where he was hanging out with the rest of the band and greeted everyone. After a few minutes, The Musician and I found a place to sit and catch up. I told him about Asher and Jack. He told me he was newly married, which felt like a punch to the gut even though it had been years since we'd been in touch. It was more evidence of what would never be between us, never mind that I, too, was already married with a family.

An hour or so later, after watching him give an interview, we rolled out our yoga mats on the pavement next to the tour bus. I started out sitting in half lotus pose with my eyes closed, willing my nerves to settle. I tried to focus my mind with Ujjayi breath, a breathing technique that engages the throat and nostrils and is meant to be centering, but it was no use. The ambient noises, the machinations of their tour, and his presence next to me were too much. I gave up the breath and resigned myself to moving through poses in near-complete distraction. I couldn't believe I was there with him, again.

The Musician had to go and do a pre-show meet and greet, so he directed me to his dressing room to change. I was glad to have a moment of peace and quiet to compose myself and breathe again. I took a quick shower and dried off with paper towels—all I could find—and slipped into a dramatic open back dress, my fullest feather earrings, and my favorite red-gold lipstick. Despite my nervousness and the lurking shadow of reality—how fleeting the joy and relief of the experience was bound to be—I was consumed by excitement. I felt so special being there as his guest, a world away from my husband and child at home. When the first bass beats poured from the speakers, I ran from the wine line to my seat a few rows from the stage.

Watching him perform, I was overcome. Listening to his words, I felt as inspired as I did the first time I saw him play. When he jumped offstage and ran into the crowd, I followed him with my eyes, rapt. I could hardly believe when he approached me, took my hand, and twirled me in a circle as he sang, gazing into my eyes. Was he singing to me? It didn't matter. My heart felt so full. I felt a happiness I hadn't in years, like a part of me that had been lost had returned.

Over the course of the concert, listening to his lyrics, gazing back at him onstage, I felt like someone else. Or maybe it was the beginning of feeling like my former self again, the woman I was before life happened, before I'd become Mom and Wife.

After the concert I stopped by his tour bus to say goodbye. He texted he'd be a minute, so I waited across the parking lot in my car. I didn't want to stand there like just another fan because in my mind, I was special. This was and had always been part of my obsession—out of thousands of fans, he had chosen *me*. Well, I was pretty sure he had "chosen" lots of women, but I wasn't thinking about that as I sat there in my car, staring at the swinging doors of his tour bus, waiting for him to emerge. Instead I thought about his last text to me: "I want to see you before you go."

He wanted to see me. Nothing else mattered.

When he came striding off the bus I stepped out of my SUV—our family car—and walked toward him. Our approach to one another felt slowed down, as in a film sequence: him, moving confidently, certain of his intent, and her, smiling timidly, acquiescent and eager, but unsure.

When I got close, he extended his arms and folded me in. He held me tight and kissed the top of my head. I looked at him with tears in my eyes, feeling like there were a million things I wanted to say, a whole relationship yet to be had, knowing that none of it would ever be.

I wanted to tell him how much he meant to me, and how much his music had gifted me, but I didn't know how to explain, so I just said, "Thank you doesn't seem like it's big enough."

"Yes and thank you are the biggest words there are."

The words came so fast they sounded insincere, or at least not personal. I let them sink in anyway.

Determined to spare my dignity, I thanked him again, gave him a final hug, and let go before I wanted to. We held hands until the last second, reaching toward one another as I walked away. It was a cinematic touch, but I wasn't sure it meant anything at all. I had never known what meant something with him and what meant nothing.

He gave one last wave and then turned to some fans who were waiting for an autograph outside the fence.

I walked back to my car laden with the grief of what would never be between us, of the young woman I'd been, of the uncertainty I felt about how to improve my marriage. I felt fragile under the weight of my emotions, like I might shatter at the tiniest bump or startle. Barely holding it together, I drove out of sight of the tour bus to a small grove of trees where I parked and finally released the sob that had been building since I'd watched him dance his way on stage hours before.

Watching him had reminded me of what felt like a distant youth. Seven years before I was living a free life in San Francisco, doing as I pleased. In the years since, I'd had two babies, grieved the death of one, nurtured the other, gotten married, and become bound and committed to a lifestyle that, I was beginning to realize, stifled and bored me.

But I loved my family; we had a great life. Marriage and family was the life I'd always wanted. It was the life I'd chosen.

That night I wanted something else. Worse, I wanted something—someone—I knew was bad for me. I had been close enough to see the profound insecurity behind The Musician's power and allure. But I wanted him anyway because I still didn't have the thing I'd always sought. I wanted to feel that I was important to him the way he was to me. It wasn't conscious, but on some level I believed his validation would raise me from the self-doubt and shame I'd carried since childhood.

I'd taken enough psych classes to recognize why I was vulnerable to this kind of thing: a young woman with an unavailable father will seek to replicate her paternal relationship with unavailable partners in hopes of redeeming the lost experience of her childhood. I was a textbook case.

Knowing this did nothing to change it.

Raindrops began to dust the windshield as I dug in my purse for more tissues and mentally chastised myself. How could I feel sorry for myself when I had a great husband at home waiting for me? He'd given me his blessing to come tonight—many husbands probably would have said no.

I would have had to lie, and to be honest, I probably would have. But Jack let me go. He even seemed happy, knowing how much it meant to me. Why didn't I feel grateful?

Because I wanted more. Years before The Musician had introduced me to a part of myself I'd been trying to find again ever since, a part that was awake and alive and fearless. I was inspired by his creativity and self-expression, and I wanted to be the woman I felt like when we were together. Not the insecure part, but the part that had permission to be herself, to be fully, wildly expressed.

Also, the sex. As the raindrops ran down the windshield, I longed to know again the same intense eroticism, the same intimate revelation, the same deep connection and vast expansiveness I had experienced with him in the times we'd been together. The ache for these things in my chest and stomach felt like a hole in me. A void.

And I still had no idea how much more was at play beneath my awareness, that in addition to the unthought known, there was an unthought *un*known at work that was even more significant. My dad's absence, abuse, and neglect had created an attachment wound I had been striving to heal—one way or another—for my whole adult life. I thought my issue was with Jack, but the real issue was within me.

When I returned home from the concert I went straight to our bedroom and looked in on Jack. I guessed he'd long been asleep, but I wanted him to know I was home safe. I walked to his side of the bed and gently rubbed his hip. He roused quickly.

"How was it?" he asked, making space for me next to him.

"Amazing," I sighed. "It was really good."

I sat down in the gray square of light shining through our bedroom window. I knew he'd want to hear more but I didn't know what else to say. I felt emotionally exhausted and unable to offer a more articulate summary.

Or maybe I was afraid I would give something away. Maybe I just needed time to process the complexity of my feelings.

There was one moment I couldn't stop thinking about, the hug we shared when we said goodbye. Maybe I just wanted to hold the magic a little longer for myself.

"Amazing?" Jack asked. "That's all you've got?"

Begrudgingly, I elaborated. I figured I owed him that much.

"Well, it was really nice to see him and hear the music. I liked a lot of their new stuff. You probably wouldn't have, though."

Jack wasn't much of a fan. Whether it was a matter of personal taste or had something to do with the feelings Jack knew I still harbored for The Musician, he was not impressed.

"Anyway, it was fun to be there and remember my time in that life," I continued.

I didn't mention the post-concert sobbing, of course. How could I explain my despair to Jack? I'd never so much as intimated that I didn't feel fulfilled by our life together because the truth had only recently dawned on me. I assumed it would hurt him, and even the thought of hurting him made my heart ache. I couldn't conceive of it. He'd given me so much.

Anyway, what did I possibly have to complain about? We loved each other. We had fun together. He was a great dad. I assumed it was the plight of every woman who was married with kids to feel unfulfilled to some degree, and that being an adult meant sucking it up or pushing it down. If the option was to hurt Jack or ignore my longing, I'd have to go on ignoring it.

"That's great," he said, closing his eyes. "I'm glad you had fun. And I'm glad you came home." He rubbed my bare knee and settled back into bed.

"I'm going to get in the shower," I said. I leaned over and kissed him goodnight. "Thanks for being so cool about tonight. I really appreciate you being supportive of my wanting to go."

"Of course, baby."

By the time I returned from my shower, a quiet had settled over our darkened house. Asher was sleeping soundly in his room and the dogs were asleep in their beds at the foot of ours. It was going on 2AM. I pulled back the thin duvet and top sheet and slid, naked, onto my side. Jack was already asleep again, breathing a soft, endearing rhythm. I was careful not to disturb him. He had to get up to do his radio show in less than three hours.

I closed my eyes but couldn't quiet the thoughts in my head, so I rolled to my back and stared at the ceiling, wired by the events of the night. I revisited the hug in my mind over and over, certain it was the most perfect hug that ever was. The thought simultaneously delighted and devastated me. I had looked forward to the concert all summer; it pained me it was already over.

I toyed with regret. What was I thinking going to that show? How did it ever seem like a good idea to dredge up old feelings? *I shouldn't have gone.* We shouldn't have done it. It lasted too long. It meant too much. It meant so much—it did to me—that I wondered if it constituted a betrayal of my marriage vows. But it felt vital. That hug was an oasis.

"Yes and thank you are the biggest words there are," he'd said.

What had I said yes to by seeing him again all these years later? I had no idea.

My phone chimed with the arrival of a text. I jumped to silence it so it didn't wake Jack. As I flipped off the sound, I looked at the message and shivered with a years-old excitement. It was him.

The message was a picture of me that his photographer must have taken earlier that day while we were doing yoga; I hadn't known she was there. How do I characterize that picture? I look…powerfully meditative. Erotically composed. Ferociously sensual. He included only one word.

"Mmmmm."

My stomach fluttered with an exhilaration that ignored decorum and common sense.

"Mmm hmmm."

I knew the reaction it would elicit.

"I wanted to kiss you so bad tonight," he texted back.

I felt a bittersweet pang in my chest. I had wanted that too, so much. Would I have let him kiss me? Absolutely.

A part of me knew I should just say goodnight and put my phone away. But another part, a wilder part consumed by need, replied instead.

"And what would you have done next, after you felt the warmth of my lips and tongue on yours?"

"I would have grabbed a handful of your hair and pulled your head back, and wrapped my hand around your throat so gently, and kissed you again, long and soft."

I set my phone down and put a hand over my mouth to quiet my breath. Suddenly every nerve in my body was alert and waiting. The top of my head grew light and an ache rolled through my low belly and hips. My back arched in blind invitation. My mouth ached for something to fill it.

Sexually, this felt like the most exciting thing that had happened to me in years. As conflicted as I was texting another man from the bed I shared with my husband, and as scared as I was he was going to wake up and deduce what was going on—and with whom—I didn't want to stop. So, I didn't. I picked up my phone.

Within a few more exchanges our texts were loaded with desire and included more body parts and verbs. Soon I was touching myself the way he told me to and describing what I would do to him given the chance, just like we'd done years before. Prolonged pauses in our messaging meant we were getting closer to climax. Several dozen messages and more than an hour later, he asked me to delete the evidence and we quickly said goodbye.

Flushed and ashamed, I set my phone next to me on the bedside table and tried again to steady my breath. I couldn't believe what I had just done with my husband asleep right next to me.

I felt proud to know I could still turn a man's head—and not just any man. The thought made me giddy with ego. But I was conflicted by my desire. Why didn't I want Jack like that? Why didn't we ever talk to each other that way?

Any guilt and uncertainty I felt about the hug seemed trivial now, compared to this actual betrayal. I felt terrible. Also: empowered. I definitely didn't want to do something to hurt Jack. But seeing The Musician had reminded me of a vital part of myself I had desperately missed.

It's not so bad, I told myself. After all, Jack slept through the whole thing. *If it doesn't impact our relationship, what's the harm?* Jack probably still had feelings for some of his exes, I reasoned. So what if he texted them, or even sexted? What was the big deal if I never found out about it? *What I don't know can't hurt me*, I thought. I decided the same was true for Jack.

Lying there waiting for sleep, I relished that old familiar rush of freedom. That part of me had dashed off, springing like a doe in wildflowers.

Another part of me—a part I wanted to cling to—stayed, hovered close to the line, more comfortable near the predictability of packed lunches and made beds.

Still another part of me hated myself.

It didn't occur to me how these were each parts of the same whole.

13. Little Lies

I've told plenty:

1. My phone number is…
2. I'd love to go out again.
3. It's not you.
4. I agreed.
5. We didn't have sex.
6. I don't feel bad about it.
7. Our sex life is fine.
8. Everything is under control.
9. This is what I want.
10. All my needs are met.
11. I don't think I could ever be with a woman.
12. I'm so happy.
13. My sexuality isn't that important.
14. I'm not in love with him.
15. I don't care.
16. I'm not addicted.
17. I don't want it.
18. I'm not scared.
19. I don't need you.
20. This is not about self-worth.

14. Graceland

Jack and I had been together—happily, for all intents and purposes—for nearly six years when I started sexting with The Musician after the concert that night. Asher was almost four.

Though I was initially scandalized, gradually it began to feel less wrong. It was energizing to have a thing that was just mine. Anyway, Jack knew I still had feelings for The Musician, a point I used to justify our occasional contact (whenever he turned up looking, if I'm being honest). It was fine-just-fine—that's what I told myself. It never occurred to me this secret corner of my life might have begun to undermine the foundation of my marriage. Nor that by meeting those needs elsewhere I was undermining the intimacy I professed to want with Jack. It's hard to be close to someone when you're simultaneously hiding something from them. But I'd been telling myself that what Jack didn't know couldn't hurt him for long enough that I'd begun to believe it, which made it that much easier to take things a step further when an opportunity presented itself.

I was meeting my friend Reese in Colorado—we were going to see The Musician play a show. Reese and I had booked an Airbnb, which is where we met the afternoon of the concert. The apartment was on the top floor and it was sweltering, so we opened the windows and went outside while the space aired out.

As Reese and I sat talking, a burgundy pickup pulled into the dusty parking strip. The driver got out and walked through the gate, feet from where we were sitting, acknowledging us with an authoritative nod.

Something happened in those thirty seconds. Was it the nod? His bare chest? Some alchemical fusion? I had an instant crush.

The guy disappeared inside for a few minutes and reappeared with work gloves. He gathered tools from the side of the house and began tilling the garden fifty feet from where we were, generally appearing to ignore us as Paul Simon played on a small speaker turned way up. The guy—The Gardener—mouthed the words to Graceland as he worked. Reese and I were mostly silent, watching him move. Or she may have been talking. I wasn't listening. I needed to study him, the first stranger I'd really looked at since I married Jack—the first man that gave me that kind of pause.

He had a shaved head like Bruce Willis. He kind of looked like him, actually. The absence of hair on his head revealed its perfect geometry, the bones at pleasing angles I'm not sure I'd ever seen before. His neck was maybe a little longer than average, or perhaps this was an illusion created by the nakedness of his broad shoulders and back. His muscles were evident under the slightest bit of cushion. He wore his shorts across his hips—not low-low, but low enough to reveal those abdominal muscles that point straight down. He had a faded black t-shirt hanging out his back pocket and holey checked Vans on his feet. His chest was covered in a light golden fur. He was tall. I estimated my eyes might reach his lips, or maybe his throat. He was perfectly proportioned and looked a little dirty. I knew he'd smell like sweat. The thought of it filled me with want.

In a low voice I admitted my crush to Reese. Also married—monogamously—she swept me back inside to get ready for our night out.

The next morning, after rising from our post-concert fog, we bumped into The Gardener on the porch. After chatting for some time (with lots of eye gazing and flirting), he invited himself to join me and Reese for brunch, which turned into spending the day together. We microdosed mushrooms and went to the Denver Zoo, then capped off the excursion with a bottle of rosé in his garden.

Certainly, it was out of my norm to spend an entire day with a man that was not my husband, but I was fairly confident Jack would be okay with how the day was unfolding.

84

One reason for this trip was to recharge—to exercise my autonomy outside the trappings of routine family life.

At some point during the afternoon, I asked The Gardener if maybe he could take me to the airport. That way Reese could get going home before it got too late. I pretended I was just being practical.

When it was time to leave we wrested ourselves from the peaceful garden and went in to grab our bags. I had to get to the airport, and Reese wanted to start home.

"So good to see you!"

"You too!"

With my bag on my shoulder I gave her a final squeeze goodbye and clicked the door shut. It was just us two standing in his living room. We had ten minutes to spare before we had to leave for the airport.

I'd been wearing my luggage as if to confirm our imminent departure. I realized when I looked at him I didn't have to say anything, I just had to put down my bags. We smiled at one another. He crossed the room and stood in front of me.

Looking up to meet his eyes, I regarded the fullness of his lips for the first time and the tiny chip in his front tooth. Without saying a word, he took off his shirt, so I did the same, then pulled off my jeans, which I left inside out on the floor. I was nearly naked and we were still standing with only eight minutes left.

He lifted my chin and kissed me gently. Then holding me behind the small of my back, he walked me backwards to his bedroom, our kissing ramping up in intensity.

He lowered me onto his unmade bed and we wasted no time: mouths, hands, laughter, and the button of his cutoff plain-front chinos rubbing hard against my pubic bone. I felt breathless but restrained. Things were happening too fast for me to justify each transgression.

I was more comfortable allowing him to act on my body than I was taking any initiative with his—passive engagement seemed less incriminating. I tried to ignore the blooming sense of scandal in my heart and mind and told myself it was harmless. I barely touched him. He never even took off his shorts.

At three minutes past "we're late" we rushed to put on clothes. He said he wanted more time. I did not. More time would make it impossible. I desperately wanted to be naked with him, but I didn't dare. *That would be crossing a line.*

All the way to the airport I was wiggly, sweaty from the hot seat of his truck, wet from our roll in the hay, and anxious about what I'd just done.

When I got out of his truck I told him I wasn't going to look back, because once I got out of his truck I was leaving this in Colorado. I didn't see any point in drawing out a goodbye and didn't intend there would ever be another hello.

As I approached the terminal and the automatic doors opened, I couldn't help it. I looked back. He'd gotten out of his truck and was standing there, on the far side, leaning on the hood. Just like Jake at the end of *Sixteen Candles*, he smiled and waved. If I was single, I would have swooned. I would have rushed back to him for one more kiss or blown off my flight entirely and spent the night with him. Instead, I turned and rushed to make my flight.

When I arrived home that night Jack met me at the door. Asher was already asleep. As I stood in front of Jack, greeting him, I felt an urge for his body, a rare thing between us.

THIS! I thought. *This is what they're talking about.*

I'd heard that in nonmonogamous relationships, the energy created with a secondary partner (or partners) could invigorate the primary relationship. *It's true*, I thought. It was like a dead battery getting a jumpstart. The fling with The Gardener turned me on. The juices were still flowing as I took Jack's hand and walked him to the bedroom.

Every time it gets a little easier.

Three months later, thoughts about my secret life—The Musician, The Gardener—had begun to occupy more than just a corner of my psyche.

They were an illicit distraction that spared me from feeling the sorrow of my unthought known, and the despair of my baby who was never coming back, and the restlessness of my midlife ennui. I was beginning to separate in subtle ways, though I couldn't see what I was doing, nor how I was accelerating.

I had decided to get a tattoo in Vox's memory. I had a few small ones, but I wanted something big. Something defining. I wanted to make a statement, though I'm still not sure to whom. Was I sending myself a message about who I was, or who I wanted to be? Was it about the size of my loss? Was it for Jack? Maybe I was trying to convey something sinister about his wife. A warning? I don't know precisely. I was operating on impulse.

The tattoo artist was a body builder with a full beard who wore metal t-shirts and black combat boots. Unsurprisingly, he was covered in tattoos. If it weren't for his youth, well styled hair, and artsy glasses, I thought he might have passed for a Hell's Angel. His Otherness was intriguing. What would it be like to be fucked by a man with pictures all over his skin?

The day of my tattoo I arrived fresh from the shower with wet hair that I made sure smelled like flowers—I wanted to engage as many of his senses as possible. Soon after I arrived I had to take my pants off so he could access my hip, where I wanted him to put it. Removing my pants entirely seemed easier (and more flattering) than pushing them down, so I took off my jeans, and then my underwear, too, because they would have been in the way and it was a perfect excuse to indulge my inner exhibitionist and bare my naked ass. The Artist seemed unfazed, regardless of how loosely I wrapped the sarong I brought as a cover up. Clearly, he was used to women pony prancing their bodies in front of him.

The first day he completed the outline of the whole design—a hummingbird with a bouquet of gladiolus flowers. I loved watching it come to life; I hadn't anticipated how much I would like big art on my body.

It was like watching an animal molt—a hermit crab, or a snake. But instead of a loss, it was a gain. My skin, my body. Under his needle I was becoming something new.

I asked him questions while he worked to distract myself from the pain and discovered he was ten years younger than me. He had a girlfriend who got on his nerves, he said. They'd been together awhile. I saw later when I Insta-stalked him that she was tiny and vampish and young enough that she probably understood Snapchat.

I brought a pinch of Vox's ashes to the second session so I could put them in the ink. The Artist sat quietly to the side while I prayed over the gritty gray powder before dropping it into the tiny plastic cup he was about to fill with black stain. As he got to work, I asked if I could touch him. Like it happened all the time, he said sure. This gave me something to fixate on besides the astonishing pain of the needle. Gradually, I worked my hand up his leg and under his shirt. I hooked my fingers over his jeans and moved them over his stomach, slowly. Neither of us acknowledged what I was doing.

By the time he finished my tattoo it was late afternoon. I'd been touching him for hours; it felt like we'd been through something. So even though I was running late to get home and help Jack clean the house for the dinner party we were hosting that evening, I suggested to the Artist that we get a drink at the bar down the street.

"Yeah," he said.

We walked through the darkened door and sat side–by–side on spinning barstools and I felt like his girlfriend, even though he already had one. We both drank a Dewar's on the rocks—double—because that's what he ordered, and when the bartender asked me what I wanted all I could think of was the vodka martini or Chardonnay that I usually drank, but both of these seemed too bougie, middle-aged white lady for how I wanted him to perceive me, so I just said "same."

We didn't have that much to say so we didn't stay long, which means we drank fast, which is why I was maybe a little tipsy and more likely to say what I did as we walked back: "I want to kiss you so bad."

88

He turned on his heels and ducked into a doorway. I followed him, observed him waiting for me.

Without thinking, my lips were on his. Immediately I calibrated to his tenderness. Despite my desire to swallow him whole, I was soft and restrained. I felt the clandestine electric for a long moment, until sense got the better of me. Someone might drive by and see. It wasn't until I got into my car that I considered what just happened.

"OMG," I texted him.

"Wait don't leave yet"

My stomach dropped. "Okay, sitting in my car."

When he came around the corner a minute later, I gave a tiny honk of the horn so he would know where I was. I watched him get in, deftly adjusting the seat, looking oversized and a little awkward in my Mini Cooper. When he leaned in to kiss me again his eyes betrayed something desperate I hadn't seen before. His mouth over mine, our tongues searching one another, he reached into my pants. As his fingers slid inside me all resistance gave way. I tried to open my legs so he could move in me but he pulled away and put my hand on his crotch.

It was so foreign. For a moment I forgot what to do. Or maybe I sensed the boundary I was about to cross. Sexting was one thing. Allowing another man to do something to me…that was something else. But actually touching another man? It felt like a new threshold of wrong. And yet I continued. I kissed him again and remembered: stroke it.

I moved my hand over his lap and followed the shape to his right hipbone. I imagined opening his fly and climbing on top of him and drawing him deep inside me. I wanted it so badly I was shaking.

I had to go.

We kissed again, urgently. I told him I'd let him know when I was ready for more ink and he said he'd get me right in. He got out of the car like a sentence with no punctuation. When he peeled out of the parking lot before I had even buttoned my pants, the mom in me texted to tell him to drive safely. I put a piece of chartreuse spearmint gum in my mouth, thinking about our smells on each other.

He replied, "Gonna have to park and bust a nut You made me so hott"

Flattered, breathless, and out of my mind, I drove home and served dinner to our guests.

15. Time After Time

The effects of grief are different over time. It's easier at first, in a way, when you cry a lot, because you're aware of how much you're still hurting. Over time, you begin to recognize strands of yourself in the life happening around you, and you begin to engage once more. You don't forget the loss, but you forget to consider how it might still be ruining you on the inside, undermining your best efforts at something greater than survival.

> You forget not how to exist, but how to live.

16. Risk It

By the time I finally suggested to Jack that we open our marriage, I'd been wondering about it for two years. In hindsight it seems ridiculous that I was more afraid to explore the subject with him than I was to cheat, but maybe it's not surprising. Broaching the topic of nonmonogamy was a step closer to acknowledging the unthought known, which I was subliminally convinced would be ruinous, so I continued to stay as far away from it as possible.

And then I reached a tipping point, which was brought about by a series of events that helped me step from the shadows of adulterous shame into the light of consensual nonmonogamy.

The first thing to happen was that I went to the movies. More specifically, a documentary called *Beyond Naked*, which is about four people, including my sister Mari, who accept a challenge to ride their bikes naked in the Fremont Summer Solstice parade, an annual tradition in Seattle. Because she starred in the film, Mari got to attend the premiere. She invited me as her plus one.

Before the lights in the theater went down, Mari leaned over and whispered, "The filmmaker is the guy with brown hair sitting in front of me and a little to the right."

I nodded.

"That's his girlfriend in front of me in white," she said. Then, "His wife is sitting on his other side."

My breath caught in my throat as I processed her words.

The film was engaging—funny, endearing, sad, inspiring—but I remained preoccupied for the duration by the man and two women sitting in front of us. I was so intrigued.

At the afterparty Mari mingled about while I receded into the shadows, observing. Over water crackers and cubes of cheese I watched the filmmaker and the women he was there with.

I drank my share of wine, and Mari's, too, then took to looking at the art in the back room of the space, not wanting to appear antisocial but completely enthralled by what I had seen. One man, two women…this could just as easily be one woman and two men. *Two men!* The thought had never occurred to me before, but it sounded sublime.

A month later I was chatting with a work associate who mentioned a friend of his who was opening her marriage. His friend had some sexual trauma in her past and wanted to explore having sex with women as a potential means of healing. He seemed upset about it. I wondered if he was worried it would ruin her marriage, or if he was maybe a little jealous. He had gotten married young when he and his wife were both virgins, and his wife had stopped wanting sex. As we delved deeper into conversation it was apparent this had been going on a long time. He was beside himself with grief. How could he get his needs met without betraying his wife and his covenant with God? (But wasn't acceptance of a sexless marriage a betrayal of himself?) I sensed his desire to explore other options. I wondered if it was his unthought known. I didn't ask.

Soon after that conversation, I signed up for an ayahuasca retreat. Mari had gone to Peru seven years earlier for a ten-day experience and had told me all about it: rustic accommodations in the middle of the jungle, a bitter medicine she drank every other night, psychedelic experiences that she said could heal my body, mind, and soul. I was intrigued when she talked about it, but figured it sounded too far out—and too far away—for me. But when she mentioned there was an opportunity to join a ceremony in a rural area a few hours from my house, I found myself suddenly interested.

My intention was to gain some awareness of what I wanted to be doing with my life. I'd been feeling resistance about my reiki practice. To make it worthwhile financially, I needed to see more clients, but I didn't want to, and I couldn't explain why not.

Did it have something to do with how much I'd been drinking lately—my "fuck it" solution to the vague ambivalence I'd had about life since Vox died? Or did I feel guilty knowing I was out of integrity in my personal life? Either way, I felt unqualified to be counseling others.

Jack was planning to take Asher to the car museum during one of the afternoons I was away. He was great about planning activities for them to do together and he never begrudged me the time I spent on my pursuits.

The closer the retreat got, the less present I felt with the two of them. I was writing in my journal and meditating daily, trying to get into the right headspace for the epiphany I hoped was coming. I needed something to replace the thrill I was getting from sexting with The Musician. I was desperate for a way to address my restlessness without the risk of changing my marriage.

I'd been so edgy lately I wasn't sleeping well. For weeks I'd been waking up in the wee hours tormented by self-doubt and longing. The secrets I was holding—The Musician, The Gardener, The Artist, the unthought known—were getting heavier. When that much of your energy is going somewhere else, it has consequences, and I guessed that Jack probably sensed it. I didn't feel as close to him as I had before I started stepping outside the mutually assumed boundaries of our marriage. I didn't want to go on lying to him, but I didn't know what would happen if I told him. I didn't want to give up control. I didn't want to be the bad guy. I didn't want to risk the truth if it meant he would leave me.

So I decided to try an ayahuasca retreat, where I planned to get myself sorted out once and for all. What was I going to do with my life? How was I going to address my restlessness *in a constructive manner*? These were the questions I intended to answer.

I realized during the first of the two ceremonies that I didn't want to take care of people anymore. I decided right then to close my practice and stop teaching yoga—ironically, the two things that made me feel the most like myself.

My excuse was that I was tired of taking care of others, which wasn't unfounded. But I think it was more than that. I knew if I quit seeing clients that it wouldn't matter if I wanted to have a martini on a weeknight and chase it with a glass or two of wine. I wouldn't have to worry about maintaining a clear energetic field. I'd be able to do whatever self-indulgent thing I felt like. Instead, I decided that I would restart the *Eat Like a Yogi* cookbook I'd begun when I was living in Berkeley.

And that was the extent of my personal epiphanies, because the rest of the time I was distracted by a woman, one of the first people I met when I arrived.

"Hi, I'm Jessa. You can call me Jess."

My field of vision narrowed to her long black curls and blue eyes like kyanite. Her raspy voice and waist to hip ratio reminded me of Scarlet Johansson, but that isn't what stopped my heart. It was something in the way she said her name as she shook my hand. There was a gentleness about her. Also a fire, and a mystery; she seemed like she had lived lifetimes. I knew we were going to be good friends.

People mostly kept to themselves—this was the unspoken retreat protocol—but I noticed her all weekend. It was impossible not to, because—it became increasingly apparent—she was there with two men: her husband, Bobby, plus her boyfriend. *Two men!*

I wondered about the function of each of them for her. I studied them from various corners of the room and took mental notes. I noticed how she alternated between engaging with each of them. The way her ass looked in a pair of Spandex covered with Tetris shapes. Also, that sometimes they all hung out together, including Bobby's girlfriend, who was also there. Four people, three relationships: wife-husband, wife-boyfriend, girlfriend-husband. I had never considered there could be such an apparent absence of animosity among people who shared love for the same woman and the same man.

The last morning of the retreat I asked Jessa if she wanted to go out together for a cigarette—I had noticed her smoking the first afternoon as I unpacked my car. She agreed and reached for her jacket.

"Okay, this is really tacky, but I don't have any cigarettes," I told her.

Smoking had been an occasional, off-and-on-but-mostly-off thing for me since I was in my twenties—usually only when I was sad. I smoked after my first divorce. I smoked when I lost my job in San Francisco. I smoked when Vox died. I always liked smoking, as much as I hated it.

"It's okay," she said warmly. "I'm happy to share."

We sat and talked and smoked, but one cigarette wasn't enough for us to clinch the friendship, or there was just too much to say. This would be the first of many chain-smoking sessions we would perform, dwelling in the space of contemplation. Dwelling on dwelling itself.

As we talked we discovered, among other things, that we had similar attachment wounds from childhood (this is my phrase for it now; at the time I would have described it as, "we were both kind of fucked up by our dads").

Also, I learned that we had the same reaction to the retreat guide. We both knew better but nonetheless found ourselves struggling not to want to seduce him. He was a crown jewel: an abundantly powerful, deeply grounded, deftly competent man who kept his demons behind him and radiated masculinity. And he was French. We both responded to his presence with a similar, embarrassing desire: corruption, seduction.

What that looked like in practice was going braless in my tanktop. Extended periods of stretching or "yoga" that revealed my very flexible hamstrings or the ribbon of skin between my shirt and yoga pants when I raised my arms. Contrived reasons to ask him a question. Hyperawareness of his presence and my movements around him.

What I really wanted was for him to see and validate me. I wanted to be important to him because he was a man I respected. And since sex was the best way I knew to get a man's attention, that was my default. I hated that I was this way, but I had no idea how to change it, and the fact that he was uncorruptible made me feel worthless and rejected. I was humiliated by my desire for his attention, by my need.

Jess and I instantly became our own fan club. Our first date after the retreat was a week later. We met at a playground to occupy our kids. She wore a tank top with no bra. Never a bra. I felt the same longing to touch her breasts as I did her ass in the Tetris Spandex she had on at the retreat. It made me ache a little in a way that felt shameful, because I had never been sexually attracted to a friend before. I didn't know how that might impact our friendship. I had never examined the notion that my sexual orientation was maybe more ambiguous than I always assumed, and I had no idea that I had internalized homophobia. So I held my secret close and kept my eyes lifted.

While the kids played, Jess and I delved into the highlights of our lives before each other—only the most interesting, heartbreaking, enduring stories at first. The canon would emerge over time.

The thing I was most curious about, at least initially, was how Jessa and Bobby opened up—how it started, how it was going, and how it all worked. Basically, I wanted to know…*everything*.

I asked Jess. "So how did you do it? Who brought it up?"

"Well, it kind of just happened one night when we had a threesome with a woman we knew…"

"What?! How did the threesome happen?"

Before I was curious. Now I was rapt.

"We came back from a night out. She wasn't sure if she wanted to drive home so I said she should stay. Bobby was still up so we had drinks and one thing just kind of led to another."

"And then what happened?!"

Jess laughed at my eagerness, but I was serious. How do you change the shape of a relationship just like that? What about when multiple relationships are involved?

"We started dating her, actually. It was really fun. And that led to more conversations between me and Bobby and we decided to try dating other people separately."

If I had a trained ear, I would have heard the subtlety in what she said: *Not all extramarital activity is created equal.*

There is the kind of nonmonogamy you do together—sex clubs, parties, group experiences, swinging. And then there is dating separately, without your spouse or partner. These are very different things with very different requirements in terms of the emotional ante. One is a friendly bet; the other is an all-in gamble.

But I didn't know about this yet, so I failed to pick up on the nuance. I have since learned. Going to a sex club together—to watch other couples, to fuck each other in a somewhat public environment, to feel the thrill of being propositioned—this likely seems quite radical to a couple that was formerly rather vanilla. It would have to me and Jack. But in the grand scheme of consensual nonmonogamy, a joint activity of this nature is relatively safe, like dipping your toe in to check the temperature of a swimming pool.

A threesome, or swinging when your primary partner is present—in other words, swapping partners—is a little scarier. Now there is another person—or other people—to account for. There are ways to mitigate the physical and emotional risks, however. For example, drawing a boundary at a soft swap, which typically means everything but penetrative sex. This is wading in the shallow end with your hair still dry.

Then there is dating separately: a cannonball into the deep end without swim lessons or a life jacket.

At each stage there is danger to consider, and also the potential and means of recovery if something goes awry. Jess and Bobby inadvertently did something very right in the way they opened their relationship. They started slowly and worked their way in. They learned how to swim before taking the plunge.

But I didn't hear the difference in what Jess had said. All of nonmonogamy, as far as I was concerned, was a vast unknown. I had no ability to differentiate between everything the term represents, and I had no clue how clueless I was. I figured since I knew a few terms and had a basic intellectual understanding of them, I was ready.

I thought back to my beginnings with Jack. The shape of our relationship had changed a lot in the time we'd been together—we were friends who became lovers who became parents who became married.

Between that and our age difference we were already an unconventional couple. Certainly, we could withstand another metamorphosis. I had basically already said it: if he was 80 and I was 55 and he didn't want to or couldn't, could I seek…relations…with someone else, somewhere else?

Did it matter if the time had come fifteen years early?

Did I know all along this was going to happen?

Probably.

Eventually, I rallied my courage. We were lying downstairs in the guest bedroom, post-coitus. *This is the moment*, I thought to myself. Despite all my previous pondering, I had no idea what I was going to say.

What came out was, "Can you believe we haven't had sex with anyone else for eight years?!"

Almost instantly I remembered Jack had been married to his late wife for more than 20 years, faithfully so.

"Er, I guess you probably can believe that," I stuttered, "being that you've been monogamous for much longer…"

He made light of my comment and said that yes, in fact, he could believe it.

Then, "Is there something more you want to say?"

"Well…"

I was looking at the ceiling. He was next to me, on his back, too. It was easier this way than looking him in the eyes.

"I was just thinking that at some point…I'm probably going to want to have sex with someone else," I said. "I mean, if we're married for another 20 years or something. At some point something will probably come up. You know what I mean?"

I did not tell him something already had come up, or that I was thinking about this as something I would like a lot sooner than 20 years down the road. I did not say these things, but Jack is a good listener, and he knew what I was afraid to say: I wanted to open our marriage. I was asking him for permission to have sex with other people.

I would like to tell you how he responded—what he said, what he looked like, feelings he expressed—but I don't remember. Or maybe he didn't say or reveal much at all; that wouldn't have been unusual. Jack was generally less inclined than I was to talk about or interrogate his feelings.

It's also possible I don't remember his reaction because I had pinned my hope of redeeming our marriage on the prospect of opening it. At the first indication he was agreeable, I might have stopped listening and concluded that was it, it was decided, we were in an open marriage.

Or maybe Jack responded with ambivalence, or even veiled enthusiasm, because he was as curious about nonmonogamy as I was? I really don't remember.

What I do remember is that we stayed in bed awhile longer that night, talking about the prospect of nonmonogamy impassively, almost hypothetically. And I remember the enormous relief I felt that Jack hadn't responded with any great concern. Maybe he would have if I'd said what I actually wanted, and why. Or maybe he was secretly relieved, too.

You might think a couple that is curious about dating other people would take their time and approach the concept slowly, with curiosity and care. Right? Well, we didn't do that.

Or, it might seem like a couple that is opening their relationship would seek counseling with a therapist who is trained in such matters, no?

We didn't do that, either.

A couple who is considering opening their relationship would of course insist on Real Communication about Hard Things—talking long into the wee hours about their desires, their fears, and what could happen if things don't go well—would they not? They probably should. But we didn't.

Because I was still avoiding the unthought known. If we talked about our desires and fears, if we aired the fullness of our thoughts and feelings, I didn't know how I could avoid admitting that I didn't feel any significant sexual chemistry with him and never really had. Also, I was eager to start dating.

We read some books, like *Mating in Captivity,* by Esther Perel, *The Ethical Slut*, by Dossie Easton and Janet Hardy, *Opening Up,* by Tristan Taormino. Well, actually, we bought the books (and hid them when the babysitter was coming). Jack might have read them all. I meant to, but ultimately I think I only read some of *Opening Up*, and all of *Mating*. I think that's the one I finished.

I can't remember, honestly. By the time I got this far in my quest, I didn't want to read. I wanted to have sex and I couldn't wait. I have since met couples who considered it *for years* before they opened up. For Jack and me it was a matter of weeks.

Before we took the final plunge and declared ourselves "open," we scheduled a date night to talk specifically about what our agreements would be. Basically, what were our rules? How were we to behave in this brave new world, without the assumed structure of monogamy to order things for us?

Our date was at a bar down the street from our house. It wasn't a bar we cared about, which was maybe why we chose it. We had no sentiment tied to the place. There was no chance of ruining one of our favorite spots if the conversation went sideways. Neither of us bothered to dress up much. It was date night, sure, but this was a working date.

We chose a spot at the far end of the bar, where we would have more privacy. We ordered martinis and joked about how this conversation required something strong. The drinks were set before us. We shared a toast—something about loving each other and great adventures. And then Jack announced he had something to say.

Jack is very low-key. It was unlike him to be this assertive, so I was a little taken aback by the emphasis in his voice. I listened closely. He wasted no time.

"If we are going to do this," he began, "then I want to have sex with a man. I know what it's like to have my dick sucked but I want to know what it's like to suck a dick."

It's possible my jaw dropped open, or that I grunted like a baboon, or that I fell off my barstool. Time folded back on itself. We had crossed a threshold.

17. Don't Wanna Fight

If you're the type of person who can learn from someone else's mistakes, here are some things to consider before you open your existing relationship:

1. Have you done your own personal work (developed self-awareness, healed past traumas, been to therapy or the like, etc.)?
2. Do you have a secure attachment style?
3. Do you have good interpersonal boundaries?
4. Are you good at communicating your needs?
5. Do you have excellent ongoing communication with your primary partner (without requiring a fight)?
6. Are you and your partner mutually interested in opening?
7. Are you and your partner in agreement about opening up as a way to enhance the bond between you?
8. Have you and your partner addressed any fundamental issues that exist in your relationship?
9. Have you and your partner communicated about what you are hoping to gain by opening your relationship?
10. Have you and your partner discussed and determined, hypothetically—without the specter of an imminent date with someone else—what your agreements and non-negotiables are relative to seeing other people?
11. Are you and your partner in agreement about what you will do if opening up doesn't go well for one or both of you?
12. Are you committed to the relationship for the long haul?

If the answer to any of these questions is 'no', you might consider addressing these issues *first*. (Jack and I would have failed at least half.)

18. Dirty Work

A few weeks after our date at the anonymous bar we headed off on a family vacation, making sure to pack our small library of nonmonogamy books to read poolside. I was not only celebrating the vacation, but the clarity I had gained about closing my reiki practice. The week before we flew out, I moved out of my office. It was a relief. I didn't realize until I stopped seeing clients how much pressure I had been putting on myself to be perfect for them. If I was going to be wading around in their energetic field during a reiki session, I thought I better be as close to perfect as I could be. Which didn't make me any "better," I just felt worse about myself. Especially as I was becoming so preoccupied by (and ashamed of) relationships outside my marriage.

I was celebrating something else, too, if only privately. The Musician was going to be performing that weekend near the resort where we were staying. I'm not sure why I didn't come right out and admit that I engineered the whole thing, that I had planned our vacation to coincide with their tour. I guess because I still hadn't realized: there is nothing more powerful than the truth.

Instead of coming out with it, I mentioned it obliquely to Jack as we were brushing our teeth the first night of the trip.

"I saw in the paper The Musician is playing this weekend," I said, turning on my electric toothbrush.

"This weekend, huh?"

I suspected this was Jack's shorthand for, "I don't believe this is a coincidence."

I talked around my toothbrush in reply, "I know. Isn't that crazy!"

This was my shorthand for, "Thank you for not making me admit that I did this on purpose."

We didn't talk about it again until the morning of the show as I was stirring scrambled eggs on the stovetop.

"Are you planning on going tonight?" Jack asked.

"Yeah, I'd like to, if you don't mind. It would be fun to see those guys."

The Musician and I had been sexting on and off for nearly two years by this point. I'd seen him at four or five shows during that time with only brief contact, because his wife had started joining him on tour. We ignored each other when she was around, but I liked that we shared a secret.

Jack was always cool with it when I wanted to go to one of his shows, which I appreciated. It was generous of him to give me that space, and he didn't seem too bothered. It never occurred to me he might not admit if his feelings were hurt because he never said anything of the sort. Actually, he seemed somewhat amused. I never considered that what I took for amusement might have been masked uneasiness, and I never asked how he felt about it. There is so much we avoided addressing; I see that now.

"Okay, that's fine. Ash and I will find something to do around here. Maybe I'll take him to the lazy river or something."

"Oh, okay! That sounds sweet, honey."

I tried to keep my voice still and calm, void of any inflection that would give away my excitement and nerves.

"Just be back by sunrise," he said, teasing.

"Haha. Well thank you!" I walked over and gave him a quick hug and kiss. "I promise I won't do anything you wouldn't do," I added.

"Ha! I don't believe you but have fun."

I wanted to jump and scream and celebrate. I'd been thinking about it for so long, and now I had a golden ticket to do the wrongest thing you can do as a married person, a point that I imagined absolved me of guilt for my prior transgressions.

But I didn't jump and scream. Instead, I slipped into our bedroom to text The Musician that I'd be at the show.

"Can't wait to see you later!"

His reply, "Yahoo! How many for the list?" didn't tell me what I needed to confirm.

"It's just me," I texted back. "And you…are you solo?"

"Yes." Then, "See you later!"

It was so on.

That afternoon I left Jack and Asher at the pool while I ran back to our room to use the restroom. When I sat down to pee, I was crestfallen. My monthly. I had been waiting all week for it to start—apart from when I was pregnant it had never been late. And now here it was, seven days past due.

This was a problem. Did you know there is such a thing as an Ultra tampon, which is a step up from Super Plus? They were made for periods like mine. I had definitely been planning on having as much sex as possible with The Musician. But I was imagining romance and candlelight, not a bed that looked like a murder scene when we were done. There was no way.

Maybe it's for the best, I figured. He was married, after all. Although I was certain I wasn't the only woman he was in touch with, so I didn't feel too bad about it. He'd never been monogamous, at least not since I'd known him. Anyway, isn't the cheater the one at fault? I wasn't sure. Or maybe it was more convenient to feign ignorance.

My vague justification was that I had pre-dated his wife. Meaning, I met him first. As if that meant anything more than chronology. Perhaps it should have been obvious to me by how thin my justification was that my pursuit was beyond justifying. But that would have been an inconvenient truth, because then I would have felt bad, and I wanted to feel good. The blame, I decided, remained squarely on him. After all, I'd gone to the trouble to secure a hall pass. I was free and clear.

After the show that night I was wandering backstage looking for a bathroom and found one in a back corner. When I opened the door to come out, there he was, looking at me with his head cocked. He pushed his way in like a tidal wave.

As soon as the door was closed, he started kissing me. In no time his hand was under my dress, though I could barely feel him since I was wearing a thick maxi pad, practically a diaper. I mentioned I had my period; he was unfazed.

We groped each other wildly, aimlessly, until sense got the better of me. There were people outside the door. What if his wife found out? It seemed like he should be more careful. Also, we were making out in a windowless bathroom with a musty mop bucket in the corner.

"Where are you staying?" I asked. "I'll come meet you later."

He gave me his room number. "Don't come before midnight."

We straightened ourselves and walked out like everything was fine-just-fine and merged with the crowd at the afterparty. I was happy to be there. The afterparties were almost always fun and full of interesting people, and I relished the anticipation of what was to come. An hour or so later, the party wrapped up and the band piled into the van. I made a point of saying goodbye, then got in my rental car and texted him, "See you soon!"

When I knocked on his hotel door, he let me in and went back to his phone.

"I'm just finishing up some things," he said, lying back on one of two queen beds.

"What are you working on?" I asked, sitting down on the bed next to his.

He didn't answer, just kept staring at his phone. A cloud of foreboding gathered within me as I remembered in the silence how cold he could be. But I was too affected—overwhelmed and excited—to acknowledge the shadow.

I looked around the room. His stuff was everywhere. A lamp was resting against a wall in the corner, a rock and roll cliché that made me wonder. How had it gotten that way? Why hadn't anyone stood it back up? It was hard for me to wrap my head around a lifestyle in which lamps were overturned and never set right.

From the outside the hotel had looked sort of quaint and charming but, now that I was looking more closely, I could see it was kind of gross. I wondered how old the mattresses were. For so long I'd been fantasizing about the next time we could be together. I had imagined the Four Seasons. This was definitely not that.

"Okay," he said when he finished working.

He set his phone on the nightstand and looked at me, waiting. I moved to where he was laying down.

"Hiiii…" I leaned in to kiss him. He ran his hand under my dress.

"Does your man know where you're at?"

"Yes, I told him I was going to see you. He told me to be home by sunrise."

The Musician raised his eyebrows. He didn't look like he believed me.

"We're in the process of opening our marriage," I added.

"Oh. What's that like?"

I talked for a minute about this and that, trying to sound like it was all mutual and well-considered, but he didn't seem to care much about my answer. I kept talking—rambling, really—because I was uncomfortable. Finally, I brought it to a point.

"It really stuck in my mind when you said a while ago that my desire is a gift."

When he'd said it via text months before, I was irritated. My desire, which I could only think of as *him*, felt more like a curse than a blessing. I didn't want to want him. But the more I'd thought about it, the more I decided he was right: desire is a gift. It reveals what you value and the experiences you long to have. Desire gives life shape and purpose. Without desire, there would be no pursuit.

My problem wasn't that I had a desire. It was that I was largely unaware of what was driving it. I didn't know what I didn't know.

The Musician nodded in a way, as if to affirm his belief in the statement, but he didn't engage any more than that. Until that moment it hadn't occurred to me that he wouldn't be happy to hear that Jack and I were opening up.

I hadn't considered that our arrangement of extramarital shenanigans only worked for him as long as I, too, had something to lose. If my husband already knew, who's to say I wouldn't expose him?

Or maybe it was less of a thrill for him since I had permission...maybe he got off on corrupting another man's wife? I admit I felt something of the same. Sure, his wife got to share with him in his big, exciting life. But he still wanted to fuck me. It made me feel powerful to corrupt a man of his stature. I'm embarrassed to admit that was ever a source of pride.

If I had listened to my heart instead of my will, I would have recognized in my discomfort a feeling that I was not only betraying his wife, but that I was betraying myself. If I had listened to my heart, I would have known I should say goodbye and head home. But my desire for validation was greater than the shame I felt about what I was doing, so I stayed. It wasn't the first time I ignored my better knowing at my own expense, and it wouldn't be the last.

The Musician started kissing me again. I kissed him back. Soon we were both naked, except for my underwear.

We rolled around and groped without meaning. I ended up straddling him, facing his bare feet. Things proceeded quickly: he pushed aside my lacy booty shorts with his fingers and used his thumb on me. I fingered my clit and came hard facing the expanse of the barren room, basically alone with my desperate gasps. The pleasure was short lived.

I moved to his side and kissed him tenderly. "I've waited so long for this," I whispered. I was hoping he would share the sentiment, that I would find some solid ground in mutual affirmation. Instead, he glanced at me and silently guided me down. After a few minutes he handed me a jar of Vaseline.

I started with one finger and he encouraged me on. I used a second finger and then a third. Within five minutes of my orgasm, my four fingers and thumb were covered in petroleum jelly and moving inside him.

I had never done anything like this before, had only vaguely heard of fisting. And it did nothing for me. I felt nothing.

Actually, I did feel something, and it was revulsion. Not about the act itself, but how empty it all was.

Still, I tried to make it good for him. I wanted him to want to see me again.

As time wore on, I deflated smaller and smaller. I didn't expect this was how the night would go, not at all. I had hoped I would feel a sense of deep connection with him, the way I did years before. But that night I felt like a nobody. None of what we did felt like we did it together, except maybe the cheating part.

Once I asked him to look at me. I thought it would connect us. I thought if we made eye contact, he might remember there was magic between us. He had told me in our texts he wished we had ended up together, and I believed him. I wanted him to see me and remember that feeling. Instead, he just opened his eyes and looked my direction, vacantly, then closed them again, like he didn't understand what I meant.

Finally, he got himself off. Finally, it was over.

I washed my hands and changed my tampon. I felt sick with emotion; he was matter of fact. When I got back to the shelter of my rental car, I attempted to reassemble myself using the rearview mirror and dome light; I did not look fresh or clean. I cried the entire forty-five-minute drive back to the resort, overwhelmed with disappointment and shame.

If I had known Jack would be awake when I got back—that there would be a power outage that caused the appliances in our condo to beep and wake him up, and that he'd be standing there resetting the clocks, naked and surprised, when I walked in the door—if I had known that I would have made more of an effort to clean the tears off my face. I would have reapplied my smeared lipstick.

I did my best to pull myself together in the awkward moments that followed, him explaining groggily about the power outage, me forcing a smile and blabbing about the after party as if that's where I'd been all night.

It didn't matter that I had Jack's permission to go. I was so humiliated…I could never have told him what happened. As we laid down to sleep, Jack leaned over and gave me a kiss.

"I'm glad you had fun, sweetie. And I'm glad you're home."

19. bad guy

Since I was so young when my mom left him, story is the principal way I got to know my dad. The earliest story I know about him vis-à-vis my own life is that he was annoyed when my mom went into labor with me on a Saturday night because he was tired and didn't feel like driving from Ellijay, our rural Georgia town, to the city hospital in Gainesville.

The next story in my chronology is of him punching a bedroom door while my mom held me, an infant, in her arms. She said he destroyed the door while I screamed.

There is another story of him burning down his trailer for insurance money. There are so many stories. But the worst I ever heard was when I was eleven and got caught in the crossfire of a fight between my brother, Alex, and my oldest sister, Ellen. Alex was trying to get my mom to let Mari and me go with him to Georgia to visit our dad that summer. Ellen forbade it. The fight got louder and louder, until it finally culminated in Ellen screaming at him:

"Because I don't want him doing to them what he did to me." The whole room was shocked into silence. My brother's girlfriend swooped in and took Mari and me outside. No one ever spoke of it again.

Since I only know these stories secondhand, and my dad never did anything *that* bad to me, I always had a hard time believing my feelings about him were justified. If he had done to me what I'd heard he'd done to Ellen, or if he had hit me or starved me or burned me with one of his cigarettes, or if I could remember more of what happened at the bathtub when I was five, I think it would have been easier to qualify his abuse and believe my feelings were valid. But since he didn't, and I couldn't, I spent my whole life reasoning that it wasn't that bad. It could've been so much worse.

It would have made sense if Ellen felt the way I did around him—small, overwhelmed, afraid—because she was a victim of what seemed like real child abuse.

But for the most part she remained his advocate and supporter, which confused me. If my dad was so bad, why did she even talk to him anymore? I didn't understand she was in the same denial I was. Neither of us wanted to admit our dad was an abuser. What would that mean about us?

Since I couldn't understand, and no one ever talked about it, I concluded it must be okay. Not for other people, but maybe in our family? I guess I deduced it was the family way: ignore it. Refuse to name it. Carry on like it didn't matter.

This must be how I learned to ignore the rumble of misgivings in my gut when something didn't feel right. Maybe this is how I learned to close my throat despite wanting to protest, how I learned to ignore my truth to protect someone else's feelings.

Could it be I also learned to distance myself from intimacy to avoid vulnerability? Seems right: I stayed in my head so I wouldn't have to feel. But even in my head I knew it wasn't normal. I knew I had a bad dad, and I felt ashamed. I suspected my bad dad had fucked me up at least a little, but I hoped I could compensate by acting normal. I was determined to pass as a normal girl.

For most of my childhood I only had to deal with my dad when he called, usually drunk. It weirded me out how my mom would act when she heard his voice. Her anger and frustration unnerved me. I knew I wasn't supposed to like him either, and I didn't, but I indulged him anyway each time he called and slurred his way through the same little dialogue he always said:

"You know what?" he'd ask me.
"What?" I was supposed to say.
"I love youuuuuu!"
Then I was supposed to say it back:
"You know what?"
"What?" he'd ask.
"I love you, tooooooo!"
"Aww, baby."

113

It was always the same thing. I acquiesced to his charade and then passed the phone to one of my siblings.

Apart from his phone calls, my contact with him was limited to the few times he sent Christmas gifts. They were always bizarre in some way, not quite right. One year he sent fake Cabbage Patch Dolls. Another he sent Mari and I matching argyle sweaters with arms that must have been three feet long and necks too tight to fit over our heads. His gifts always smelled like old cigarettes.

When I was twelve my dad reappeared in my life. By then he had gone through another divorce and was chasing some woman who lived in Oregon. As far as I know, that's the only reason he turned up in the Pacific Northwest.

From twelve to sixteen our visits with him were all the same.

"I was thinking we could do some clothes shopping," he'd say when he called. (Is there a better way to get a teenage girl to want to hang out with you than to offer to spend money on something important to her?)

"Come on," I'd say to Mari when he honked his horn from our driveway. There was no way I was going by myself.

After Mari and I got through the obligatory hug in the driveway—he always squeezed too hard—we'd climb into my dad's white pickup and drive to the Tacoma Mall, where we would wander into Gap or Natural Wonders, my two favorite stores. We'd have a budget of $20, or maybe $40 if the construction trade had been booming lately. Mari and I went to the dressing rooms alone.

"Model it for me," he'd call to our backs.

We'd pretend we didn't hear him, then crowd into a corner stall behind a locked door.

I was too young to parse the complexity of my feelings, at once happy for something new to wear but conflicted by what I had to do to get it, because I didn't want to spend time with my dad. But I felt obligated. I'd remind myself that he was it—I only had one dad—and continue going through the motions.

After all, I wanted the new sweater or shirt or whatever I could afford with the budget he'd given me. I was a teenager, trying to sort myself out and define who I wanted to be, and how I wanted to be perceived. Tangible expressions of self were vital.

Another reason I went with him: I pitied him. Occasionally I would consider something about him, like the way we have the same eyes and identical thumbs, or the way he could build or fix anything, and I'd feel a unique affinity and sometimes even a fondness. He was, after all, my dad.

After he took us to the mall we'd drive to Denny's, Shari's, or the local favorite, Cattin's. Their menus were nearly identical, and so were their waitresses, which is presumably why my dad took us there.

"Can I take your order?" Vicki or Sharon or Debbie would ask, poised with her notepad and straining a smile.

"Steak and eggs."

My dad always ordered the most substantial entrée on the menu. Sometimes he'd order two. Somehow, in spite of his voracious appetite—maybe because he labored all day—he remained trim.

Once Mari and I ordered our Shirley Temples and pasta or sandwich or whatever, my dad would have come up with some way to engage the waitress again. He might motion to her with his two thick fingers, gesturing for her to come closer. Or he'd leer and compliment some part of her body in a hushed tone, as if we couldn't hear him from the other side of the table and didn't know which curves he was referring to. I'd watch and wonder if she, too, felt disgusted by the cigarettes on his breath, booze in his pores, and wafting remains of cheap aftershave.

Sometimes it worked, and he'd leave with her phone number. If she rebuked him in any way, he'd turn on a dime.

"Bitch."

He said it with acid on his tongue.

This was how I got crystal clear on what seemed like one of life's most basic lessons as a girl: to be of value to the world—to the people that mattered, at least…to men—was to be sexually acquiescent.

If I wanted to be liked, if I wanted to be pleasing, if I wanted love and attention, then I better give him what he wanted. And that was, obviously, sex.

20. Into the Great Wide Open

My night with The Musician hadn't gone well, but that didn't dissuade me from wanting to start dating as soon as we got back from our trip. I was eager to have new experiences. Also, to blot out the terrible memory of that night.

I didn't want to join a dating site. I'd done it years before when I was single and remembered it was a lot of time and effort for little reward. Instead, I hoped I would meet people organically. Jack had gone ahead and joined a couple sites—one to meet men, one to meet men and women—because it was harder for guys, at least that was Bobby's opinion.

Bobby insisted that for every ten dates Jessa had, he had only one. I found that hard to believe, handsome as he was. Bobby was an All-American football player from Nebraska. He was well proportioned and muscular and had the sort of masculine vibe I thought must appeal to a lot of women, with brown, chin-length waves that suggested he might read poetry. If he had trouble on dating sites, I wondered how Jack would fare. Were there many women closer to his age willing to date nonmonogamously? (Were there many women of any age that wanted to date nonmonogamously?)

Jack signed up but remained low-key in his approach. He was in no rush. I, on the other hand, was actively looking for opportunities. So when Jack and I went to the movies and I ended up randomly sitting next to the director of the film my sister was in, I took it as a sign.

"Oh! Hi! Are you…? I'm Mari's sister, we met at your film premier. How are you?"

I introduced him to Jack and he introduced me to his wife. We chatted for a few minutes before the lights went down and I suggested we meet up for coffee. Knowing the little bit about him that I did, specifically that he had been polyamorous for some time and was a cool person, I figured he'd be a great person with whom to practice dating—he was intelligent, dynamic, and a skillful communicator.

I didn't know yet what I was looking for because I didn't know even the basics of nonmonogamy. For example, people generally identify one of two ways: they are either polyamorous (poly) or a swinger. These are broad categorizations that don't nearly capture the variety of nonmonogamous expressions, but it's helpful to know this basic difference.

Poly folks are open to or seeking multiple loves. They want some degree of emotional bond in multiple, simultaneous relationships.

Swingers are open to or seeking a variety of experiences. They want to have sex with different people without necessarily maintaining ongoing relationships. (Swinging also often refers to couples who swap partners...context is everything.)

The Filmmaker was poly. He had a wife and girlfriend with whom he split his time, literally living with one of them for half the week and the other for the remaining half. It had been that way for years. I asked what they did about Saturdays; he told me they took turns.

I went out with the Filmmaker several times, each date better than the one before. On our last date (though I didn't know it at the time), we went for a hike and had a picnic at the top. On the way home we stopped at a lake for a quick swim in our underwear. We kissed and held our bare torsos to one another, the first explicitly sanctioned contact I had with someone who wasn't my husband. It was a turn-on, and only the slightest bit threatening. I picked up Asher from preschool that afternoon with the sun-kissed glow of a secret known only to me, my date, and my husband.

There was one issue, however. The Filmmaker's girlfriend was not polyamorous. Neither was she a swinger. In fact, she was monogamous, a point I struggled to understand. My brain was still programmed with black and white binaries, and the fact that a monogamous person could happily date a nonmonogamous person was a mindbender.

The girlfriend wasn't keen on my arrival (I guess it was okay when she was the interloper?). I got spooked that getting more deeply involved would lead to someone's heartbreak and I ended the relationship, ineloquently, before we got past second base.

A month later, Jack and I were out to dinner for his birthday when an attractive man introduced himself as our waiter. We chatted with him as he came and went. He said he traveled a lot and shared a couple interesting anecdotes. Jack and I joked over dessert about me asking him out. So when Jack went to the bathroom and the waiter asked if there was anything else I needed, I said, "Yes please, I would like your phone number."

I told Jack what I had done when he got back and we laughed about it. It felt like a novelty, something the two of us were in on together. He didn't seem the least bit bothered.

The Waiter was a year younger than me. As I thought about this on the way home from our picnic date, I heard the question in my mind: *What would it be like to be with someone my own age?*

Instantly I heard, *I would feel like I had my whole life ahead of me.*

It was a startling realization. Riveting, really, the potential. It was the first time I had a felt sense of what I missed out on by marrying a man 25 years older than me.

The Waiter and I messaged about getting together again, but I was unmotivated. It was fun to go out with him. It was interesting to kiss someone new and tell my husband about it. But I must not have been that attracted to him, or he didn't trigger me in the right way.

For the most part, our summer was quiet. I still wasn't interested in online dating, and Jack wasn't seeing a lot of action. I was working diligently on *Eat Like a Yogi*, which I turned into a food blog within the first few weeks. Asher was home from preschool and just about to start kindergarten. I was glad to be home so I could be near him even while I was working on a new recipe or editing an interview.

In August, Jack went east for a reunion of radio people he had worked with decades before. While he was there, I knew he was likely to see an ex-girlfriend. I told him it was okay with me if he wanted to spend time with her. They went to dinner and he explained our arrangement. The way he told it when he got home, she seemed offended by the suggestion. She told him we were playing with fire.

"Nah. What does she know?" we said.

The next opportunity to make out with someone was unintended and unexpected. It was early November. I was at home, bored, on a Saturday night. I knew Bobby and Jessa were going to a costume party so I texted and asked her if I could meet them for a drink before they went to their party.

I burst out laughing when I saw him. The party theme was superheroes and Bobby was dressed in a bright green spandex bodysuit with a bunch of "R" accessories. He was the Riddler. Jessa was wearing a lacey bustier and had a question mark drawn on her face in eyeliner. She was The Question, a DC character I'd never heard of.

It wasn't until our drinks arrived that they told me it was a sex party they were going to hosted by an organization called Kinky Salon. I had (recently) heard of these parties. Jack and I even talked about wanting to go to one in Portland—I didn't know they were in Seattle, too. After our first drink, Bobby and Jessa asked if I wanted to join them. We wondered if I'd be able to get in.

"There's only one way to find out!" Bobby concluded.

I texted Jack that I was going to join Bobby and Jess at a party for a while. I didn't say what kind of party it was because I didn't want him to be concerned when I didn't even know if I could get in. It's possible I also wanted to spare myself a big talk in the middle of a fun night out. I knew Jack well enough to know it would be okay to tell him after the fact.

When we arrived at the party we explained to the guy at the front table, who was dressed like a priest, that I didn't have a ticket. He said it was okay. I handed him my money but he said not to worry about it. I didn't know I had become his mark.

The Priest went over the rules, explaining the layout of the space, how the bar worked (BYOB, but they hold your bottle/s for you behind the bar), what to do with soiled linens, etc. He mentioned there would be a drag show at 11:30PM and talked extensively about consent. Then he pulled back the heavy purple curtain.

Right away I saw, in one corner, a man tied to a cross, gasping every time he was flogged by his partner. A woman on a swing in another corner was being stuck by her partner's monstrosity—(ENORMOUS! I had never seen one so big)—every time he rocked her back and forth. It was a jarring transition from the world outside. I was enthralled. I had no idea whether it was polite to watch so I kept my eyes up and moving around the room, where I noticed many duos and trios and quads and more in various stages of…canoodling. Everyone, at least everyone who was still dressed, was in costume, except me.

I quickly realized that although I had nothing to put on, I could take off, which is exactly what I did. This left me wearing a black lace bra, a black thong, and a fuzzy, off-white jacket with a pair of black booties.

It was liberating. I felt unabashed walking around the party of strangers with my ass hanging out. No one seemed to mind—or notice, for that matter, not in a shaming way, at least—especially not The Priest, who I ended up kissing, if only because he looked so eager standing in front of me. After chatting and kissing for a few minutes he invited me into the Dungeon. It sounded like exactly the kind of adventure I'd been wanting to have, so I went.

The Dungeon was dark and pulsing with cheesy techno. To the right of the door was a set of shelves with buckets of condoms and lube and stacks of clean folded sheets. Baskets of dirty linens lined the wall underneath. Two dozen or so mattresses defined the remainder of the space.

It was astonishing—I had NO IDEA what the good people of the Emerald City were up to.

We found a spot in the back corner, passing lots of shapes and Bosch-like contortions on the way, which might sound skeevy and gross and weird, but it felt shameless and joyful and liberated. I had never given myself permission to explore with abandon the way the people around me seemed to be, and it was thrilling to step out of my comfort zone. It never occurred to me that for many people there it may have been a lifestyle—that the party was not vastly out of their norm like it was for me, that they were always so free with their sexuality.

If it had occurred to me I might have been inclined to think that anyone who lived "that way," who fucked "indiscriminately," who made a hobby out of kink, must have been traumatized, that something must have been a little wrong with them, that they maybe had questionable boundaries and morals. And the irony would have been lost on me. I was straddling two worlds and two belief systems yet completely lacking self-awareness.

We laid down on clean sheets in a corner where The Priest worked *very* hard at fingering me, which was particularly surreal given the clerical collar and heavy metal cross around his neck that kept grazing my face. Jessa pointed out later he was probably trying to get me to squirt. This didn't occur to me because I'd never done it. I just figured he was sort of clueless, which might also have been true.

Jack woke up when I got home. "How was it?" he asked, rolling to face me.

"It was okay…" I started to get undressed. "Did Asher go down alright?"

"Yeah, we had a good night. He ate a good dinner and then we played Hullabaloo and watched a Paw Patrol. Tell me about the party." I met his eyes, then looked away.

"Well, I wasn't even sure I'd be able to get in…"

"I'm sensing there's more to this story?"

I pulled my bathrobe on and sat down next to him. "Remember how we talked about going to one of those parties by Kinky Salon in Portland?"

He sat up, alarmed. "It was a sex party?"

Quick to try and assuage his anger, I explained my thinking—that I wasn't even sure when I'd texted him earlier that I could get in, I didn't want him to worry, I wasn't sure I'd stay even if I did get in. After several tense minutes of back and forth and lots of questions about what went down ("I made out with a guy a little"), we settled it. He had the last word, reiterating that he would have preferred to know. It wasn't a fight, but I felt bad for compromising his trust.

Knowing what I do now, I would handle it differently. I would sit myself down and instruct myself to lean into every single conversation I didn't want to have. I would advise myself to tell the *whole* truth, to overcommunicate until mutual comfort was a given, and to check in often with Jack. I would suggest questions like:

How are you feeling about things?

Is there anything you want to talk about?

How can we be better partners to one another while we're exploring this new frontier?

And I would insist that we not proceed until we were both comfortable with every development as it unfolded. It might have made no difference—once the train left the station it started gaining steam. But if I could do it over again, I would have tried to be better and, as soon as I was aware, to say the hard things. They were about to get harder.

21. Situation

Jack's first serious date was a cold night in the middle of December a few days before our fifth wedding anniversary. The things he told me in advance:

>He met his date online.
>His date was 27 and liked older men.
>They were going to meet for a drink to see if they clicked.
>His date was, for the first time in Jack's life, a man.

"Okay!" I said nervously as he was getting ready to leave. "Have, um, fun! Don't do anything I wouldn't do."

There wasn't enough this statement excluded.

I asked if they were going to have sex. Jack said it was probably just a meet and greet. After he left, I focused on Asher.

"Daddy's meeting a friend for dinner, honey."

I didn't bother with the protein-vegetable push at dinner time. If he wanted mac and cheese with tortilla chips and a plain hamburger bun, fine. I tried not to look at my phone while he ate dinner. I tried to rally my spirits after he finished by singing the bath time song we sang most nights.

"It's bath time, it's bath time, it's time to take a bath…"

Objectively speaking, I was glad for Jack that he was going to get to fulfill his curiosity, or at least he'd get to savor the potential. I was curious what would happen. I wondered what his date was like as a person. But I was also nervous.

Asher played in the water while I sat on the closed toilet seat, staring at my phone, scrolling Facebook while I waited for Jack's text.

"Mom," he said.

"Uh huh…"

"Mom," he said again. "Mom, look."

"Yes honey. Uh huh."

"Mom! You're not looking. Look!"

He had made himself a bubble beard, a trick we had laughed about often. It was less charming now. I was distracted. He tried it again. I did my best to muster a giggle.

After Asher was down, I busied myself making jewelry in the basement office. We were having a holiday art sale at our house that weekend. I already had more inventory than I had room to display, but I needed something to keep my hands and brain busy. When I wasn't messing with beads or pliers, I was on my phone again, swiping left or right or responding to messages on OKCupid, which I finally joined before I quite meant to.

Drafting an OKCupid profile, it turns out, means creating one. As in, the profile is live from the time you enter your email address and make up a screen name. There is no "Save and post when I'm good and ready," option, which is how my first peek around led to me creating an active profile, and shortly after that, a host of potential partners. It felt loaded with possibility. Swiping was intoxicating, and an absolute time suck.

A couple hours had passed since Jack left. I thought we had agreed he would check in. I texted him.

"Everything cool?"

"Yup," he replied. "He's cool. It's mellow."

Okay, so they weren't going to have sex. I was relieved. I didn't know it but I needed a little more time to get used to the idea of him being with someone else. Whether it mattered if the someone else was a man or woman, I couldn't honestly say. It probably bothered me more that it was man, because I was afraid Jack might decide he preferred being with men and I assumed that would mean he would leave me.

It's also possible I was bothered by Jack's date for less sympathetic reasons.

"I think you're homophobic," Dianne said when I brought up Jack's date in my session with her later that week.

"I don't think I am. I have gay friends. And I'm curious about women. We celebrate Pride every year!"

"I have gay clients who are homophobic, Minda. It's the environment we all grew up in."

She was right, though it would take me awhile to sort it out for myself. I didn't know yet that there is a difference between internalized and externalized homophobia, nor the ways each is toxic.

It's also possible I was unnerved by Jack's date with a man because I envied his liberation. I had long fantasized about a sexual experience with a woman but lacked the courage to realize it. Because: homophobia.

For all of these reasons I did not feel rational about Jack's date with a man. I wasn't proud of it. I was trying to be super chill and even. But I was unsettled. Which is why, for the moment, I was relieved. He said it was mellow.

Three hours later, my body hurt. I'd been alternately curled over my worktable or my cell phone for so long that I was getting tunnel vision. I needed to get up and stretch and breathe some fresh air. Jack had been gone nearly five hours. He hadn't messaged me since, "It's mellow."

I didn't feel mellow, but I was still trying hard to be cool. If it was midnight and I hadn't heard from him, I decided, I would text him that I was going to bed.

Minutes before the hour, my phone dinged. "On my way, see you soon."

Knowing I wouldn't be able to sleep, I waited up. When he got home, he came right downstairs. He stood in the doorway looking like I had never seen him, like he thought he might be in trouble. It didn't occur to me that what the moment called for was empathy, that Jack might need a safe space to land and process what he'd just experienced. I would like to have been able to receive him with such care, but I'm not sure he trusted me to. I'm not sure I was capable.

"Hi," I said.

"Hi," he replied automatically.

A lot was said in the silence that followed as his initial reticence turned impish. Clearly there had been sex.

"I guess we'll talk about this in the morning?"

He appeared relieved. "Okay. I'm going to get in the shower."

At the mention of a shower, I gripped the blunt-nosed pliers I was holding tighter. I wanted to shove them through the wall. I wanted to throw all the million tiny beads on my table at him and his stupid grin. I wanted to scream in his face like a hurricane, "What the fucking fuck?!"

I knew my impulse to anger was hypocritical and unfair. I had been out on a lot more dates than he had. I'd messed around with other people. I went to the sex party and only told him about it after the fact. Jack hadn't done anything wrong. He violated no agreement. I knew I had no right to be furious, but that did nothing to change it. Anyway, I wasn't actually furious. I was scared.

What would it mean if my husband was bisexual, or gay? It was such a huge unknown. It was true that I was curious about women, but I knew it was mere curiosity. I would never leave Jack for a woman.

Also, I had just seen a new side of him. It was deeply unsettling to realize I didn't know my husband as well as I thought I did.

Instead of addressing my feelings, I said quietly, "Okay. I'll shower upstairs."

We often showered together but given the circumstances I did not want to be naked with him.

When we got in bed it was quiet. He confirmed it was more than dinner but insisted he only took so long because he had to stop for a martini on his way home. And he didn't like the ambience at the first place, or he wasn't ready to come home yet, or something. He wasn't sure why but after the first martini he stopped at the bar next door and got another one. He was hammered.

We agreed as we turned out the lights that we'd take a walk the next day. We'd talk about it all then.

The next morning was clear and bright and cold enough we could see our breath as we walked Asher to school together, then set off with the dogs. It was almost officially winter and the trees were bare.

Our house was a couple blocks from a large park on the Puget Sound waterfront, which is where we decided to go that morning. I felt more robust than I had the night before—calm and composed and genuinely curious about Jack's date. My insecurity was, for the moment, tempered with optimism. As we eased into the conversation, I told myself this was all part of the adventure we were having together. I was glad to have a husband who was open minded and willing to pursue new experiences. And ideologically I believed this. But my heart wasn't in it.

The trail passed between a large stand of oak trees on one side and a steep cliff that dropped off into the water on the other. This is where I finally said, "Okay, spill it."

"What do you want to know?" he asked.

"Uh, everything?"

Jack described meeting at the guy's place.

I interrupted him. "Oh, so you didn't meet at a restaurant?"

"Oh, uh...no."

Turns out we were both having a hard time telling the whole truth.

(This would have been a good time to stop and ask ourselves why that was. Were we really sure we felt okay about what we were doing? Why then, the resistance to the truth?)

After cocktails, Jack said they smoked a little pot. They kissed, then moved to the bedroom. He got less specific as things progressed. I got the picture.

"And how was it?" I asked.

"I loved it!" he effused. "It was so hot!"

I stopped walking, the phrases echoing in my ears. *Loved it. So hot.*

In the half an hour it took us to finish the walk he used both phrases several more times. His enthusiasm was unnerving. I couldn't tell if it was about having a new partner, a new experience, or an experience with a man, specifically.

For days after his date I continued to ask him what it all meant, but it seemed he didn't know; he wouldn't or couldn't say. When his answers didn't satisfy me, I got more demanding.

"Are you gay? Bi? What?"

I didn't mean to hound him. I just needed to know what happened to my husband. He was different, like he'd discovered a secret world, and he seemed to be staking a new claim to his privacy. He didn't feel like mine anymore. And Jack had never been that excited about our sex life, never effusive, not remotely. Although, neither had I.

22. Don't Think Twice, It's Alright

A week after I joined OKCupid I was receiving more attention than I could manage, which I had heard was common for women. Within a week there were several men with whom I was corresponding, but one I was particularly excited about. I was extremely attracted to him, for one thing, and intrigued by his description of himself. I liked his messages. His intelligence was striking, and he had many cultivated interests. We made a lunch date for the plainest day of the plainest month, a Tuesday in January.

I found parking in front of the Seattle Art Museum, less than a block from the restaurant, which I decided must be a good omen. I was early for once. My date didn't seem like the kind of man that suffered flighty women showing up late for a first date. I'm not sure what about his messages gave me that impression, but he struck me as exacting.

I was nervous as could be but didn't bother with yoga breathing the way I did when I met Jack. Since Vox died, I had largely withdrawn from any spiritual practice. My interests in yoga had narrowed to the physical, to what it did for my body.

I was still in my car texting Jack that I was on my way to my date when a form fluttered in my peripheral vision. A white BMW convertible had been parked in front of my SUV. Its driver was moving between our vehicles toward the meter. My date. I gasped, hand to mouth, enthralled.

With shallow breath and my stomach rolling somersaults, I paid for my parking, said a quick prayer to the Universe of Gods and Whatever, and made the walk from my car to the restaurant door, where I knew he was waiting for me. I felt awkward for no reason as I walked in and saw him immediately, looking down at his phone. For reasons I didn't understand at the time, my steps toward him felt painfully self-conscious. When I stood before him at last, he looked up. I kissed him on the lips, startling myself. He was unfazed.

"I'm Viktor," his voice was warm and moderately accented.

"I'm Minda," I stammered, overcome. My attraction to him was overwhelming.

I followed the hostess to the table and imagined his eyes on my back. Did he notice my outfit, so intentionally curated?

I'd chosen a black cashmere turtleneck sweater, black stretch jeans, and black booties. My hair was in a top knot with barely a smear of makeup—mascara and colored gloss. I was striving for something prim and conservative, a sexy librarian. Or maybe a nerdy outcast that doesn't know she's pretty. I was imagining a contrast, setting up the moment, eventually, when I would let my hair down in a dramatic tumble, like a shampoo commercial.

I took the seat inside, a bench, and he sat across from me. I watched him over my menu as he perused his. He looked self-assured and effortless: button-down shirt, light jeans, and a weathered leather moto jacket that tied it all together—several shades of grey. His shoes were blue suede. All of it looked imported (Italy, not China). The silence between us was electrifying.

I noticed lots of other things about my date now that we were up close. His crown of black curls, graying at the temples just so. His eyes of true blue, not the kind to change colors depending on what he was wearing but a true, honest blue. His full lips framing the most beautiful straight, white teeth. He wore a sterling Star of David on a short chain around his neck. His skin was the color of sunlight at the magic hour.

Already I was idealizing him, making assumptions and projections based on little concrete knowledge, but I didn't realize it at the time. In my fantasy mind he was everything I ever wanted. I could tell we had chemistry in spades.

The server arrived at our table and we ordered our drinks and entrees. I chose a veggie roll, certain it wouldn't fill me but uncertain if my nerves would allow me to eat at all.

Viktor appeared to be as tall as he claimed in his profile, 190 cm, which made him taller than more than 98% of American men. He didn't seem like the sort of man to misrepresent himself. His profile also stated that he had genital herpes, which I thought was remarkably forthright.

When he removed his coat, I confirmed his broad shoulders and narrow waist—this was not an illusion in the cut of his jacket. His chest was muscular but not bulky, his limbs long and elegant.

He'd been with his employer for 25 years, which seemed remarkable given he was only 46 and had two advanced degrees. He told me he enjoyed his work. It was challenging and had a lot of flexibility, he said. For example, he'd gone in early that morning, knowing he'd be out for awhile in the middle of the day. He didn't have to get back until 3:30PM, he said, when he had a conference call, which he was planning to take from home. The hint was lost on me.

My date himself was an import: eastern Europe, by way of Canada. It was important that he was Canadian, because this created a bridge from the mysterious separateness of a country I was taught in grade school was my enemy, through the friendly fields of Canada, to my doorstep. No American was as interesting to me as an eastern European, or as intimidating. He moved to the US for graduate school—business and computer science—and was offered a job upon graduating. He'd lived in Seattle ever since.

From his looks to his intelligence to his life story—what I knew of it—I was dazzled.

Our food arrived. I did eat, but I did not taste. I was too preoccupied by my company. We talked easily, although I was reacting a great deal more than I was initiating. I didn't mind this. It was nice to let him take the wheel. This was not a common dynamic for me.

The server, recognizing people had to get back to work, brought our check before we finished eating. When our dishes were cleared Viktor set his credit card on the bill. He waved me off when I offered to split it. I thanked him and smiled.

He looked at me directly then, his hand still resting on the check. As perfectly as if he'd rehearsed it, he said, "I'm enjoying my time with you. I would like to continue our conversation. I live about fifteen minutes from here. If you'd like to join me, I'd love to host you at my house for the early afternoon. As I said, I have a couple hours before I have to join a conference call. If you're not comfortable, we can reschedule for another day."

I sputtered internally, wide-eyed.

My body, first to respond, was thrilled. "OH FUCK YES!"

My body was already out of the seat, snatching my purse in a sprint to the door.

My brain, not as quick on the draw, demurred. "It wouldn't be proper."

I was in my late thirties, which meant I had steeped in the sex negative culture of my country for nearly four decades and internalized the mixed messages—(though I doubt I have to remind you)—"'Purity' signals 'virtue'." "Women aren't supposed to like sex." "Sex is for his pleasure." "If you like sex you must be a slut."

My brain sat back in the seat, pulled my purse onto my lap, and crossed my arms over my chest.

My heart was the quietest and most withholding.

"What is going to happen if you do this?" she whispered.

I smiled and began, "Well—"

He interrupted me. "Take your time and think about it if you wish. Ask your husband if you must. I'll be right back."

He leaned forward halfway across the table for a kiss. I was sitting with my legs crossed, which made it awkward to reach him—I had to grab the sides of the table and lift myself to meet his lips. It was the subtlest of adjustments, but I felt bumbling and foolish.

I wasn't used to feeling so self-conscious and didn't understand it. I generally knew myself to be articulate, poised, and confident, but that's not the way I felt with Viktor. With Viktor I felt inexplicably unsure of myself, somewhat like…a child. I felt overwhelmed by his presence and a little wobbly.

Which isn't to say I didn't like it. On the contrary, the energy between us stirred something in me that left me yearning and eager to please.

I would never have imagined this degree of complexity was possible with a man I just met, but in hindsight, I can see how much was in play. As soon as I put my esteem in him, he became a man with the power to validate me. And then he had something I wanted even more than sex.

With him gone from the table, the decision was mine to make alone.

What I wanted to do was go to his house and spend every minute until 3:29PM being fucked senseless. I knew I would have to tell Jack, though, if I was going to go. I would have to get his permission. I knew without a doubt that going home with someone after a thirty-minute date for probable sex most definitely fell in the category of Ask First.

My desire was also clouded with uncertainty about the potential pleasure—would it make me a bad person? Was it wrong? All of my programming told me it was. What would it mean to share something with this stranger that I didn't have with my husband? Also, was I worthy—did I deserve to have an experience for the simple virtue that I wanted it? These were among the many thoughts obstructing a clean yes.

It seemed impossible an exchange could be so simple, and so mutual. Was it safe? Going with him felt so exciting it must be dangerous. But I felt safe. Viktor was experienced—he had been consensually nonmonogamous for years. He knew how to have a lover and what to do with one. Also, he was a father. He had a partner of several years. He wasn't just some guy. These were all points for the 'Yes' column.

I didn't think to talk any of this over with him because I was titillated by the unspoken, and nothing he said would have made the decision any easier. I knew exactly what I wanted—my belly had been rumbling with pointed lust since I saw him in front of my car. My conflict wasn't one of desire, it was one of morality.

Was I a bad person?

Was I a bad wife?

23. Stuck in a Moment You Can't Get Out Of

I was 21 years old, sitting in my university's Counseling Center, seeking help for my exceedingly stressful marriage to my increasingly controlling husband. I was at my wit's end. Nothing was changing. It was never getting any better.

A week before I turned up at the Counseling Center, Ethan and I had agreed not to swear at each other anymore when we fought. Three days after that we were installing the front door of the house we were building. I was standing outside, on the deck, and Ethan was inside, in the kitchen, yelling instructions around the doorframe. We had to shim it into place so the door would be perfectly level and even. I was trying to hold the heavy door very still when it slipped, pinching my fingers. I yanked my hand back.

"Fuck!"

"Hey!" he yelled.

"I'm sorry, I can't hold it like this."

Eyes welling, I looked at my fingers and shook my hand out. Three knuckles were skinned, already purple, and the one in the middle was pulsing blood. It hurt to bend them. My eyes welled up and I squeezed my three fingers with my other hand, willing the pain away as tears rolled down my cheeks.

"Is there somewhere you'd rather be?" Ethan asked tersely. "You know I could probably do this better without your help."

Trick question, but I caught on right away—there was no right answer. Regardless of what I said he was going to yell at me. I tiptoed forward. "No, I want to be helpful. I'm trying, I'm sorry, it just slipped."

I had to stifle the sob rising in my throat. My fingers hurt, but his lack of concern hurt more.

He continued to pester me. I tried to placate him, but he just got madder any time my tone sounded anything but acquiescent. I knew I couldn't win.

The argument culminated with him bellowing, "You know what, Minda? Fuck you! FUCK! YOU!"

This was why I was sitting in the counseling office that day, talking with a kind gentleman counselor, Al. I was hoping he would confirm for me that I wasn't crazy, that Ethan's behavior was out of line, or even that it constituted what it felt like: abuse. I doubted there was any solution to my troubled marriage other than divorce, but I didn't want to admit my failure. I had known it was a mistake to marry him in the first place, but I didn't know how to get out of it, and didn't know who I could turn to for help.

Al was bald on top, with long white hair on the sides pulled into a ponytail. He seemed like he probably used to be a hippie. I felt safe with him. Which is to say, I didn't feel like he was sexualizing me.

Al started the way therapists often do: "Tell me what brings you in."

Soon I was rehashing the argument, explaining the background of my relationship with Ethan. I'd been talking for ten minutes when Al surprised me.

"Do you want to be married?"

"What?"

"Do you still want to be married?"

I looked up for an answer, but nothing came.

Al continued. "If you don't know whether or not you want to be married, it doesn't mean anything for you to stay, does it?"

I looked left for someone else to answer for me. No one was there. I looked back to Al and bit the inside of my lip. My chin quivered.

Al grabbed a box of Kleenex and said, "Take this." I took it.

"Did it mean anything for you to take the box from me just now?" he asked.

I didn't know what he was getting at, so I didn't say anything.

"Let's try again." He motioned for me to hand him back the box.

"Minda, would you like a Kleenex?"

I had been crying off and on and my nose was running. I did want some Kleenex.

"Yes, please."

He handed me the box again.

"That's great," he said. Slowing down, he continued. "You wanted a Kleenex, so you acted on your own behalf. You made a choice for yourself. It's a different thing when you take the Kleenex I offered because you want it than it is for you to take the Kleenex because I told you to. Do you understand? If you take the Kleenex because I told you to, you haven't made a choice."

I nodded slowly.

"In other words, if you don't make a deliberate choice, your resulting action means nothing."

He let that sink in and continued.

"I will ask again, a different way. Do you want to stay married to Ethan? *Is that your choice?*"

There are so many choices I had assumed in my young life. Of course I would go to college. Of course I would get married and have children. Of course I would be like everyone else...I would be "normal."

There are many choices I had assumed in my adult life, as well. But once I began to reconsider monogamy, I began to reconsider them all:

Did I want to live in a city or a town?
What kind of job would please my soul?
What kind of car would it delight me to drive?
What kinds of people did I want to associate with?
How did I want to spend my free time?
Who did I want to have sex with?
Did the life I wanted require a lot of money, or would I be happier with less?
How did *I* feel about my body, regardless of cultural inputs?
What were the dreams I longed to fulfill?

Did I want to be married?

What did I want?

And how much of my life was a reflection of what I had learned women like me—white, affluent, liberal, educated—were supposed to think, believe, and value versus what I actually thought, believed, and valued?

What was my authentic yes?

Yes, I was beginning to learn, leads where life means for us to go.

Yes, one of the biggest words of all.

24. Take Me to Church

Thirty-five minutes after we had arrived at the restaurant I was sitting in my car, texting Jack. I told him my lunch date had gone well. I said I was going to maybe join my date at his house for a couple hours, if that was okay? Jack asked if we were going to have sex. I knew it was likely, almost certain. But I said that I didn't know. Radical honesty was still just a concept for me, not a practice.

Jack texted back, "I think you do know. Go ahead. Have fun!"

I told him I would be back around 4PM because my date had a conference call at 3:30PM, so I was certain I'd be on my way by then.

"Okay. Be careful!" he said.

At first glance his house looked like all the other houses in the neighborhood of large Craftsman homes lining a maze of cul-de-sacs on a hillside. I was surprised by the commonness of his taste, until I noticed the front door, large and heavy with a circular iron knocker in the middle, like a castle, or a dungeon. I knocked. The door swung open and there was Viktor, beaming in the doorway. He had changed into a brightly colored concert t-shirt and a pair of loose printed hippie pants in every shade of the rainbow, a sort of casual flamboyance.

As he invited me in, I noted several pairs of shoes near the door—women's and men's—and slipped mine off. Next to the shoes there was an imposing Steinway, colossally shiny, practically playing its own song. A sign on top, near the keys, requested people kindly keep their beverages off the piano. It was the first of many indications that they entertained frequently.

"I've played since I was a child," he said, gesturing to the piano. I was impressed but not surprised.

He expounded for a moment about his favorite composer (Rachmaninov) and the superiority of the piano concerto in the classical music genre (I had no opinion, except that I was not particularly keen on opera and preferred jazz). Wrapping his soliloquy, he asked if I would like a tour.

I let out a tiny gasp on first sight of the kitchen.

"We designed this ourselves. Marin did all of this," he said, gesturing to an ornately tiled wall behind an enormous bronze range.

He said his partner's name as if we were acquainted. I wondered about her. Was she an artist? A designer? What did she look like? How did they meet?

He poured us each a glass of wine, which we carried downstairs. He showed me an enormous dressing area filled floor to ceiling with costumes, coats, dresses, hats, and shoes, and said something about people fucking there when they hosted parties.

Around a corner we walked into the kitchen of an adjoining apartment. He had mentioned this space, which they called the Escape Room, when we talked about where we could meet, since I could never host with Jack and Asher at home. (This can be a challenge for nonmonogamous people—where does the sex happen if you're both partnered? If there are kids? If there is no money for hotels?)

Back upstairs, as if he had read my mind, he asked if I would like a robe to change into.

"Yes, please."

He disappeared into a room he never mentioned—I assumed it was their bedroom—and returned with a black velvet robe lined with red satin that featured a massive dragon on the back. He thrust it toward me in a bulky wad. I paused.

"Oh!" he said. "Allow me."

He held it open from the shoulders, inviting me to put it on as if he were offering my coat following dinner out. He thought I had paused because I was expecting courtesy, but no. I was standing frozen in time because I had a feeling my life was about to change.

For the first time in eight years, I was about to disrobe and have actual penis-in-vagina sex with someone new, a man who wasn't my husband. The robe was my invitation to undress.

I felt everything but calm.

I removed my sweater first, careful to turn my head so my chin didn't catch on the turtleneck. This was a trick I learned at a striptease class in my 20's at a girlfriend's bachelorette party. The instructor said to turn your head when you take off your shirt so it doesn't catch on your chin and make you look clumsy. I'd never forgotten it, just like the sex tips I read in Cosmo when I was young. I absorbed anything I thought would make me better in the way I valued most.

The sober silence as I finished undressing lent an intimate feeling, and I wondered what he was thinking. Did he like what he saw? I was relieved to step into the shelter of the robe and tied it snugly around my waist.

I hadn't paid much attention when I came in, but as I began to feel more comfortable, I saw a space I hadn't noticed yet. Across from the piano, behind the front door, was a large lavish lounge area that was overwhelmingly Red, the color I would come to know as his. There was a shaggy red rug in the center of the dark wood floor. The walls were a shade more deeply saturated than blood. Two low sofas on either side of the rug faced one another as if they were having a conversation in crimson velvet.

The room had been thoughtfully designed for socializing and sensualizing, an observation that moved me. Above one of the sofas there was a massive painting of colorful geometry. In two corners there were elaborate Moroccan lamps. The rest of the room was filled with the sorts of objects that could entertain you and a group of friends for a conversation or a weekend: unusual books and sculptures. Inlaid chests covered in silk scarves and several trays of candles in every height. The items spoke of open minds and travels beyond. It was enchanting.

"Do you like our chill space?" he asked jovially, searching his music to find something just right.

"I do."

I tried not to sound too eager. All of this seemed normal to him. It was decidedly not to me. Most of the furnishings Jack and I had acquired came from Crate and Barrel or the like...IKEA. The art we'd purchased together was limited to a few pieces. The imagination we'd put into furnishing our whole house would fit into the bathroom of this one.

Satisfied with his musical selection—something by Ruslan Dudaev, I learned later—Viktor and I sat down across from each other on the floor of the chill space. Through the thin fabric of his pants, I couldn't help but notice that he was not wearing underwear. Heat rose in my chest and cheeks.

He held up a bong and asked if I wanted to smoke. I did. This was a faster reprieve than wine. I welcomed any change that would make me feel less nervous and more strange, that would transport me from married motherhood and middle-age monotony to something unfamiliar and new. He passed me the bong to start but I declined.

"Go ahead," I told him. I knew if I didn't pace myself, I'd be too high to drive home.

He lit the bowl and passed it to me. I took the tiniest hit and passed it back. He took an enormous rip, coughed, and handed it back to me, smoke filling our bubble. I took a little more and coughed. He took one more and maybe another. I was still coughing. He set the bong to the side. The smoke cleared.

"Now come here so I can eat your pussy."

He said it so directly, without a trace of shyness or self-doubt, that I was completely disarmed. Thrilled by his command, my breath caught in my throat as we locked eyes. I couldn't believe what I was about to do.

I began to move toward him, but he stopped me.
"Wait!"

He disappeared briefly and returned with a furry scarlet blanket that he spread over the middle of the sofa where he wanted me to sit.

"So it's extra comfy," he said.

In the moment, his delight made him seem more boy than man. The contrast of his intelligence, worldliness, and giddy excitement charmed me completely.

I relocated myself on the legs of a fawn, unsure my next right move. I couldn't just sit down and spread my legs. It seemed indelicate, unfeminine. He made short work of my shyness, placing a hand on each knee and glancing up for visual consent. When he noted my rapt attention, he spread them wide, rubbing his hands down my inner thighs. I was still wearing underwear, at least. Not for long. Holding them at my hips he said, "I like these."

Thank god, I thought. I had avoided the disgrace of dreary underwear.

And then, like a surgeon conveying a procedure to his patient, "Now I am going to take them off."

I was exhilarated and the tiniest bit queasy as he pushed my knees back together so he could remove the last thing standing between me and my midlife, sexual re-liberation. I lifted my hips.

With an unobstructed view he looked at the broad daylight between my legs, which hovered somewhere between open and closed. He smiled and pushed my knees all the way apart. He leaned closer and blew cool air over me.

When I ran my fingers through his curls he looked up to meet my eyes. His expression was certain and playful. I smiled. Maintaining eye contact, he licked me with a wide tongue from bottom to top, then paused. He blew more cool air over my moistened parts and licked me again.

"The more spit I use, the wetter you'll get."

His movements ramped up gradually, gaining in intensity until he was gorging himself as if he were ending a fast. My inhibitions faded as his enthusiasm became more and more apparent. I had never been with a lover who seemed to take so much pleasure from going down on a woman…on me.

I had no worry of taking too long to orgasm, no concern he didn't like the way I looked or smelled or tasted, no sense that I wanted something he didn't really want to give. Without these things, I could drop in and let go. After a few minutes he paused for me to come. As soon as I could tolerate more sensation, he was moving in me again—his tongue and lips, his nose and chin, his rolling fist, his whole face. It was humbling and it was glorious. He made me small and darling. I would do anything.

He rose to his knees and ordered: "Get on your back."

The sounds he made when he spoke, his vaguely unusual choice and placement of words, his foreign accent—I couldn't get enough. He motioned toward the rug.

I stood up from the sofa and he transferred the blanket to the floor to make a nest for us. He found three pillows and stacked them intentionally. All of my senses were awake—watching, listening, tasting, smelling, feeling, memorizing.

I paused for a breath and a sip of wine to wet my cottonmouth. The music was electronic, pulsing.

He said it again, "Get on your back."

"One more sip," I said of my wine, testing, challenging him with my smile to make me.

"Get on your back, bitch!"

Startled, I complied. And for another hour Viktor had his way. He opened my body to his world and dimensions beyond it. He raced with me to the furthest edge and capably walked me back.

I wasn't used to a partner with such confidence and skill, and I don't mean my husband. I mean ever. In his hands, under his weight, straddling his hips, I felt a part of me called into being. I had never felt more fully alive. With his mouth, hands, cock, skin, and heart, Viktor made me into something new. I became a woman whose desire had been fulfilled.

The only interruption was when I realized I should set an alarm—Jack was at home and I would need time to shower before I went back.

When I told him I needed to grab my phone he said, "Let me do it," and he did. We resumed.

We were paused and breathing heavily when the alarm went off. My head and hand were on his chest. I had come so many times that I lost count. I was exhausted and sore and rapturous.

As we rose and reorganized ourselves, profound uneasiness set in. I felt queasy again. It was maybe post-coital tristesse, or sub drop—the feelings of sadness and anxiety that can accompany an endorphin crash after an intense sexual experience—but I didn't know about those things yet. I only knew I felt vacant and disoriented and something akin to grief.

Minutes earlier I was roaming an enchanted garden of delights. Now the room just looked alien. I craved the comfort of my home. I wanted the reassurance of my husband.

I started to feel panicked but tried to breathe through it: this was not a man who was going to talk with me about my feelings. That is not what we were doing there.

After a quick shower, I dressed quickly. He had located my bra and underwear and set them on top of the pile I'd left two hours earlier. It reminded me that this was not an isolated incident for him. He knew what to do next. I had no idea.

We were both acting with efficiency that bordered on abruption. I wanted to get out the door as fast as possible, lest I overstay my welcome. I didn't know how I felt, on balance, or how Jack would feel about what I had done. The thought of my husband made me unsteady as I pulled the fitted collar of my sweater over my head. I didn't want to face him, but longed for the comfort of him.

I turned to Viktor. We hugged and thanked each other for the time. I had no idea what he was thinking, much less feeling, or if I would see him again. We hugged once more, said goodbye, and he closed the door behind me. I walked to my car and got in, closed the door. I was back on home turf. The reality of it was crushing.

"Holy fuck," I said to the air. "Holy fucking shit."

I had learned in high school science class that for every action, there is an equal and opposite reaction. Was it a worthy trade—soaring, interstellar flight for the pit of ashes now gathering in my stomach? I couldn't say.

I buckled my seatbelt and pushed the button to start the car. And then I made a startling, dreadful realization: I absolutely could not drive.

I reconsidered the route to his house—there were so many twists and turns from the highway. There was no way I could navigate home, not even with Google telling me where to go. I couldn't conceive of it. I couldn't even say with confidence that I could follow the steps to get my car out of his driveway and re-parked across the street.

I'm drunk, I thought. *Or stoned?* But I hadn't even finished one glass of wine, and I was very sparing with how much I smoked, for this reason, and that was two hours ago. Nonetheless, I clearly could not drive. My executive function was offline. My endorphins were exhausted. I had exceeded the capacity of my machine. I was Humpty Dumpty.

I glanced at the time: it was 3:26PM. There was no way I was going back to Viktor's door, to interrupt him from his work to tell him I couldn't drive home. What was I going to do—take a Lyft? Home was 15 miles away.

There was no way I was going back to his door.

I tried again, gripping the wheel at the 10 and the 2. I put my foot on the brake and the car revved. That wasn't right. I looked at the gearshift; it was in "N." I couldn't even think what "N" meant. I'd been made stupid.

And this is how I came to learn what the phrase means: mind-blowing sex. It always sounded so good. I had never considered there might be a downside.

For every action, an equal and opposite reaction.

I took the Lyft. I texted Jack on the way to tell him that I had to leave the car. He asked if I was okay.

"I'm fine," I texted, which was all I could manage in the moment.

He asked how it was. I didn't bother censoring myself.

"It was like international hyperfucking with an almost computer."

It didn't occur to me how Jack would feel about it. Nothing occurred to me. My mind, and the rest of me, was blown.

25. Panorama

There are so many reasons you might pursue an open relationship or decide to date nonmonogamously. Here are a few:

1. It's exciting.
2. It's fun.
3. To accommodate mismatched sex drives.
4. You don't live in the same city or region as your primary partner.
5. The two of you keep different schedules.
6. You want to learn tips and tricks you can bring back to your partner.
7. You want to do things in bed that they don't.
8. You feel stuck and want to shake things up.
9. Sleeping with someone else may inspire new affection/appreciation for your existing partnership.
10. You identify with the ideals of nonmonogamy.
11. You feel unfulfilled sexually with your current partner.
12. Your partner is unable to perform sexually.
13. You're curious what it's like to have multiple lovers at a time.
14. Your partner says they no longer desire a physical relationship for whatever reason.
15. You want to experience someone else's body.
16. Relationships of all kinds are a great way to learn about yourself.
17. You are bisexual or bi-curious and want a same/opposite sex partner.
18. You crave closeness with multiple people, perhaps simultaneously.
19. You lack experience sexually and want to broaden your horizons.
20. You and your partner lack the polarity needed to balance your exchanges (both submissive or both dominant).
21. You want to experience the energy of a new lover to reinvigorate other areas of your life.
22. Your partner's partner/s might add friendship or affection to your life.
23. Variety!

24. Someone you've always pined for has become sexually available to you.
25. You want to claim sexual agency for yourself.

26. Come Back

A few weeks after my first date with Viktor, Jack and I booked a room for my birthday at a fancy hotel an hour from our house. Asher was staying with my mom while we went wine tasting and out to dinner. And we'd left plenty of time for what I hoped would be lots of epic fucking.

I'd had two dates with Viktor by then. The second was similar to the first—an afternoon at his house between conference calls. Except on our second date he had an orgasm, then held me close to him, and still, for the longest time. It felt profound, like there was something unspoken emerging between us. In those moments, being held, I felt absolved of all suffering. I didn't want to be anywhere else ever again.

Viktor had mentioned that afternoon that he was "borderline Asperger's." Among the common characteristics of some neurodivergent folks that also described him: profound intelligence, demonstrating little to no empathy, particular area/s of interest, and unusual capacity to focus intensely on one thing. These, and others, described him to a T. The one criterion he didn't meet was an inability to maintain relationships over a period of time. That, he explained, he was good at, and it seemed true. He and Marin had been together five years, and he had friends and lovers he'd been close with for even longer.

In the same way a person who loves an instrument might practice for hours to become very skilled, Viktor had trained himself to be an exemplary lover. Not only had he mastered what to do and how to do it, but he was remarkably good at controlling the energy of the space. In every other aspect of his life, his lack of empathy was evident. But in the bedroom, he was incredibly sensitive and aware.

Eventually I would ask him how he got so good at sex.

"People tend to be good at what they love."

Pressed to explain the way Viktor affected me, I might have supposed it was his skillfulness, or his fascinating mind. The other explanation I might have given for what was quickly becoming a borderline obsession with Viktor—his sex, at least—was that mystical alchemy I was determined to call forth with Jack. Chemistry.

This was precisely my goal when we scheduled our hotel date, to cultivate wild attraction. To that end, we'd brought a vast supply of equipment that we hoped would help us to expand our repertoire and stimulate some hot, dirty passion: a pre-rolled joint, bubble bath, massage oil, a bottle of wine, lube, sexy snacks (grapes, chocolate, raspberries), nipple clamps, a vibrator, a paddle, a dildo, and a strap-on harness. I kind of hoped it didn't come to that because pegging was not especially my favorite thing to do. But if it was requested, I would oblige. Jack and I considered ourselves GGG—Good, Giving, and Game. It only seemed fair that I should offer tit for tat.

We checked in at 3PM. Our dinner reservations weren't until 7, which gave us plenty of time to fuck first. Why do people wait to have sex until after they've gone out to eat, when they're full, maybe a little drunk, and likely bloated? If your intention is to get laid, fuck first—a bit of wisdom that, like the phrase GGG, we gleaned from listening to sex columnist Dan Savage's *Savage Love* podcasts on road trips while Asher was asleep in his car seat (well before he ever parroted the word fuck).

We smoked a little pot and got in the bath. We talked comfortably and rubbed each other's feet. After a while the water had cooled and the bubbles all burst, so we got out and dried our bodies. Jack turned on the fireplace and laid down on the king bed. I returned to the bathroom and put on a black lace bodysuit I bought for the occasion (while thinking about Viktor) and a pair of black heels.

It was rare that I dressed up like this for Jack. Lingerie felt contrived with him—I didn't know how to wear it without feeling self-conscious. But I loved the notion of wearing something specifically to create a feeling of sensuality and sumptuousness. It made me feel beautiful, luxuriant, and sexy.

I imagined as I was dressing that I was showing up to a lover's house, instead of my husband in the next room. It was easier to try and relate in a new way if I imagined we were different people.

I returned to Jack in the bed and told him I wanted to give him a massage, which he was happy to oblige. I warmed the oils in my hands and took my time. When I finished, I asked him to roll over. In a moment he was nice and hard. I got on top. I was dry from the pot, so I spit in my hand and wiped it over my twat in one quick motion.

The sex was pleasant and more lavish than usual. Each of us took more time with the other's body than we normally did. We fingered and grinded and licked and sucked and I said filthy things and tried to make it good.

But honestly? It was an effort. There was no flow. This was not how we related.

Jack rolled me on my back and fucked me with my legs over my head, holding both ankles with one hand so he could use the other to squeeze my nipple. I watched him with passive attention, looking for a way in, a way to connect. His actions were pleasing but we weren't moving together. We were two people trying to please one another. We were acting.

Within a few minutes I started to notice he wasn't really with me anymore. His attention had waned; his awareness was gone. He seemed not that into it. I tried to resist the conclusion that it meant something larger—that he wasn't into me, that I had done something to turn him off, that he preferred a male partner, that he was avoiding deeper intimacy. These were all reasons I guessed, because I couldn't understand. I didn't understand where he went, or why.

I tried to make it sexy when I whispered to him, "Come back to me."

"I know—I just got in my head, didn't I?"

It wasn't the first time something like this had happened. A few months earlier Jack and I were both home one afternoon with about an hour before Asher needed to be picked up from kindergarten. We hopped into bed.

Jack came before I did, right about the time I was fully warmed up, which meant I was still plenty horny. I wanted to be close with him. I wanted to have an orgasm. But I sensed his attention waning, which presented a dilemma. I could get up and carry on with my day as if I was satisfied, but that sounded frustrating, and I knew I would feel resentful. I could wait until he got in the shower and then finish myself off with my vibrator in secret before joining him...that's what I usually did.

(Why in secret? Because shame. I felt ashamed I wanted that pleasure. I worried my sex drive was too high. I didn't feel deserving of my husband devoting his time just for me to get off. And I didn't want him to do it because I asked; I wanted him to want to.)

The third option was to speak up for my desire. Dianne had been encouraging me recently to allow myself to be vulnerable, and I knew this was exactly the kind of thing she was talking about.

"Unless we practice vulnerability," she had said, "we become hardened. Where we lack vulnerability, we can't be known."

I didn't want to become hardened. And I wanted to be known by Jack, just as I wanted to know all of him. I knew I had to risk being vulnerable if I wanted to foster a more intimate connection between us, but I didn't know what to say. I gathered my courage and ignored my embarrassment at the transactional nature of my request:

"Will you suck on my nipples while I masturbate?"

Without missing a beat, Jack agreed and tucked in next to me as I reached for my vibrator. He kissed my left breast and licked my nipple a little. He pinched my right nipple with his left hand. It was exactly what I needed. As I started to approach orgasm, I turned to kiss him.

He was staring at the ceiling.

My desire vanished like a popped balloon. Instantly, I felt devastated, exposed, and foolish. I got out of bed and grabbed my robe.

Jack said something apologetic, but I couldn't hear it through my embarrassment. I tried to stuff it down in the shower and left early to get Asher, but I couldn't stop thinking about it. I felt ditched. I felt ridiculous. I had opened myself to him and he seemed barely interested.

I wondered if it was that thing they say about men after orgasm, that their brain goes stupid for a period of time. Then I wondered if that wasn't just a bunch of bullshit made up by the very same men who always came first and then rolled over and fell asleep.

If I wanted things to change then I had to address the problem. So for the second time that day, I leaned into my vulnerability. I went right to him when I got home—he was sunning himself on the back deck—and told him how I felt.

"Abandoned. I felt intimately abandoned."

I was relieved by the ability to articulate my experience, even if the word sounded cliché. I hoped that by putting my finger on my felt experience he would understand, and if he understood we could address it. We'd find a way to solve it.

Again, Jack apologized sincerely. Again, I asked him to explain. But he couldn't tell me what happened for him in that moment, nor others like it. He didn't know where his attention wandered off to, or why, at least he said he didn't. Or maybe he just didn't want to tell me the truth. Maybe he was afraid he'd hurt my feelings.

Back in the hotel room, deflating rapidly, I said it again, "Just come back, baby. You can fuck my ass, or I'll fuck yours…" I thought sex was the problem, so I suggested sex as the solution.

When he didn't engage, I patted the bed next to me—"Come here…"—and tried to reassure him. I touched him lovingly and kissed his shoulder and chest. I didn't want him to feel discouraged, and thought maybe if I touched him the right way we could get something going again. I could feel him blaming himself. I told him it was okay, not to worry, we'd have fun working on it. And I meant it. I wanted to mean it.

Inside I was despairing. I didn't know how we could be different with each other. I didn't understand why an incredible sexual connection didn't flow naturally from our sincere love. And I didn't understand why he wouldn't tell me what the problem was. Was he withholding, or unknowing? Or was he avoiding his own unthought known.

27. I Just Want the Girl in the Blue Dress to Keep On Dancing

Four girlfriends were out to dinner, laughing about life, when one of them disclosed that she had recently started dating a woman.

"What?!" the others exclaimed. "Why?!"

"Because I'm gay!" she said boldly.

This was news to the others, who had long known her to like BBM—big black men.

"What?! Have you, like, actually had sex with a woman?" They twittered with a mix of surprise and interest (and in at least one girl's case, envy).

"Yes!" she said with an eyeroll, waiting for them to catch up.

The surrounding girlfriends said things like, "Oh really!" and, "Oh, wow!" and, "But wasn't it weird to eat pussy for the first time?"

To this she replied, "Wasn't it weird the first time you sucked a dick?"

She had a point. I never forgot this conversation, because it was the first time it occurred to me that it might be possible for me, too.

When Jack and I opened our marriage, it was the first time in my life that my lifestyle didn't match social norms. I had always felt like a free spirit on the inside. I was drawn to art and expression and sought freedom as one of my highest values. But when it came to my personal life, I gravitated to safety. I stuck to vanilla. I insulated myself with heterosexuals and let everyone believe that was me, regardless of the mild dissonance I felt as a result.

This should have been all the evidence I needed that I had internalized homophobia. If I was "cool with gay people," which I genuinely thought I was, then why would it have felt so shameful to admit that I was bi-curious? What bad thing did I imagine would happen if I expressed my curiosity?

I was afraid I would be shunned. Female friends would think I wanted to have sex with them. Men would fetishize my attraction to women. The silent majority would think I was different from them…not "normal." I may have grown older but on some level I was still the same adolescent, striving to pass.

So I never let those thoughts leak from my fantasies into the light of examination. I figured it was an urge that would remain unexplored, because I was too ashamed by it. I think I believed that my attraction to women was not a matter of sexual orientation but a result of my hypersexuality. Naturally it followed that once I got myself tamped down, set quietly back in the box, it would go away.

It's very possible I still have some things to unpack here. But what I realize now that I didn't know then is how a grown adult can still feel uncertain about their sexuality, and how they want to express it. And many of us, locked into stable relationships, will continue to exist and wonder without ever doing anything about it.

Maybe that's okay with you; there are all kinds of things people wonder about and never act on.

Or maybe, like Jack, you'll decide to answer the call of your sacred desire and take the initiative to explore.

Or maybe you'll get lucky, like I did, and an opportunity will land, quite literally, in your lap.

When we met spontaneously to go bowling on a Sunday afternoon in late January, a week after my birthday, none of us had the slightest inkling where the night was headed. It was me & Jack, Jess & Bobby, and our kids—their two and our one.

We decided after bowling to go back to our house and order Thai food, stopping on the way for the beer and wine we'd drink after the first round of cocktails. We arrived home, fed the kids, ate the Thai food, and had some more drinks. Suddenly it was nearly 11PM. None of us was sober. We discussed our options and decided they should spend the night.

Once we got the kids settled into their improvised beds, Jessa and I rejoined the men, who were mixing another round in the kitchen. We talked about online dating. We laughed about online dating. We turned up the music. Soon Jess and I were interpretive dancing on the kitchen floor while the men stood talking at the other end of the room. We were more stupid than sultry, more sloppy than skillful, but we were having fun, slowly working our way around the corner into the dining room.

Jess crawled toward me like Baby in the Lover Boy scene of Dirty Dancing. I laughed. She looked feral and feline in her indigo sweater. No bra, which was typical, and always drove me crazy because it made me want to touch her.

Before I saw it coming she went for my face, locking her lips on mine, pushing me to the floor with one hand on my sternum, moving to straddle me as she did. It was not unwelcome, but it was a surprise. Before it fully registered in my mind, we were making out, the men still laughing and talking in the kitchen.

The first thing I reached for, finally: her breasts. The second my hands formed to her shape I felt quenched and softened. Desire rolled through my body like a thunderclap.

She yanked my jeans open and pulled them off. She did the same with my shirt, over my head. When she removed my underwire bra she told me to never ever wear that awful thing again. I felt a little small at this, that I did something wrong. That I was a bad woman for confining what was perhaps most explicitly female about my body.

But I was encouraged, too. With her declaration it felt possible all at once to release the whole of me from confinement: the adult woman in the midst of a sexual awakening, the new mom who was tired and afraid to admit something vital was missing, the bereaved mother devastated by loss, the young co-ed who longed to know what this would be like, the little girl who learned too early how to please. All of these women lived inside me.

Within a few years of graduating from college, I noticed I felt a pang of jealousy about women who experimented or had sex with women during their college years. My own college years were spent with Ethan, enduring his control and abuse. He might have divorced me right then if he knew about the crush I had on the girl that sat in front of me in my *Sex and Society* class, with her pale blue eyes, small tits, dancer's frame, and translucent white blouse over worn old Levi's. I didn't understand what I felt about her, but he might have.

I didn't go to parties in college; instead we spent every weekend laboring on the house we were building eight miles away. It was his dream, and he was never nice about it. All of my college graduation money went to buy windows and plumbing fixtures.

My envy of the sexually liberated co-eds I heard about and read about and probably even knew had little to do with sorrow about my own sad college years, however. Instead, my disappointment was rooted in the belief that I had missed out on a free pass, a rite of passage, when sexual mores are expected to be tried and tested and experimentation is what you do. It seemed like it would have been easier to suggest to a girlfriend in drunk college that I wanted to be naked with her than it would be to tell a milfy PTA mom about my latent curiosity. It seemed easier to find someone to do it with then—when everyone is young, curious, horny, and single—than to try and convince an exhausted middle-aged lady that her curiosity was valid and no harm would come from it.

By middle age you know, or at least suspect, that harm can happen accidentally, and there is much more at stake. I never imagined the other women at school pickup or in the grocery checkout or sipping their coffee one table over might feel the same way I did. I never considered that every single person experiences their sexuality in their own unique way, or that most of us have questions and curiosities and things we'd like to try, however buried these thoughts may be. So I never approached a lady friend. My curiosity remained curled and sleeping like a dog in its bed, waiting for the keys in the door.

It's not that I never, ever indulged my curiosity. When I was in second grade, I developed an elaborate kissing game with a girlfriend, one of my classmates, that involved kissing through a pad of gauze. The rule was that we kissed. Apart from the feel of clammy cotton and the first spark of heat between my legs, that's all I remember about it.

(Incidentally, this was the first thing that friend—whom I had long since lost touch with—said to me when I saw her at our ten-year high school reunion: "Remember when we played that game hahaha at your house hahaha and humped with a rolled up towel between us hahahahahahah…?" She had four kids by then, with a man. I had forgotten all about the towel.)

I also touched my friend Andie's breasts over her sweater once when I was in ninth grade. I was straddling her. She had played with women before—or girls, they must have been. It felt like an initiation. But before my hands breached the acrylic hemline of her sweater, my sister came home. We stopped and ordered a pizza. I never forgot how touching her made me ache.

That girl, Andie, was bad news. My mom knew it and tried to warn me against her. In the spring that year, when our friendship broke up over a boy, she wrote on the blackboard of my Algebra class that I was a dyke. I knew nothing about "dykes," but the way it was written in stark white chalk and block letters made me know it was something to be kept secret. I was mortified, certain I'd be wearing a scarlet letter for the remainder of junior high over this thing I didn't understand and lacked my own permission to explore.

Jess stuck her fingers inside me and stroked me with a soft rhythm. I felt overwhelmed with desire. I imagined as she kissed me doing to her the things I had fantasized about someone doing to me. I moved my hips in invitation, scared to make too much noise. Our kids were asleep; our husbands still talking in the kitchen. Did they know what we were up to? I didn't know.

When the men appeared from around the corner, drunk and amused, they asked if we would be happier in a bed. We reluctantly agreed, although I didn't really want to move. I didn't want to change anything except the feeling in my body, which I wanted to turn up past eleven. I wanted the feeling between my legs and at the end of my tits to be magnified until I transcended the boundaries of flesh. It felt possible. I was not sober.

I floated to my feet and swayed toward our bedroom, where we climbed on top of our king bed, the four of us. It was quickly determined by someone else that I would be the center of attention.

This wasn't how I fantasied a threesome, or foursome. I imagined less focused attention and more bodies moving all together in various acts of depravity and pleasure. This was far from a complaint, merely a revelation. It was my first lesson in how these things can work, how they do. It was my first time with a woman, and my first experience of group sex.

"Minda's the rockstar," Bobby said enthusiastically, burying his face between my legs.

His mouth was different than Jack's. Not better but different. Maybe better in the moment by virtue of being different. I closed my eyes and let them take me with their hands and mouths and tongues, working me into a frenzied orgasm so loud it woke their daughter down the hall. Bobby yelled back that we were watching a movie. All of us barely noticed.

It was Jess's turn. I kneeled over her, a man on either side of her body. I didn't mind their presence. I also wouldn't have minded if one of them took the opportunity to seize me from behind—in fact, one of the most lasting impressions of the night would be how much I wanted it—but the men were preoccupied with this girl-on-girl and I couldn't blame them.

If I could have, I would have watched us, too. I would have watched myself as I crouched between her legs for my first taste of another woman.

I would have looked for my expression to change when I smelled her, and I would have noticed my enthusiasm wane at the detection of menstrual blood.

I would have heard Jess apologize that she'd just finished bleeding. That was the way she said it. She was a feminist with as much disdain for terms that cloak the reality of our blood as she had for underwire.

I tasted her and wondered if women all taste the same. I wondered if maybe I didn't have the right pheromone sensitivity for the smell of another woman. I wished we had showered before. I would have liked to shower with Jess. I wanted to feel the softness of her skin with my soapy hands, to glide them over her body, appreciating every curve. I wanted to savor everything unmale about her, like the way she was petite. Her small waist and tummy squish and round ass that inspired hunger and longing wherever she went. The soft timbre of her voice and sweet delicacy of her kiss.

As she reached her body to my touch and welcomed me in, I realized the good fortune of every man I'd ever been with, not because I was extraordinary but because I am female, and that is the same thing. In that moment I forgave how much energy I'd wasted lambasting my cellulite or full thighs, or wishing my tits stood up like they used to. I felt emboldened and sexy in a way I never had. I would never be unknowing again.

I was glad for the new awareness of what it must be like to share a bed with me, something I would reflect on at greater length after our friends had gone home. Among the other things I'd still be thinking about long after that night: the boundaries of friendship, the ways we use sex as power, the ultimate motivations of women who seek their worth from their sex. What was each of us seeking that night? I suspect our motivations were as varied and unique as the prints of our tongues.

I returned to thinking about my oral performance. Eating pussy was not unlike moving a largish gummy candy around your mouth, but it was more like eating an oyster—animal and mineral.

I wished I felt more enthusiastic, though I was not unwilling, either. I wanted to be good. I wanted to feel and hear and see her pleasure. I imagined her pussy was mine and made love to it the way I longed for: tongue, lips, fingers, effort, attention, time.

Jack, GGG as ever, was going with the flow, accommodating the situation. I loved that he was so game for adventures. It was fun to do this with him, though we weren't particularly engaged with each other, because that wasn't the point. Still, it was sweet to catch his eye every now and then. We knew this mutual look on our faces—("Holy shit!").

Jess and Bobby were murmuring to one another. I heard her say he was making it weird (he wasn't), and that she wanted privacy with me. I wasn't sure if I should continue. Between traces of her blood and whatever was going on between them, I was losing my mojo. I was thrilled, however, to have answered a question I had long pondered. What was it like to give a woman head? I'd finally done it. Mystery solved.

The experience did more for me than satisfy a curiosity I had long held. It affirmed my right to own my desires and reassured me I could express them without ridicule. Further, it helped me understand more about my own sexuality. Oral sex with women might not be my thing, but I loved being able to please a woman, and to feel her body and our mutual expression together. Sex is not just a penis in a vagina as I had been conditioned to believe. My sex is whatever I want it to be with a consenting partner, or partners. This experience with Jessa was my first felt awareness of that, and the first time I ever felt okay with it, that I wasn't about to be smited by some god for stepping over the thin black line of heteronormativity.

We took a break, refreshed our drinks, and smoked some pot. There were jokes about the kid that woke up (*cringe*) and about the unexpected turn the night had taken. We got back in bed. Soon Bobby and I were fucking. I wasn't sure what Jack and Jess were up to, but after a few minutes they left wrapped in blankets. I realized quickly that I was enjoying my time with Bobby more than I thought I should be, and I wasn't sure we hadn't stepped outside of some assumed agreements.

Was permission implied when you were having a foursome? What about when that foursome became a twosome? What about when the condom came off and you kept going anyway, even if only for a few seconds?

As soon as I said what we were both thinking, Bobby and I stopped and joined Jack and Jess downstairs in a big cuddle pile—naked, drunk, stoned, and happy. The next morning we managed more or less on autopilot. Let the kids skip school. We turned on a movie for them and cleaned up the kitchen. This gave me time to remember the sequence of the night before and bask in the glory of discovery.

I didn't know it yet, but when Jack and I opened our marriage I had opened a door to a lot more than merely sex with other people. It was the beginning of a metamorphosis. I had initiated a personal awakening. My desire for sensation, experience, and adventure was not the point, though I would have told you at the time that it was absolutely the point.

Because I didn't know what I was really after was an intimacy of self.

28. WAP

How did I hear about it for the first time? No one seems to talk about it but your goofball aunt or your older sister's sex-crazed best friend. If it's discussed at all it's in hushed or fearful tones—we're all so afraid to "pee." Squirting was certainly not something they addressed in my abstinence-based, public school sex ed class. My mom never even talked to me about it, and she wasn't exactly modest. She taught me about the birds and bees when I was six, talked openly with us about sex (when we asked), and had a generally body-positive approach to parenting.

Maybe she never knew about it, either?

I think I might have learned about squirting from Dan Savage, actually.

Dan Savage is a gay man. Not exactly the person you'd expect to be educating women about their bodies.

I wanted to experience it. I thought of myself as sexually competent and GGG and so on but I'd never done it, and once I heard about it I felt like I was being left out of a secret. Imagine if you'd never had an orgasm.

"What's all the fuss about?" you might wonder.

Or maybe you would say, "Goddammit—me too!"

I brought it up in the car with Jack one day in late winter. We were on our way to dinner with friends following a pre-dinner cocktail at one of our favorite bars. We'd been making an effort to focus more on us. This was how open relationships were supposed to work, right? I didn't think we could justify seeing other people if we weren't also romancing one another, so we did. We tried.

Jack told me his experience with partners who squirted was limited, and inconsistent. It wasn't that common, he said, but he'd heard an interview on a podcast recently that was all about female ejaculation and they mentioned a YouTube video. As he was parking the car, with a knot in my voice, I forced myself to ask.

"Do you think we could try it?"

"Sure!" he said. If anything, he seemed excited. Come to think of it, Jack never made me feel ashamed for my sexual curiosity or expression. I did that to myself.

A few days after our conversation, we looked up the YouTube video. In it, a woman is interviewing a man about his experience getting partners to squirt. Another man telling a woman how to squirt.

"Use two fingers," the guy said.

Okay. Check.

"Make a 'come here' motion against her G-spot."

I wasn't sure I even knew where my G-spot was. How was that possible? *It's my body.*

"If it doesn't happen at first, don't get discouraged," he said (I was already discouraged). "Try going faster, alter the pressure, mix it up."

On our second try, Jack and I mixed it up to some success. However, whatever good feelings I had about it—Jack's willingness, the physical pleasure, our amiable bond—were displaced by my frustration that it didn't work that well. I believed that squirting held some coveted knowledge or epiphany and I wanted to get WOKE! I was imagining the Bellagio. I was hoping to meet God.

I tried not to turn my disappointment on Jack, who I vaguely saw as an antagonist in my quest, which was not only unkind but unproductive.

Jack was born in 1954, when uttering the word "pregnant" on TV was considered offensive. His parents never talked to him about sex, ever. How was he supposed to learn without a patient partner to practice with? I mean, he was doing it for me. I wish I'd embraced it as a mutual pursuit.

Instead, not wanting to do anything to engender any more sexual frustration between us, I dropped the subject with him. I didn't want my disappointment to taint our efforts toward improving our sex life in other ways.

A week or so later I saw a Facebook Live in a private women's group I belonged to, a conversation between two women I vaguely knew that they titled, "Female Ejaculation: Demystifying the Divine." The timing was uncanny.

I joined a few minutes after they began, as they were speaking of the mysticism of squirting, calling the ejaculate "nectar" or *amrita*, a Sanskrit work that means immortality. One of the women mentioned that her lover captures it for her and they add it to the tequila they sip as part of their lovemaking ritual. This sounded completely far out and weird and I loved it. I'll have what she's having!

I listened closely to the Facebook chat. Lots of the same info I had already heard: come hither fingers. G-spot. Vary the pressure. Also:

"You have to bear down."

"You might feel like you're going to pee; ignore that."

I made a mental note.

A week or so later I was preparing for my third date with Viktor. It was going to be our first overnight. I tried to hide my giddiness from Jack as I showered and got dressed.

He had been so cool about me dating. The only time his feathers got ruffled was when I seemed too distracted by my phone. I understood; I didn't like it when his phone dinged and his attention scurried off to another person any more than he liked repeating himself because the first time he said something I was distracted by my phone. I tried to limit my extramarital communication to certain times of day, or just a few minutes here and there when Jack and I weren't occupying the same space. But it was unpredictable when I would hear from someone, and I never knew when a promising date might turn up on OKCupid. That hit of dopamine I got from swiping felt like playing slots.

I didn't want to think about Jack's feelings as I was packing for my date with Viktor; there was too much else on my mind. I wanted the night to be perfect, so I'd been keeping a checklist in my phone for a week.

I had packed a dozen condoms, a new bottle of lube, and my Bluetooth speaker. I had a changes of clothes, a black chemise, and a robe to put on if I was cold or wanted to change my look. There were extra hair ties and toiletries, a handful of tea lights, plus a protein shake and a banana for each of us in the morning, and a quart of coconut water.

Viktor had told me the week before that he would make a request. I was so excited to know what he would ask for that I'd been distracted by the thought of it all week. He'd finally texted the day before.

"I told you I would have a request for you. Black lace, please."

His wish was my command.

Before I could meet Viktor for our overnight, I had to stop by an event I had previously committed to. It was an awards dinner for women in business. One of my girlfriends was being recognized for her executive leadership and several of us were going to support her. None of my friends knew where I was going afterward. Though Jack and I had been open for a year by then, I hadn't told anyone yet. None of my friends but Jessa knew Jack and I were seeing other people.

The event gave me the perfect excuse to dress up and I did, from head to toe: hair blown out, full make up, pearl necklace, black lace body-con dress, black lace demi bra + matching underwear, thigh high stockings with a back seam, and my tallest black heels. My finger and toenails were lacquered. My brows and Brazilian were waxed.

The event was not particularly interesting, because nothing would have been interesting compared to the night I was anticipating. I stood back and looked around the room at the gathering of mostly women with the presumed satisfaction that none of them was going to have a night as good as mine. Not even the award winners. Because, while I admired their professional success, I couldn't imagine there was anything better than the epic fucking I was about to receive. I savored my little secret while I stood in line for more wine, unapologetically smug.

As soon as the winner was announced in my friend's category, I slipped away "to the restroom." I did not return.

Instead, I texted Viktor to tell him I was free. He replied he was minutes away and would wait for me outside. I collected my coat and overnight bag from the coat check and ran through the rain to his car, wheeling my small suitcase behind me. It was not unlike the day after we'd gotten engaged, when Jack and I ran through Paris in the storm with Asher in his stroller. But instead of feeling warm and filial, I felt wild and sophisticated running in my dress and heels, like a grown up in a movie, but altogether unlike my other grown up roles—wife and mother. It was one of the first times in my life I felt a sense of having arrived. It was the realization of something original that I wanted, regardless of whether or not I was supposed to. I was going to have it.

We checked in and took our things to the room. He suggested we get a drink, so we headed back downstairs and found our spot in the bar on an ornate cushioned bench. I relished the anticipation of the night ahead as I reflexively sipped my martini faster than the other drinkers in the place. Halfway through he asked me to join him outside while he smoked a joint. I smoked a little. He smoked a lot.

Before the joint was gone he leaned into me, just behind my left ear, and whispered in his Slavic accent, "I'm going to ask you to do something and I want you to pay attention."

I held my breath, nodded, and smiled at the street ahead.

He pulled out two ribbons, each about a half meter in length. There was a slit at the end of each, like a buttonhole. He showed me how he could pull the ribbon through the slit to make a loop—a satin handcuff.

"Now I want you to put your hands behind your back," he instructed quietly. "You are to be subtle; no one should be able to tell anything is unusual."

I smiled again and looked around. There was a doorman twenty feet away, and a dozen or so patrons in the bar who could see us through the windows. They paid us no mind. To everyone else this was just another Thursday night.

I did as I was told, gamely but subtly extending my arms behind me. He left me like that—waiting—while he took his time finishing his joint.

After he threw the roach on the ground, he reached into his coat pocket again for the ribbons. He slipped the first cuff over my right hand and tightened it just enough. Then he did my other wrist. He was talking behind me as he tied the ends of the ribbon together in a thick black bow. His voice was barely above a whisper.

"I'm going to take you up to the room, and you will be made to wait."

"I will retrieve our cocktails when we go in; we'll take them with us upstairs. You will have to ask me if you want a sip, because I'm not going to free you until I'm ready to have my way with you."

Then he repeated himself, "You are to act as if nothing is out of the ordinary. Do you understand?"

My nod was subtle and elated. I could feel my eyes twinkling. The fact of his assumed permission to treat me this way was intoxicating. His assertion of dominance revealed his desire—he wanted me to comply. My compliance meant his approval. His approval was my reward.

We did exactly as he said. He held my tied hands as we walked through the front door, as if this was simply our novel way of holding hands and not an erotic ruse. He collected our drinks while I waited with my back to a wall. When we returned to the room, he set down the drinks and walked me to a corner by the window.

"You'll have to wait here," he said, "while I get things set up. If you would like a sip of your martini, please tell me and I will get it for you."

I tried to be coy and pretend I was suffering, but on the inside I was singing and twirling like I was Julie Andrews in *The Sound of Music*.

"I brought surprises," he said from across the room, smiling and holding a brown paper bag. Seeing his teeth made me want to kiss him. Instead, I stood in place and watch him fan out a bunch of condoms.

"For starters," he said, setting them around the room.

Next, he pulled out a candle, which he brought over for me to smell.

"It's a sex candle. You can use the melted wax as massage oil."

After he lit the candle he pulled out a small, inexpensive ball gag.

"Also, there is this."

My eyes widened. In a previous moment of inspiration, I had asked if he had one, and he said no. I didn't even know it was something I wanted until I heard myself ask. Now that he'd gone and gotten me one, I felt some trepidation. I'd never worn a ball gag before. It seemed so…kinky.

I had a feeling in my stomach like peering over a cliff. This wasn't two hours in the light of day. We had all night, and it could go any number of ways. I felt physically safe with him but somehow endangered, too. I didn't know it was a psychological precipice I was sensing, because I was pushing an edge I didn't know existed. Maybe this was the reason our dates seemed to affect me for days afterwards, a psychic hangover that physically ached.

He unpacked his clothing and toiletries.

"May I have another sip of my drink, please?"

He obliged. While he was standing in front of me, I asked if he would please untie me. I didn't want him to, but I wanted to hear him tell me no. He seemed to intuit this.

"Not until I'm ready for you," he said.

"Will you at least remove my coat?" I pressed. I would have been disappointed if he agreed.

"No," he said firmly. "Don't be such a whiny bitch."

He said it with such disdain it sounded like he might have meant it. I noted that I needed to tell him when we weren't in scene that I could do without being called a bitch. But for the moment, I let it go. For the moment I chose to focus on what I believed was his sexy intent, instead of the jarring impact.

He told me he was going to get ice and would be right back. There I stood, looking out the window, watching the neon lights across the street change colors. I was alone and calm. Pensive, even. Some part of me had surrendered. I was also beginning to get a little bored standing there, or I was still smarting from the pretend insult.

I brightened when Viktor returned. He fed me a broken ice cube and told me what a good job I did as he untied my hands. This was everything to me. He helped me out of my coat and kissed me gently, lovingly. He held my hips with his hands and ran them up my sides and over my breasts. He pushed the strap of my dress to the side and kissed my collarbone. He squeezed my ass and pulled me closer.

"You look radiant tonight. I'm so pleased with how well you followed my directions."

Radiant. The word I'd been waiting to hear since I was mired in my first miserable marriage. Radiant, like a star. His words made me glow. I slipped off my shoes and pulled at his belt.

It was hours later. Somehow, we did not tire. We had been outside once to take a walk and smoke a bit more pot. Inside, between scenes, we talked and cuddled. Then he'd tell me something new he wanted.

"Now get on your knees and suck my cock. I'm going to take your picture."

And just like that we'd be moving again. The photos I would save for the "best of" collection in my phone's Hidden folder.

After another vigorous session we rested on the bed. I was on my back, leaning against a bunch of pillows, completely naked, watching him. I could watch him for hours, the wild ableness of him. He was so competent at everything he did—my favorite quality in a man.

He instructed me to touch my pussy while I waited for him to choose new music, then took over for me when he returned, kneeling between my legs. He spit on his fingers and smeared them over me, top to bottom. He slid two fingers inside as he started to kiss me. It felt as good as if we had just started.

My body hummed with pleasure as he picked up the pace. Soon he was working me deeply, sliding his fingers in and out, three or maybe four, opening me. He pressed his other hand over my lower abdomen. Every sensation drew a gasp or moan as he changed tempo or drilled my cunt deeper still. I could hardly keep up with my breath. The buildup of pressure and intensity was a pained ecstasy.

In the back of my mind I heard my own mental note: "Bear down, it feels like you're going to pee, ignore that."

I wanted it so much.

As Viktor worked me closer to orgasm I started to have the feeling of transition during childbirth, that primal loss of control, that animal state, of body overtaking mind so there is no choice but surrender. My legs fluttered, wide and open. I was panting and groaning and gripped by a potent, unfamiliar pleasure. I felt a resistance similar to childbirth, but rather than physical, it was an emotional resistance: the shame of my body and its natural ways, the longing of unmet desire, the erroneous beliefs about what I did and didn't deserve. All that I had been holding, the weight I had been carrying, for so many years. In that moment, I had a choice: shame or pleasure. Protection or trust. Resistance or surrender.

I bore down slightly and felt a fullness I never had before. Something was happening. I was ready. All that was left was to let go.

I had to let go.

The second I did I was flooded with warm liquid that gushed from a cave within. When it came, he began fucking me so vigorously with his hand that liquid sprayed everywhere—my legs, his face, my stomach, his bare chest. He didn't stop, and neither did I. His enthusiasm made it safe to let go completely. I wanted the feeling to last forever.

Viktor continued until I was empty and we were both soaked. At the end I was speechless. Awestruck. Profoundly satisfied and unbelieving: that was in me all along.

We laid side by side for several minutes listening to jazz piano. I was non-verbal. No words could suffice.

I felt an urge—a compulsion—for Viktor's body. Not his sex but his weight. I pulled at his arm with a little grunt. He seemed to understand and laid on top of me, kissing softly my cheeks and chest and neck. My eyes were closed, my cells still vibrating, but I was coming to. I was making my way back. I needed him to anchor me to complete my return.

"So you're a squirter," he said after a time, nuzzling my cheek.

I summoned my voice, which came out as feral laughter. "I am now—"

"You have not done that before?"

I was simultaneously embarrassed and proud to tell him that no, I had never squirted before.

We spread an extra blanket over the soaked bed and laid down to sleep, pleasantly exhausted. I felt as if I had expelled years of emotional sludge—shame, rejection, fear, sadness—and exposed a new self, untarnished by trauma and grief. I couldn't believe such an experience was possible from a sexual encounter. All that remained was profound peace.

I was barely awake when Viktor left to make his morning meetings. I took my time getting up, noticing the ways I felt different in my body, and snapped a couple sexy photos to send Viktor with my thank you text. I was deeply calm. I felt more…intact, somehow, like something missing had been returned. I felt emboldened, proud, and at home in my body in a way I never had. My thighs didn't look full, they looked powerful. My tummy didn't seem soft, it seemed lush. My frame didn't feel big, it felt enduring.

Rising to meet the day, I felt like a different person. I couldn't know yet the long-term impact of that night, but I was, almost certainly, standing taller.

I texted Jack from my Lyft on the way home to tell him I'd be back soon. He asked if I had fun. In reply I sent one of the photos I had taken—a picture of me tucked into bed, one nipple peeking over the sheet, a supremely serene expression on my face.

The memory of this guts me now—I can't believe I was so insensitive. But at the time I was so entranced that I didn't reason. The photo, I thought, was a way to give him insight into my experience; you could see it all over my face. But it never occurred to me how it would feel, or what that would do to him. *My husband.*

He didn't acknowledge the photo. Instead, he suggested we debrief over lunch at a café near home. An overnight date—the first for either of us—was a big deal.

One of our agreements was transparency, so I answered all his questions. I was glad to process it a little and tried not to be too gleeful in the retelling. Dom/sub dynamics weren't something Jack and I had ever explored, so I felt a little like I was telling Jack about a trip I'd been on, a new world I had visited. He seemed curious and interested.

I did withhold one part. I didn't tell Jack that I squirted. I knew that might hurt him since we hadn't been so successful at it. Also, the experience revealed so much to me, but I hadn't had time or space to contemplate what it meant or integrate the new awareness. I wanted it to be only mine, at least for a little while.

As we were clearing our dishes, Jack added, "Can I ask one more question?"

"Of course."

"Did you squirt?"

When I told him yes, I couldn't help but notice him flinch for the briefest second—the kind of expression no one but his wife would have noticed. I didn't know how to ask him if he was hurt, and I wouldn't have known where to begin to make amends, so I didn't address it.

All he said was, "I knew it. I had a feeling that was going to happen."

I didn't know how to tell Jack that it felt like a personal revolution, so I said nothing more. The rest of the day I marveled at the deep calm that had settled in me. Also, deep sadness. It was, I guessed, the cost of soaring so high—the inevitable crash. I listened to Bon Iver and looked at the pictures we took. I didn't hear from Viktor. He was at work. He had a life.

Soon I figured out how to do it for myself. I read that it helped to sit up, knees wide. Also, that it was easier if you'd already had a clitoral orgasm, so I took care of that using my vibrator and then set to work exploring with my hands. Sure enough, it worked. It was one of the proudest days of my whole life.

Before long it occurred to me: what if women were designed to ejaculate with the same frequency as men?

What if women are designed to ejaculate with the same frequency as men?

That changes everything.

29. The Greatest Love of All

Babies die but they remain in your heart. Even when it's been two or four or six years. Even when you have another baby, who wouldn't exist if your first baby had lived. Even as your second baby grows into an extraordinary being that who somehow surpasses everything you ever imagined about him, you think about your first baby and wonder. You are devastated by the goneness of him, and it's worse, because now you've witnessed what you missed out on by not getting to see him grow. You imagine the two of them together—brothers—and the fact that this will never be will gut you in a way that feels like violence. You will feel it viscerally, as if someone blew a hole through your most tender parts with a point-blank bazooka. You will feel always that part of you is missing. You will feel the tears that live behind your eyes in every single moment. You will feel a sob behind every breath you take. You will feel you belong on the other side of life with your baby as much as you belong on this side of life with your living boy. This will never go away. Escaping this life won't feel like a good idea, exactly, because you know what that means, and you could never bear to leave your living child without a mother. But if something should happen, something that you could not help, and you ended up on the other side sooner than expected, it couldn't be such a very bad thing, because whether or not you're ever going to see him or know him again, at least once your time here is finished, you'll get to know. The pain of uncertainty will be erased and the terror of vulnerability that life requires will finally be laid to rest.

30. Trouble

Jack's first girlfriend after we opened our marriage was a woman named Kat who had an orgasm when they kissed in the parking lot after their first date. Two, actually. She came twice while standing on asphalt next to a Toyota Prius. He wasn't sure that's what was happening so the second time he checked to make sure she was alright.

"I'm just really sensitive," she said.

When he told me about it after he got home, the best I could muster was an eye roll. *No one has orgasms like that*, I thought. I didn't bother saying it out loud because he hadn't asked for my opinion. He didn't seem to care what I thought.

Less than two months had passed between when I met Viktor and when Jack met Kat, but to him it might have felt interminable. He never begrudged me the experience I was having with Viktor, but he did express concern—would it ever happen for him? I tried to encourage him that someday the tables might be turned—he could be dating someone he was really into while I had no interesting prospects. But the evidence seemed to support our conclusion—online dating is easier for women, especially when it came to nonmonogamy. In our experience there were more men than women who were willing to date knowing they weren't the only one, and without the expectation of a wedding ring at the top of the escalator.

I was glad Jack met someone he liked. I felt happy for him to have a new friend, and I felt less guilty about my feelings for Viktor now that he would get to explore something new, too. They'd been out a couple times but not slept together yet. I wasn't looking forward to it happening, but I knew it was coming.

Whenever I thought about it, I tried to brace myself by turning the tables mentally. I'd had a great time with Viktor, but I still loved Jack very much. If that could be true for me then surely he could go out with Kat and have fun with her and love me all the same. I repeated this in my mind over and over and over again.

None of my friendships was mutually exclusive; who said sex had to be? Why did having sex with someone change anything? Wasn't it just an activity, like playing cards or dancing, with fewer clothes and more sweat? Surely Jack could feel something with and for Kat without those feelings undermining what was between the two of us. Intellectually, at least, I believed this was true. But my emotional body seemed to have something else to say about it. The thought of Jack having sex with someone else made me feel physically sick.

It was a Tuesday night and I was leaving for my second ayahuasca retreat the next day. I would be gone until Friday. It was unfortunate timing—Jack had given me concert tickets for our recent wedding anniversary to a show that was that Friday night. When the retreat was announced and I realized the conflict, I was disappointed. I didn't want to miss my opportunity for a night out with my husband, but the retreats didn't happen very often and, especially given how much was changing in and around me and us, I felt like it would be a good idea to get away and go within.

Jack was understanding and said he would find someone else to take to the concert.

"Please not Kat," I said. I suggested someone else he could take.

My intention wasn't to be controlling, or at least I didn't want to *seem* controlling—I just felt superstitious about him using my anniversary tickets for a date with his girlfriend, like it would energetically taint our marriage or something (but sex with someone else wouldn't?).

I had been cleansing in advance of the retreat for two weeks: no sex, no wine, no martinis. No American Spirits, no sugar, no salt. No meat, no caffeine, no fermented products...it was a long list. The organizer recommended eliminating these things lest we obstruct the divine assistance we were seeking. I had been almost completely observant of the restrictions because I was almost completely committed to my betterment.

For years, in the wake of Vox's death, *almost* was the best I could muster. I was *almost* committed to life. That part of me with a bias for survival wanted to thrive. The best the rest of me could muster was a shrug. Fuck it.

The cleansing diet made me realize how many substances I used on a daily basis to affect my mood and energy (and appease the "fuck its")—caffeine, sugar, and, as nonmonogamy was getting more complicated, nicotine. Also, alcohol, typically a drink or two (or three) a night. The more I drank the more I smoked—never without guilt and self-loathing, but I did it anyway. Without these crutches I felt sensitive and raw.

The suggested cleanse meant I had to make all my food because there was next to nothing you could buy in a grocery store that came without added salt. I was fluffing a batch of steaming quinoa when Jack walked into the kitchen.

"Did you look at the calendar?" he asked.

Immediately tipped off by his curt tone, I braced myself.

"No, what did you plan?"

"I'm having an overnight with Kat on Friday."

A subzero chill ran up my spine.

"Are you taking her to the concert?" I asked, steadying myself, eyes down.

"Yup."

I heard no contrition in his voice. To my ears, he sounded defiant. Energy surged through me as I grasped for something to say.

It's common, I've learned, for people who grow up with trauma to develop a hair trigger when they sense their boundaries are being crossed. It's an attempt to protect the wound from being reinjured. In the same way you baby a broken bone with ice and elevation, or caretake a bad headache with a cold compress in a dark room, I had learned to defend my emotional wounding with self-sufficiency, invulnerability, and—if push came to shove—a strong offense.

But in an intimate relationship, there are spaces you can't protect. I needed Jack's love, and the threat of him withdrawing it felt crippling. But he didn't know that. I didn't even know that yet. Our lack of awareness and our mutual failure to be honest about what we were really feeling was undermining our foundation. But neither of us could see it yet.

The argument that followed his revelation quickly reached a stalemate. I didn't want him to go with Kat, he insisted he was going to. I got furious and stayed that way. He remained defiant. I interpreted his actions as prioritizing his desire to have fun with Kat—to have sex with her—over my feelings. At the most basic level, it felt like he was choosing her over me. That's what I told myself, and I was devastated. But in defense of my vulnerability, I was enraged.

I didn't know at the time how intolerant I was of relational strife because Jack and I had never had a real argument. The lack of confrontation in our relationship allowed me to preserve the belief that we had excellent communication and were a perfectly harmonious match for one another.

It never occurred to me our lack of conflict was likely a sign not of harmony, but all that we were avoiding.

With the argument in deadlock, the house felt cloistering. My mouth dry and fiery, I was too livid to talk about it any longer.

"I'm leaving," I said to Jack, brushing past him in the kitchen.

"You're not leaving." It sounded like an eyeroll.

"I meant I'm going to the store."

By the time I got in the car to return home I was nominally calmer because I had spent the entire walk through the grocery store reasoning to myself that Jack would, of course, apologize as soon as I got home and tell me he had cancelled the date. Of course he would. He would greet me at the door and tell me he was so sorry and that he had come to his senses. And together we would decide on someone else he could take to the concert, if he really was so set on going, and he could see Kat the next week or something.

But that's not what happened. When I walked in the front door, he was nowhere to be found. The air in the house still felt thick and heavy. Nothing had changed.

Twenty minutes later he cornered me in the bedroom where I was folding clothes. I told him he was being careless and thoughtless and passive aggressive. In reply, he mocked me. The swell of anger in me felt hot enough to burn a house down.

Our first real fight revealed a lot about each of us. I have a temper, can be very focused and intense, and take any affront personally. Jack is generally more easygoing, conflict-avoidant, and tends toward passive aggression. He isn't triggered in the same way when he perceives he's been slighted.

If we had ever been in a fight before, maybe we would have learned these things about each other and learned to work through our differences together. But this was a first, and neither of us was thinking clearly or calmly. Eventually, we went to bed, a concrete silence between us.

Three days later I was on my way home from the retreat, which was in a remote area north of Seattle. As I approached the edge of civilization, my phone dinged with a new text. It was Jack. His message said he was planning to take Kat to "…that Queen Anne hotel, unless you have a problem with it."

Well of course he fucking knows I'll have a fucking problem with it, I thought. That Queen Anne hotel was the same place Viktor and I had our first overnight date a month before.

I wrote him back with all the strength I could muster from my tender state of being: "I AM NOT IN A PLACE TO HAVE THIS CONVERSATION. I ABSOLUTELY DO NOT WANT YOU TO STAY THERE. PLEASE FIND SOMEWHERE ELSE. ANYWHERE ELSE. SPEND $1000 ON A SUITE, I DON'T CARE."

We didn't have $1000 for him to take his girlfriend on an overnight, but I absolutely did not want him to stay at the same hotel where I had such a profound experience with Viktor.

I couldn't understand why he'd want to, anyway. Well, I couldn't at the time. It seems pretty evident now—understandable, even? He wanted to even the score.

When I arrived home, I walked through the front door and dropped my bags on the cold tile. I stared at him with lasers in my eyes. After an emotionally fraught week and difficult retreat, I was exhausted and weepy.

I did not greet him or give him a hug or anything else. There was only one question on my mind.

"Where are you staying tonight?" I demanded.

"We're staying at the place in Queen Anne," he said defensively. "It's next to the venue. And the reservation is non-refundable."

I took Asher as calmly as I could and went to Jess and Bobby's for the weekend. I couldn't conceive of how he could go enjoy his date after what had transpired between us, but that's exactly what he did.

We would be struggling to overcome the events of that weekend for months to come.

Weeks before, Jack and I had scheduled a date for that Sunday night. After two days to cool down, we decided—haltingly—to keep it, ultimately agreeing that we could use the time to debrief the fight, my retreat, and his date. A public space would force us to maintain decorum, which we managed, barely. My anger felt like hatred towards him. I couldn't fathom how he could be so cruel. His actions felt specifically designed to inflict pain. In my mind, that could only mean he didn't love me. It meant Kat was more important than me, his wife. It meant that I was now responsible to take care of myself in all the ways I used to rely on Jack.

In reality, it didn't mean any of these things, but I couldn't see that. I was in fight or flight, and I picked fight.

Contributing to my sustained reaction was Jack's apparent lack of remorse. His apology sounded defensive and laced with anger. If he wasn't begging my forgiveness, there was no way I was going to back.

"Tell me this," I demanded drunkenly as we were getting ready to leave for home after dinner. "Do you have better chemistry with her than you do with me?"

Just like that, I released the unthought known into the great wide open. Jack hemmed and hawed before answering in the affirmative.

"What?" I badgered him. "Was that a yes?"

"Yes!" he repeated.

"I fucking knew it," I sneered.

I acted like I was hurt by what he said, and to a degree, I suppose I was. But inwardly, I was also glad. Our lack of chemistry was a two-way street. It wasn't my fault. Neither of us felt sexual urgency for the other.

In the car on the way home my rage worked its way into my feet and fists and I pummeled the inside of the car as I screamed from the netherworld, surprising even myself. When he pulled over abruptly, yelling at me to stop, I snapped out of it, suddenly aware, deeply ashamed, and full of regret.

31. New Rules

I know this now: before you open your relationship there are a number of useful things to consider in terms of your agreements with your partner. You might even want to create a contract and sign it, if only to validate your mutual understanding and affirm your commitment to upholding what you both agreed upon.

If we had it to do over again, these are some of the things I would want us to consider:
1. What are your shared values underlying your new lifestyle?
2. How much notice is required before a date with an outside partner?
3. How quickly do you agree to respond to your partner's texts when you're out with someone else?
4. How much communication with outside partners is acceptable when the primary couple is spending time together?
5. Under what circumstances is it unacceptable to communicate with an outside partner (e.g. while you're in bed together)?
6. What are the check-in points of escalating with a new love interest?
7. Is it okay to fuck on the first date? Or is kissing okay but for anything more you need to check in? Etc.
8. What is an acceptable rate of progression/escalation with a new interest?
9. How much money can be spent on a date with someone outside the anchor pairing?
10. What sex acts are permissible—is anything explicitly off the table?
11. Are overnights acceptable?
12. How many dates per month are acceptable to each partner?
13. How much does each partner want to know about the other person's experiences with other people?
14. How do the two of you each feel about privacy versus secrecy, and how do you define these things within your relationships?

15. How are birthdays and holidays celebrated with secondary partners—time, gifts, etc.?
16. Are sex toys acceptable? Other props? Are these separate for each partner?
17. Can you wear your sexy lingerie/underwear/etc. for other partners?
18. Is group sex an option, and how much notice is required of someone additional?
19. What requirements are there relative to pre-screening for STIs?
20. What requirements are there relative to barrier protection—is a condom/dental dam required for oral sex? Gloves for manual stuff? Condoms for anal? Vaginal?
21. How will you handle an STI scare?
22. At what point do you want to know that your inside partner is developing feelings for their outside partner?
23. Are there any circumstances under which a "veto" of another partner is acceptable?
24. How will you handle it if you see someone you and your partner know while out on a date with someone else?
25. Is it acceptable to spend time with outside partners where sex is not the focus (going out, hanging out, socializing with other people)?
26. Are you going to come out as a nonmonogamous couple? If so, what are you going to tell your kids, your friends, your wider community?
27. Is it okay to go with a partner to places that are special to the original couple (e.g. restaurant, park, theater, museum, etc.)?
28. Is it acceptable to talk with your primary partner about challenges with outside partners?
29. Is it acceptable to talk with outside partners about challenges with your primary partner?
30. How do the anchor partners support one another through the breakup of another relationship?
31. How will you handle it if one partner decides they no longer want to be open?
32. How do you reconnect with one another after having a date with someone else?

33. Will you introduce outside partners to your children?
34. What are acceptable ways of meeting new partners—online sites like Tinder and OKCupid? …Craigslist? …bars? …activities (climbing gym, salsa dancing, etc.)? Mutual friends?
35. Is it okay for either partner to date someone who is monogamous?
36. Is it okay to take a trip with another partner? Of what duration? Who takes care of the kids?
37. If you decide to wait and see about some of these things, how often are you going to check in about how things are going, to address any uncertainties or update the agreements between you?
38. Is it okay for an outside partner to come to the primary couple's home? To occupy their shared bed?
39. If not, where will dates take place?
40. Do you ask one another for permission, or forgiveness?
41. What constitutes a breach of trust and how will you handle it?
42. When there is conflict, will you automatically default to honor the person with the least comfort in the circumstance or do you each have to make your case?
43. If one partner is in need and the other partner is with a secondary partner, does the partner in need have a right to interrupt their time together for a phone call, text, etc.?
44. Are you open to revising your agreements/commitments with your anchor partner to accommodate another person?

This is just a start.

32. Believer

Or maybe you don't want a whole list of agreements to make things brittle. Maybe you and your partner are so aligned, and have such deep trust in one another, that you don't need to outline a thousand if/then scenarios. Maybe you can just talk to one another and act in good faith, and check in often, and say the hard things, and find your way forward…together.

33. Bitter Sweet Symphony

After the night I freaked out in the car, Jack and I started couple's therapy with a sex-positive psychotherapist. We figured that was probably the first requirement—find a therapist that was accepting of nonmonogamy as a viable model of relationship, who had some insight as to how to help people trying to navigate it for the first time.

Jessa had recommended him, although the relationship she'd sought counseling for—not Bobby, but a boyfriend—had ended, which was not exactly a ringing endorsement of the therapist's skill. But it didn't occur to me at the time to research therapists with Jack and choose someone together.

Over time it would become increasingly apparent that, whatever his methods, they weren't working. But once we were invested with him, it seemed like too much work to start over. Were sex therapists that common? I didn't know. So often we handicap ourselves with questions we fail to ask.

One useful thing about the therapist was that he helped us identify that Jack and I both fell on the submissive side of the Dom/sub (D/s) scale. In other words, we both preferred the other person hold the power during a sex scene. We both wanted to be dominated sexually. This similarity in our sexual dispositions explained a lot: Jack and I lacked polarity. In the same way positively charged protons repel other protons, and negatively charged electrons repel other electrons, Jack and I, on some level, repelled instead of attracted one another. Thinking about it this way helped me think about our lack of sexual harmony as an objective fact. It's just who and how we were. It wasn't anyone's fault.

I was not to blame because I didn't feel erotic fireworks. It was a simple fact, same as our biological sex, same as our birthdates.

I wanted to be dominated sexually because that was how I knew my place. As I learned when I was young, my sex and my worth were one and the same. I was to be adoring, to caretake and receive my partner.

This is the way I was erotically wired. In exchange for my submission, I gained his attention, affection, and desire for me. And that was everything I wanted. It's what I didn't know I was after when I had sought out The Musician after five years of silence. It's the reason I was so receptive to Viktor. Both of them conveyed authority and control and I ate it up. It was such a relief to be met there. It made me feel sated and calmed. I imagine it might be like a baby who cries for comfort, who is picked up, held, and soothed. For me it was like this...or maybe more like an addict finally getting their hit of smack. The cycle made me dependent. It meant I needed him—his affection, his approval, his validation—to feel okay.

If I had to be triggered this way emotionally to feel strong "chemistry" with a partner, then it's no wonder why I didn't feel chemistry with Jack. Not only did we lack polarity in our desires, but Jack was safe. He was loving. He was naturally affectionate, easy to be with, and kind, and I didn't have to do anything to earn it. In other words, he didn't trigger the attachment wound I was unwittingly carrying from childhood.

Two months after I met Viktor we scheduled our second overnight. He was having dinner with another woman before he met me at the hotel. Somehow, I didn't mind this. It didn't occur to me to wonder, let alone ask, why he planned two dates for one evening. I remained hypersensitive to Jack's actions around Kat, because that's where I was authentically vulnerable. But when it came to Viktor, I would take what I was offered. I had little invested apart from what I wanted: validation through sex.

Another reason I didn't think too much about Viktor's date is because I was so preoccupied with my plan for the night. Earlier in the week I'd had an idea. I'd never done anything like it. I was practically squealing with anticipation by the time I walked into the hotel room.

The door had barely closed behind me when I started to put away everything extraneous. I stashed the brochures, remotes, guidebook, and luggage rack. I took a quick shower so I'd be fresh as could be, brushed my teeth, and refreshed my makeup. I teased my hair until it looked artfully tousled, then cleaned up the errant water droplets and rinsed my toothpaste down the drain. The space needed to look pristine, like a furniture showroom. I wanted a blank canvas. I retrieved my phone and speakers and the elements of my outfit and put everything else away, out of sight.

Viktor texted that he was on his way.

Please let me know when you're parking, I replied.

I started with stockings—thigh high fishnets. Then a red lace bodysuit with an easy-access snap at the crotch. I had learned by then how much he liked lingerie, especially crotchless, and loved dressing for him. I finished the outfit with black fuck-me boots—knee high, pointy toe, stiletto heel. I realized I had forgotten jewelry and hoped he didn't miss it. I turned on Marconi Union—ambient sound that broke the silence but preserved our blank canvas—and tinkered with the volume. He texted he had parked.

I quickly put the ball gag in my mouth, not too tight so I could spit it out if the scene got too intense and I started to lose myself. I put the eye mask over my forehead and grabbed the handcuffs. I looked around the room for where I was going to sit. There was a chair in the corner near the curtains. I practiced sitting and decided it seemed sexier to lean than to sit. I found a way to make that work while looking natural. I was nervous he was going to walk in while I was still rehearsing.

Ridiculous, perhaps, that I was practicing my lean. I mean...*my lean*? But it was so fun! The fantastical aspects of our dates allowed me to access a new part of myself. I was discovering a side of myself I'd never developed—that I'd only tasted when I was living in San Francisco. I loved the notion I could conceive of a fantasy—create my own world—and then execute it in a scene that would deliver my fix, and then some.

That the entire ruse fed his desire for me upped the ante by an order of magnitude. Is there any greater turn on than being desired? I was living for it.

I checked the back of my hair to make sure the elastic of the eye mask wasn't pulling it up into a pouf. I cuffed my left wrist, pulled down the eye mask, then awkwardly cuffed my right wrist with my arms behind my back. Shivering, I stood in the corner of the blank hotel room and I waited. This was how he found me.

Our night together included moments of erotic thrill as well as tender connection. We took a late-night walk around the city. We stopped for sushi in a hotel bar and talked through the wee hours about our childhoods, parenting, and nonmonogamy, among other things. He showed me a picture of his grandpa.

Growing up I thought sex was the relational be all-end all, that sex was always, necessarily, a culmination and manifestation of consummate intimacy. I learned through young adulthood that was not the case. Sometimes sex was just sex, and that's what I thought I was seeking from Viktor. So I didn't know what to do, exactly, with the deepening bond between us. In spite of my increasing affinity for him, I didn't actually want anything to change. His lack of availability was part of what made him so riveting.

The next morning, we embraced in the lobby to say goodbye. Out of the blue, I very nearly said the words, "I love you." They came as naturally as if I was saying goodbye to my mom on the phone.

I willed my feet to the ground and silently reminded myself it was just a moment of feeling. I knew I didn't love him. I was only having the thing he mentioned occasionally: NRE, or New Relationship Energy. This is, essentially, the feeling of falling in love, when your brain is flooded with dopamine and the world feels idealized and perfect, but perception and judgement are compromised.

People who engage in consensual nonmonogamy seem particularly fond of the phrase, new relationship energy—I think for the way it suggests the contrast of established relationship energy.

Because it's easy to get swept up in NRE with an outside/secondary/new partner and forget you ever felt the same way about your inside/primary/existing partner. And it would be a mistake to act based on that rush of chemicals, e.g. to leave your primary partner for someone you hardly know.

In other words, it feels great to fall in love. But it's a bad time to make decisions.

According to Viktor, NRE could easily be reduced to brain chemicals, and I had it bad. I continued to insist that I didn't, however, because I attributed my enthusiasm to a sexual reawakening. What Viktor and I had was a phenomenal sexual connection and I was happy to leave it at that, even if I remained confused as to what to do about the feelings the sex created.

In the past, once I stepped into a relationship, I assumed my partner and I were riding the same escalator (at more or less the same pace): first date (possibly sex), more dates (definitely sex), seeing one another more often, spending weekends together, taking trips, moving in, getting engaged, getting married, buying a house, having kids. And I expected to ride that escalator all the way to my Happily Ever After at the top, or at least until something broke. So I didn't know what to do with the fact that I didn't want to go that distance with Viktor. I didn't know that we could invent something else on our own terms, that we could decide on a dynamic that suited us both, *and* our partners at home.

Mostly recovered from my near slip of "I love you," I asked Viktor when I would see him next. I felt less anxious between dates if I knew when I would see him again.

"Well," he said. "I was meaning to mention this earlier. I won't be able to see you for some time…"

My throat closed and my stomach lurched and the room began to spin. I tried to steady my voice. "Oh? Why not?"

"Marin and I are taking a bit of time to refocus on our relationship. It's nothing personal; it has nothing to do with you and me. It's just a matter of assuring her comfort before you and I proceed."

I tried to steady myself and breathe. I wanted more information, but it seemed inappropriate to ask. How much was I entitled to know about the ins and outs of their union?

This was how I learned two critical lessons relative to consensual nonmonogamy. The first is that, when relationships are tested, one of them has to give. Generally, in my (limited) experience, it's going to be the less established partner.

A person experienced with consensual nonmonogamy knows this is the way it goes. They understand that relationships change and morph over time, and that flexibility, patience, and tolerance is required. They know that what goes around comes around and try to engage with their partners with compassion and understanding, knowing that, in a matter of time, they might be the one seeking grace.

Lacking this perspective, I was mad. But I knew I couldn't seem like it because that would rock the boat. So my only practical options were to accept what Viktor said (and bide my time) or refuse it (and lose the most intoxicating sex I'd ever had). The choice was obvious: I had to swallow my feelings. Because regardless of what was going on for him at home, there was no way I was going to give him up.

I imagine Kat might have felt the same way about Jack; it didn't matter to her what was happening between he and I, she didn't want to end their affair. I never asked Jack to pause with her the way Viktor was with me, because I knew that I'd want to see Viktor as soon as he was available again. Also, I felt Jack's relationships were independent of the two of us. If we were going to be truly open, it seemed only fair that his connection with Kat should exist on their terms, not according to my whims. I didn't want to do to Kat what I felt Marin was doing to me, even if I didn't like how things were going with Jack and I relative to her.

The second critical lesson I was beginning to learn from the discord between Viktor and Marin—and Jack and I, for that matter—was the relevance of context, which I think of as the circumstances surrounding a person relative to various aspects of their life.

When you date nonmonogamously, you multiply the number of circumstances by an order of magnitude. I had to consider Jack as well as Viktor, *and* Marin. Plus Kat, and I even knew of one of her partners, Pete.

Kids, parents, jobs, money, health…there are so many variables that influence our lived experience at any given time, and when you are dating nonmonogamously, these can have a ripple effect on everyone involved.

Viktor and Marin were in a sticky spot. It made me needier towards Jack, which might have made him less available to Kat. Did Kat turn to Pete for the attention she missed from Jack? Did she resent me for needing more from my husband, the same way I resented Marin for putting the brakes on my relationship with Viktor?

As I continued to date, I began to wise up in terms of defining the general life context of the person I was dating. I wanted to know: how was life going for them? Were they generally happy or going through a rough patch? Were they busy or bored? Engaged or apathetic? Dating with purpose or dating for distraction?

Most critically, if they were partnered, how was the state of their relationship? Dating a person in a happy, healthy, stable relationship is far easier than dating someone who is riding a roller coaster at home, or someone who is using outside relationships as a panacea for what is lacking inside.

I don't envy the men who dated me.

"I have a lot coming up I need to focus on," Viktor concluded. "It really is nothing between you and me. I am so happy we met and you are everything I wanted."

If he hadn't been so affirming, I would have been in a panic. But we'd had an exceptional night; I knew that my little stunt had made a big impression. When he'd lifted the mask from my eyes the night before he was absolutely beaming.

We kissed one last time and said goodbye. I tried to smile. He turned toward the parking lot and I walked to the elevator—my things were still in our room.

When the elevator door closed, I pushed the button for our floor and gulped back tears. With no idea when I would see him again, I felt abandoned.

I walked into our room to retrieve my overnight bag and was struck by the stark beauty of winter morning light streaming in. Desperate for reassurance and overcome with grief, I burst into tears and said out loud, "I love him." I buried my face in my hands and sobbed. Then took a picture of the scene so I could capture the precise moment I knew that I loved him.

Desperation and abandonment. This is what I called love.

34. Little Boxes

Two weeks into our forced hiatus, Viktor made arrangements for me to meet Marin with the hope that she would feel more comfortable with him seeing me once she and I met in person. I had no template for how the visit would go. The only model I had for two women sharing a lover mirrored the basest offerings of popular culture: soap opera-style catfights with face slapping, hair pulling, and a lot of screeching. It was hard to shed the vague sense of opposition I felt toward Marin because I had no previous experience or mental framework for how we could relate.

Viktor wasn't proposing Marin and I become friends, exactly, but that we become familiar to one another. If it meant I could see him again, I was willing to try. Also, I was curious to meet her. By then I'd seen her photos on Facebook, so I knew what she looked like, but that's all. Viktor proposed to join us, which I thought would be less stressful than meeting her one-on-one. Nonetheless, I bought a pack of cigarettes the day before because I felt so frantic about the meeting and imagined it was the only thing that would calm me down.

I wore a lace blouse that I bought for the occasion. It had a choker collar and cutout at the neck. I selected it thinking it would remind Viktor of bondage in a flowery sort of way, but it felt like a straitjacket and made me sweat. I finished the outfit with black slacks and heels. It was a bizarre choice—more appropriate for the Symphony than a weekday lunch at a Thai restaurant—but I guess I wanted Viktor to perceive me as the type of woman who wore lace to eat lunch. I guess that was the woman I imagined he might adore.

Marin smiled warmly and watched as I took my seat. Our eyes met, and for a moment we were both silent. I felt frozen with tension. She commented that Viktor had texted to say he'd be along soon.

Marin was so pretty it was hard not to stare. She had sparkling blue eyes and a gorgeous white smile. Her long hair was dyed every color, ROYGBIV, around the crown of her head—a veritable Rainbow Brite. It was a stunning effect. I marveled it was even possible—something like that would never have occurred to me. I'd only done a temporary color once or twice, a dark brown on top of my darker brown.

Marin was not like the women I was used to relating with—my friends of many years, Asher's friends' parents, and the moms I saw at school drop off and pickup. Most of the women I knew had children. Fortyish. Dressed casually—yoga pants or some variation of PNW casual. Several stayed at home with their kids. Others had "good jobs," which is to say they worked for someone else and had paid benefits and upward mobility. They were almost all married to men, thus presumed heterosexual and monogamous.

Marin was in her early 30's. No kids. Divorced. Worked for herself as a freelance designer. She was bisexual and nonmonogamous and her head was a pinwheel of color. She was uniquely herself.

Sitting there, observing her, I wanted what she had. Not her boyfriend, but the permission she'd given herself. I, too, wanted to live on my own terms. I wanted to be free…not of my husband and child, but of the limitations I'd always put on myself because of who I thought I was supposed to be: Normal Girl. "Normal" was my bid for safety and security, a trap I'd made for myself.

Marin did not seem like she'd spent the day stress smoking. She did not appear worried about sweat stains on her outfit. She seemed calm, like she'd done this before, like she knew how this worked.

She saw him before I did because my back was to the door. She stood, so I did too. He appeared. They embraced. He looked into her eyes and gave her a kiss. He hugged me—it felt rushed. He paused for us to sit and then plunked himself in the chair next to Marin. As he resituated his place setting, he said something about the workday and parking, concluding "but I'm here now." He was bright, just a notch below hyper, precisely in character.

Facing them in the silence that followed I felt awkward and naïve, like a pubescent teenager cast into a spotlight that illuminated every mortifying detail of their transformation: every pimple, every body odor, every leaky tampon, every social gaffe, every uncertainty. I was nearly forty, but sitting with the two of them, I felt barely a day over 15, in the midst of a similar transformation, but with much higher stakes.

Ninth grade was the first time it occurred to me that I didn't have to be like everybody else, that I could live outside the box. I began to ask myself who I wanted to be. How did I want to look? Who did I want to be friends with? How did I want the world to perceive me? Who did I want to become?

Most of all I wanted to be myself, but I didn't know yet who that was. I thought I might like to be like Angela from *My So Called Life*. She was original, always in her feelings. Or better, Angela's best friend Rayanne—a girl with real problems, perhaps, but she wasn't going to let that keep her from smiling and having fun.

Over the course of that year, I started to morph my personal style away from a generic, preppy look to a more individualized, alternative one. I saved my babysitting money to spend on *Sassy* magazines and Doc Martens, which I wore with loose-fitting men's jeans from Value Village and t-shirts I thought were artsy (my favorite was covered in M.C. Escher drawings).

I pierced my belly button with a safety pin, dyed my hair with Kool-Aid, and shaved the back of my head with the clippers Alex left behind when he moved away to college.

I splatter painted my bedroom teal, which I thought was very original, a la Jackson Pollock.

I wrote a poem about a cigarette and gave it to Chet, the boy friend I hoped would become my boyfriend.

I interpretive danced to Fleetwood Mac and the Doors and Pearl Jam's *Ten*.

One day my friend Jenna joined in, which was the best thing ever because it meant I wasn't the only weirdo who thought that was fun. Afterward we ate Cool Whip and Wonder bread sandwiches that we washed down with her mom's peach Bartles & Jaymes.

In the spring of that year, I heard you could overdose on Dramamine to get high. I don't remember what I thought it would do for me. All I remember was that I was curious about drugs and that was one I could steal from a drugstore, which is exactly what I did.

My friend Richelle and I decided to split the pack of 24 one evening before we went to Zane's house. Zane was a boy who I kind of knew from our junior high—he was captain of the football team—whose house was near the duplex where I lived with my mom and Mari. Richelle and I took the Dramamine, then walked over. Zane and his friend offered us some pot, which we happily smoked (the second time in my life I'd ever tried it). Soon we found ourselves laying four in a row across the full-sized bed in his room, our legs sticking off the side like matchsticks—Zane, Richelle, me, Zane's friend—stoned out of our minds.

Neither Richelle nor I knew what we were in for, but Zane did. He had clearly put a lot of thought into how the night would go. The whole setup strikes me as crazy even now, but this is what he had engineered: a wooden box containing a red laser pointer was propped at an angle inside an open dresser drawer so the light would shine through an etched glass mug he had hung from the ceiling with a thumbtack. He spun the mug on its string. The red light shining through the mug produced a laser show in the corner where the ceiling met the wall. It reminded me of the time Alex took Mari and I to see Laser U2 at the Pacific Science Center in Seattle, which I thought was the epitome of cool. Achtung, baby.

Richelle and I looked at each other excitedly, like we were waiting for our favorite movie to start.

"Can you feel it?" she whispered.

"I can't really feel anything, so I think so!" We giggled.

Zane turned off the lights and turned on *Doin' It*, by LL Cool J. *Doin' It* is the kind of song that would horrify most church ladies, which is why I liked it, even though at age 15 I had no frame of reference for what it described. Next was something by Ice-T; I didn't know the song but I liked being exposed to something so different from the Indigo Girls, my favorite band at the time.

As we laid there watching the laser dance, my body started to stiffen. The feeling of strangeness in my body seemed to be accelerating. Soon I could barely move. My tongue stuck to the roof of my mouth and I couldn't lift my hands. I started to feel afraid I might have overdosed, or that my body would never go back to normal.

Zane jumped up and said to his friend, "Pantera."

"Yeah…"

I had no idea what Pantera was, but as soon as he pushed play, I felt like I'd been immersed in the soundtrack of hell. Every second grated on me like a blade scraping steel. I don't know why it didn't occur to me to ask him to change it. Maybe because I wasn't sure I could form words.

Zane's friend tried to put his hand under my shirt but backed off when I grunted no. Zane lacked such manners. Eventually he started kissing Richelle, then got on top of her. I could feel him moving against me. I heard her tell him no. I willed my hand to grab his arm so I could get his attention, but it dropped dead next to me. I slurred what I intended as daggers from my throat, "Don't have sex with her." But it came out like garbled marbles, "Derhasillepper."

The next thing I heard was a zipper. And then I heard her cry out.

I laid there, stiff and powerless, blinking tears from my eyes, the music screaming.

When it was over, and we could finally move again, we got up and walked home in a shell-shocked stupor. Richelle started to whimper on the way—one of the saddest sounds I've ever heard.

"If you get raped does that mean you're not a virgin anymore?"

"Noooooo," I told her. "You're still a virgin until you want to have sex. I'm so sorry that happened."

We were standing on the side of a busy road with gravel underfoot and streaks of head lights burning our stoney eyes. I gave her a hug, which she accepted with her arms braced in front of her body and her face buried in her hands, sobbing.

"Are you going to be okay? I'm so sorry."

I patted her back and told her over and over I was sorry. I didn't know what else to say or do, or how to help, but I knew I had really fucked up. The drugs were my idea. The boys were my idea. The need to escape was mine.

I don't remember ever looking Richelle in the eyes again. Her mom pulled her out of our junior high. That night was the last time I ever saw her.

By the end of my freshman year, I had a friend who got pregnant, one that got caught stealing, and another who went to drug rehab. In hindsight, I see that I gravitated to troubled kids because they felt safe—I knew they wouldn't judge me for my bad dad. I felt I could relate to them, and they to me. I had no idea how identified I was with my dad's failures.

Unsure what else to do and desperate to get me back on track, my mom sent me to be a Counselor-in-Training at a Christian camp that summer. It worked. Spooked by the night with Richelle and the trouble my friends had gotten into, I decided I would get back in the box. I'd go back to coloring inside the lines. No more teal splatter paint or DIY piercings. My experiments of identity and differentiation were fucking scary. I decided to be godly instead. I decided I'd be "good." "Good" and—there it is again—"normal."

And that's exactly what I did. I went to high school in the fall and made new friends with kids I thought were kind of boring, because there was no drama. They thought it was fun to go to the movies or hang out in the Taco Bell parking lot, hopping from car to car.

Up until that year, I had used the movie theater as a shield for whatever badness I was really up to—stealing sundries from the Kmart next door, smoking with Chet, shotgunning beers with older boys in the parking lot. These were things to get excited about. Now I actually watched the movie I professed to my mom I was going to see. I watched boys my own age play video games in the arcade and developed a taste for those crispy cinnamon churro thingies at Taco Bell. I started going to youth group, and to Young Life.

I had no idea how to find contentment in just being: hanging out with friends, playing sports, exploring new interests, reading, practicing activities I liked. If I wasn't feeling something intensely, I didn't guess it was worth my time. This is a common issue for people who grow up with trauma. Nonetheless, I tried to get psyched about Young Life—those kids all seemed so earnest and made life seem simple. I wanted that, even if I didn't subscribe to the rules of their god. Even if it meant I would never feel understood by the people around me.

What I wanted most of all, though—my truest longing—was for a love like the couple that ran our Young Life chapter, because they seemed so devoted and pure. I wondered if they had sex before they were married and thought they probably hadn't, which meant the husband loved the wife before they even had sex. He loved her enough to protect her virtue. This was how I thought about it. I knew you weren't supposed to have sex before marriage—(not so much a family ethic as fumes I ingested from the cultural ether)—and aspired to wait like I imagined they had. Somehow this seemed like the epitome of true love, and I wanted someone to love me like that. I didn't know what I would have to do to get it, but for starters I figured I'd go back to shopping at the Gap instead of thrift stores. I'd be cute and preppy and conventional. I'd repaint my walls white and I'd stop writing in my journal…god. What was the point of exploring feelings I didn't want to have?

My efforts to be godly and good were thwarted a year later, in the summer before my junior year of high school. The phone rang just before 11PM. My mom answered. Right away her face turned serious, almost grave. I stood close, trying to hear. As best I could tell it was my brother.

"Is that Alex?" I asked. She nodded yes.

"Is it about Dad?" She ignored my question.

"Oh Alex, I'm so sorry." My mom sounded pitiful, as sorry as could be.

"WHAT?!" I asked her. I thought my dad was dead.

She made her hand into a gun, then motioned like she was pulling a trigger.

"Someone shot Dad?!"

She pressed her lips together and shook her head no. Then she said it again. "Oh Alex, I'm so sorry."

When she got off the phone, she explained. Some guy in his building had jumped my dad the night before and beaten him up. My dad, black out drunk at the time, went to his apartment and shot him in retaliation. Later he told the police, "I shot the fucking (expletive) in the belly to teach that bastard a lesson." He sealed his own fate. Clearly it wasn't self-defense, as he would later plead.

I don't remember much else of what happened after my mom got off the phone except that I vacillated between hysterical and hyperventilating for a long time. She took me outside and tried to calm me down. I walked barefoot in circles over the black asphalt, still warm from the hot July day, crying, moaning, and asking questions that begged for a different reality. *He did what? How could he? Why?*

My most lasting impression of that night was my certainty that a new fate had been sealed for me. Life as I knew it—Young Life, normal girl—was over. My dad was a criminal, a convicted loser. It stood to reason that as his offspring, I must be, too. I wondered if I was being melodramatic when I sobbed to my mom, "No student body president has a dad who's in jail!"

I didn't feel entitled to be so devastated. It's not like we were close. Even as I paced the black ground, I wondered if I was just miming upset. Did I really care that much? I had managed through his absence and more or less ignored his existence for years. Why should it be any different now that he'd committed a crime he didn't get away with?

I blamed myself. *I shouldn't be surprised. I should just get over it.* I concluded it was something I had contrived, a sort of armchair psychology: the subject feels inferior because her paternal figure is a fuck up.

But that's exactly how I felt, and I believed I could be no better than him. I had planned to run for school office that year. I wanted to be a Daffodil princess, a coveted honor in our small town that I thought would look great on a college application. I wanted to play sports and take AP classes and get good grades. I'd spent the year before minding my manners, doing well in school, being generally responsible, going to youth group, and avoiding the new trouble my peers were getting into. I planned to go to DePauw—the school my mom meant to go to before she found out she was pregnant. I was going to be an obstetrician; I'd been dreaming about it since I could remember.

But my dad's crime changed all of that. I was and would only ever be one thing: a loser.

The following school year, I had 39 unexcused absences before winter break. I often didn't even have a reason to cut class—I just didn't want to go. When my pre-calculus teacher got on my case about missing so much school, I explained that my dad was on trial (true) and said I had been going to court to support him (not true). She looked mortified, and I got what I wanted. Her expectations of me changed. She got off my case. I continued to forge notes from my mom so I could get the blue slip I needed to get back into class whenever I deigned to return.

I didn't have to believe the narrative that nothing but poisoned fruit came from a poisoned tree. But I did believe it, consciously and unconsciously. None of my friends understood, at least none of the "good" kids.

So, I moved on. I took classes at the local community college instead of going to high school all day. I worked full time at a coffee shop and took up with my first serious boyfriend, who proposed to me after two months of dating to alleviate my guilt that we were having sex. I didn't know how else I could reconcile my overwhelming desire to have sex with the guilt I had about having it, so I said yes to the proposal. It lasted about three weeks before I realized the absurdity of being engaged at age 17. I gave the ring back. We kept dating, we kept having sex, and I continued to feel guilty and wrong, wrong, wrong.

Two years later, I married Ethan—my attempt to rebuild a shelter for myself. I knew well enough by then I'd be safer inside the box than out in the great wide open. It wasn't the love I longed for but, believing I could be no better than my dad, I hoped marriage could at least save me from myself.

I didn't realize the inherent problem with this—that being saved from myself meant I could never become her.

Sitting at lunch facing Viktor and Marin, I realized they weren't trying to be "normal." They weren't trying to be everyone's best friend. They were unapologetically themselves. I envied their liberation and felt wholly inadequate for the way I had failed to differentiate myself. To become myself. To let the colors of my own freak flag fly. I'd gone to lunch thinking I was so brave and bold and evolved with my open marriage. I tried to emphasize that Jack and I had been open now for more than a year—which was true, ish. But Viktor had changed everything, and it hadn't even been a full season since we met.

Facing the two of them, side-by-side, I considered the viability of a less conventional lifestyle. And I saw the permission I hadn't known I had been waiting for to finally be myself.

35. Backlash Blues

After Jack and I started dating other people, I began to move about the world like I had a secret. It was energizing, but could be awkward, too. Like the night Jack and I were hosting friends for dinner who confided with some disdain that they knew a couple who had just started swinging. Jack and I avoided eye contact, so we didn't smirk and give ourselves away. (Was their indignation masked envy? Maybe. Some months later the wife half of the couple confided during our kids' soccer practice that they had started swapping with another couple.)

I had never realized how much I took for granted as a married, monogamous-assumed heterosexual. I began to worry what would happen if other people found out—people tend to discriminate against people who are different from them. Would my female friends ditch me if they knew we were open, because they envied my liberation…or thought I wanted to sleep with their husband? Would Asher's friends' parents still let their kids play at our house if they knew we were nonmonogamous—or would they assume we were a part of some twisted sex cult? What if one of us ran into someone we knew while we were on a date with someone else? (This happened once, actually—Jack's co-worker saw me having a cozy lunch with a date and texted him immediately, then Jack texted me—I knew I'd been spotted before I'd even left the restaurant.)

I liked that I had started to feel different from the other moms at after school pick up. I had something—besides smoking weed and frequent masturbation—that was mine and only mine.

And dating was a great distraction, not just from the challenges in my marriage, but what opening up had revealed: I was unhappy with myself because I had never given myself permission to be exactly who I wanted to be, and the life that resulted from trying to be pleasing was not the life I wanted to live.

Therapy was helping me understand how the attachment wound I developed in childhood related to the woman I became. The consequences were subtle—not debilitating—so for years they had escaped my awareness. My whole lifetime, really. So many of us function this way.

But the price was high: I didn't trust my feelings. I believed, deep down, that life was not to be trusted, even cruel. I still felt I could be no better than my dad. But apart from bi-weekly therapy, I didn't know what else to do to "deal with it," and I hated how it felt to go there—into the sadness and feelings of despair and unworthiness buried within. So I tipped my glass, recharged my vibrator, tapped the dating app on my home screen, and kept swiping, day after day after day.

I was also using dating to avoid the shifting sands between Jack and me. Every date held the promise of escape as well as the possibility I'd finally find what I was looking for (basically, I realize now, a balm for every pain I'd ever endured, as if such a thing existed...no wonder Jack couldn't deliver). Even a bad date felt better than another night at home rehashing the same argument about Kat. Jack and I were making no progress toward reconciliation.

Apart from getting to have sex with other people, opening up wasn't working like I had hoped. The changes taking place felt like they were happening to me and Jack, not for us. We weren't growing together; we were coming apart. I was finding satisfaction—of a sort, to a degree—outside of our marriage. And I was beginning to feel like a different person. I was becoming more known to myself, and stranger as a wife.

I couldn't distract myself with Viktor because Marin was mad again. He said that any time my name came up he knew he was in for at least a thirty-minute discussion, and more likely a two-hour fight.

Oh! I thought, *so that's her game. Give him permission and then give him hell.* Kinda like I did with Jack, but I couldn't see that at the time.

I defaulted to blame. It was Marin's fault I couldn't see Viktor, and I resented her fiercely. Even though I knew what it felt like—I was to Marin what Kat was to me: the Other Woman. But I didn't want to consider Marin over my own desires, because that might lead to understanding and compassion, and I was mad and selfish.

Eventually Viktor revealed that Marin didn't believe that I was just another of his lovers. She thought he regarded me differently because we'd had hotel dates, because he took me to dinner every time, because we typically spent the night together when we did have a date—she didn't believe it was just sex.

I understood why she felt this way. I, too, sensed Viktor liked me more than he would admit. The way I understood it, he didn't want there to be something more between us. He didn't want me to be anything but another one of his lovers, because he didn't want any complications.

"I can have one relationship or neglect two." He told me that time and again.

But there were moments when he made love to me that felt like he meant it. And there was a way he looked in my eyes that felt like we were sharing something eternal. It was beautiful—exactly the type of experience I had hoped to share, and was still trying to find, with Jack. But I had found it with Viktor. It felt like our secret.

36. Mess is Mine

Jack's broken agreements around the concert and his first overnight with Kat gave us plenty to talk about in therapy. I couldn't talk about it without getting enraged. I had no idea my anger was a result of Jack triggering my vulnerability, and I couldn't see that it was out of proportion to his actions, because I felt justified—I had been wronged, and Jack did it to me. It was his fault. He was the bad guy.

The intensity of my anger rattled Jack. Where I had learned to compensate for my vulnerability by over functioning and going on the offensive, Jack tended to pull back when he felt vulnerable. I was Hulk-mode. He was a turtle inside its shell.

Meanwhile, I was also smug. *I hadn't broken any agreements. I was good at nonmonogamy. I was in such denial about my infidelities before we opened our marriage that they weren't even on my radar as such.* So I went on acting superior and refusing to empathize with Jack. If he wouldn't tell me he was hurt by my relationship with Viktor, then I wasn't going to offer him that compassion. If he wouldn't apologize convincingly and explain his actions around Kat, then I wasn't going to forgive him.

I still wanted to know, and I demanded to know: Why? Why did he insist on following through with his plans even after he knew how much it upset me? Why use those tickets for her? Why take her to that hotel? I imagined he had designed the whole thing to be as hurtful toward me as possible. The harder I pressed him for an explanation, the harder he pushed back.

"Why does it have to mean anything?"

Because of course it fucking meant something.

I had a number of my own theories about why he acted the way he did. Maybe he was striking out at me for suggesting opening up. Maybe he was hurt and wanted to hurt me back. Or maybe he wanted to experience something like I shared with Viktor, to even the score. He wouldn't own up to any of these.

Also, he still wouldn't tell me how he felt about men, which I thought I had a right to know. I couldn't accept that he might want to maintain some privacy around his sexuality, or that maybe he didn't even know. It never occurred to me how complicated and nuanced attraction can be, that sometimes self-awareness gets buried underneath social stigmas, family judgment, or our own inability to come to terms with what is real and true. It's very hard to accept in yourself what you don't want to admit, and harder still when you aren't even aware.

I was tired of asking the questions—doing the work of our relationship—by myself. But if we didn't address the issues between us, how could we ever get past them? For weeks we were in a stalemate. Any time I probed, I got the same answers: "I don't know." "You're making too much of it." "Why does it have to mean anything?"

We existed in a state of managed conflict. We co-parented easily. We moved around in the house like we always had. We chose to spend time together in the evenings, just like normal. As long as the relationship talks remained confined to therapy, we got along well. We wanted to get along. We loved each other.

Around three weeks after Jack's first overnight with Kat, he had a sort of epiphany when our therapist mentioned his actions were regressive, a nice way of saying his behavior was beneath his maturity level. That evening he shared a memory of an embittered argument he had with his dad as a teenager and noted that his feelings during our argument were similar to how he felt then.

This felt, at last, like progress. I was glad to learn something new about him. Once again, I thought knowledge would lead to understanding and understanding to resolution. I hoped that it meant we were finally beginning to make strides toward new awareness of each other, and repair. We agreed we'd talk more about it in therapy the following week.

A few nights later we were tucked into bed. Jack and I had gone to bed at the same time nearly every night of our relationship. Even when we started to struggle, this remained true.

Once in bed, Jack would read the news, preparing for his radio show the next morning. I would read a book, or—more often—my phone. Sometimes we'd play Words With Friends and rib each other playfully.

Rarely, I turned my light out before he did. I'd give him a quick kiss and roll over, turning my back to the light. This was one of those nights. After kissing him goodnight, I settled on my side, facing the wall.

"Goodnight honey," I said.

"Goodnight, baby." He rubbed my hip for a moment.

"I love you."

"I love you, too."

I closed my eyes, ready to fall asleep. As soon as I did, I heard this sentence, unspoken but clear as day, from out of nowhere:

"Ask him if he had sex with Kat without a condom."

My eyes flew open. I resisted. No. I didn't want to ask. I didn't want it to be true. But I heard the words, clear as day.

With a stone in my throat, I pushed it out, "Did you have sex with Kat without a condom?"

He was quiet for a long time. My anger compounded with every millisecond.

"Yes," he finally admitted.

In an instant I whipped around with my finger pointed in his face and hissed, "HOW FUCKING DARE YOU?"

My anger was so large I felt like I had slapped him with it. He flinched, which scared me. The look on his face said he didn't know what I was capable of. I realized: I didn't either. I was seething, boiling, erupting, furious. He looked like he expected violence.

"When?" I demanded.

"Last week."

"ARE YOU FUCKING KIDDING ME? You mean all this time we were supposedly working to regain trust, you went and fucked that fucking woman without a condom? WHATTHEFUCKISWRONGWITHYOU?!"

I was so angry it didn't even occur to me our child was asleep across the hall. I couldn't see straight. This was, I thought, the most basic of our agreements, and I had been diligent with my partners. I mean, except for those couple moments with Bobby, after we knew the condom came off and didn't stop. But I justified that so well to myself I'd already forgotten all about it. *We were wasted. It wasn't intentional.* It was different with Jack. His was a willful infraction.

"At least you had the decency not to lie about it. You know now I have to go get tested? Thanks! Thanks for exposing me to whatever she's into. That's fucking great, Jack. You endangered my life so you could get your dick wet with your fucking girlfriend. Good for you! I hope it was fucking worth it."

I had never heard myself like this. The words coming out of my mouth sounded like poison but I couldn't help it.

Jack jumped out of bed. "I'm not listening to this. It was a mistake, okay? I'm sorry. I shouldn't have done it. We got caught in the momen—"

"Caught in the moment? Caught in the moment! That must have been some fucking moment, Jack. I can't fucking believe you. I am so disgusted."

My voice was dripping with disdain. It hurt my ears to hear my own words.

He reached for his bathrobe. "I'm sleeping downstairs."

The second he said this, I panicked. The prospect of Jack walking out on me made me instantly terrified that I had overstepped out of anger. I was afraid I had broken something irreplaceable. I was afraid that he wouldn't come back.

"No, you're not," I said. "I'll go downstairs. You need to sleep well. You have to get up."

It was different if I left. I knew I'd be back. Jack was my rock, and I didn't want to be without him. Even, apparently, when he was the source of my pain. I couldn't let him leave. Not even just to go sleep downstairs for a night.

I started to get out of bed. "How could you? I really can't fucking believe you."

"You're not sleeping downstairs," he said. "Would you just take a fucking breath and stop yelling for a minute?"

We both got back in bed. I was so angry I was shaking. I hid it under the covers. I wanted to cry but I knew if I cried he would reach for me and I didn't want him to touch me. I sat silent, breathing through my teeth and holding back tears.

"I'm so sorry, baby," he started again.

"Don't call me fucking baby."

"Minda! What the hell? I'm trying to talk to you!"

"What?" I hated him.

He slowed down. "I am so sorry. If I could go back and change things I would. I didn't mean to do that. I won't do it again. I am so sorry. Please believe me that I didn't do it to hurt you."

I didn't believe him. I laid down in my spot, my back turned.

"I can't fucking believe you," I repeated. "Would you even have told me if I hadn't asked?"

"No," he conceded.

"Well congratulations on having the decency to be honest," I said, half sincere.

"Baby—Minda, sorry, god—let's talk about this in the morning. I am very sorry. I don't think you're in any health danger. Kat has been tested. She uses protection with all of her partners."

"Well she didn't with you!"

I couldn't stop. I was furious. Even if I suspected that my anger was out of proportion to the offense, I couldn't help it.

I know now that Jack's actions had virtually nothing to do with me; they weren't personal. He was acting out and finding his way. But I couldn't see that at the time. At the time his apparent disregard made me feel like he didn't care about me. I didn't matter. My brain knew better, but this was my felt sense, my underlying belief. Jack had proven it true.

The following Tuesday I got a text from my dad out of the blue saying he would be in the area on Thursday and he'd like us all to get together for dinner.

It was exceedingly rare that I saw my dad, who was released from prison after 12 years. Upon his release, he moved home with his wife, a woman he had married while he was out on appeal shortly after he shot the guy. They lived north of Seattle, and occasionally invited my siblings and me for a family get-together.

Defying our collective expectations, he remained sober after his release, which I had all but given up hope would ever happen. I never thought I'd get to know my dad sober.

For the first time in my life, I began to regard him as my father—a strange comfort, unfamiliar as it was. That year we even had Christmas dinner with our parents in the same room—the only meal I can remember ever sharing with my entire nuclear family. My brother and sister-in-law hosted. I had been looking forward to the novelty of it; I knew how much it meant to my dad.

But a few minutes after he arrived, I ducked out silently to the garage to pound a full glass of red wine. I didn't know why I was doing it, just that something in me felt very wrong. I must have imagined it would help.

Two years after my dad got out, right around the time I moved to San Francisco, he spontaneously defected back to Ohio, where his siblings and their families lived. His third wife told Mari that as soon as he crossed the state line, he went to a gas station and bought a case of beer. I got the sense he'd been more or less drunk ever since.

That was pretty much it for me. I didn't invite him to our wedding, and I'd only seen him once in the nine years since he'd left, when Jack and I hosted a family dinner because I wanted Asher to meet him at least once, to get a photo of them together. Occasionally he sent letters full of conservative news clippings (gun rights, First Amendment, pro-life stuff) and Family Circus comics, which I filed away in case Asher ever got curious who his grandfather was.

I thought I should go to the dinner because an opportunity to see my dad was rare. But the thought of seeing him made me exceedingly anxious. I had always felt this way when he was going to be around. I felt violated just being near him.

Once, in college, I didn't know I would see him, so I didn't have time to prepare myself. We were at my brother and sister-in-law's church for my nephew's baptism. I was sitting in the front pew watching them rehearse before the service. When I turned my head, my dad was walking toward me down the aisle, and then standing, looming large over me.

"Hi sweetie!" he said.

Moments later I was outside hyperventilating by a side door, trying to calm myself down. My oldest sister, Ellen, found me there.

"What is *wrong* with you?"

"I don't know. I saw Dad and I didn't know he was coming and I just started crying and I can't stop..."

"Well there's nothing wrong, Min. He's not going to do anything to you. Everything is fine. Take a deep breath. You need to calm down. There's nothing to be upset about."

She hugged me too hard, just like he always did. Eventually I calmed down.

After the baptism we all went to a buffet brunch to celebrate, tables and tables of food I couldn't taste. I was glad when it was time to leave. Driving home to my dorm with Ellen I felt anxious, disgusting, and ashamed of my body, and I had no idea why apart from a vague connection to my dad.

I wanted the feelings to go away, right away, and never come back. So after Ellen dropped me off at my dorm I went straight to the toilet and made myself puke. I gagged myself until I dry heaved and kept going until my throat was bruised and snot came out my nose.

It was the beginning of a pattern. If my feelings got too loud, I would feel a compulsion to make myself throw up, and it was all I could think about until I did. I used vomiting to manage anxiety until Ethan and I moved in together, at which point I knew I had to stop. This is one way he saved me from myself.

I really didn't know what to do about my dad's impending visit and I wanted someone to decide for me. I called my brother but got his voicemail. I tried his office but he was at lunch. I texted both sisters. Ellen said they were going—she and her husband, along with their son. Mari was going without her partner or kids.

"It's just dinner," she said.

No one seemed to understand this was a problem for me. I didn't even understand. Why couldn't I just pretend it was fine?

The following day I was no closer to a decision, but I realized why I felt so pressured to go: I was afraid it would be the last opportunity I had to see my dad alive. He had several DUIs, an affinity for firearms, and had been a heavy drinker for more than 30 years. I figured he was either going to drive himself into a tree, blow his brains out, or his liver would finally quit.

Unfortunately, the realization of why I was ambivalent about going brought me no closer to a decision. To top it all off, Jack had a date with Kat that night.

When he got home from work, he found me journaling at the kitchen table. It must have been evident I had been crying.

"What's wrong?" He was edgy.

"I still don't know what to do about my dad."

He sat down with a sigh. I told him everything about how I was feeling. This was my way, how I made sense of things for myself—talk, talk, talk.

"I'm just in a really bad way," I concluded.

"You want me to cancel my date, don't you?"

I didn't hear even a glimmer of compassion. Things escalated quickly. Before long we were yelling. I threw a fork across the room.

He finally yelled, "Fine. I'll cancel the date. Is that what you want?"

"What I want is for you to see I'm in a bad way, and to want to be there for me. How can you not see that I need you right now?"

"Well I just think it's awfully suspect that you need me *now*, when you know I already had plans tonight. You always bring up an issue right before I have a date."

"I can't help the timing—I just learned he's coming yesterday. I don't know how you can even think about going, or how you could have a good time with her when you know I'm suffering…"

I was blubbering.

"FINE! I won't go. Is that what you want?"

"NO! What I want is for you to want to help me!"

When he left for his date, I was downstairs in my office making jewelry. After the fight I had sequestered myself all afternoon and let him take care of Asher while I tried to sort myself out. I hadn't been able to stop crying all day. It was a slow, steady leak, the kind of crying you do over an impending death you are helpless to change. He expressed concern but I didn't believe him. After all, he was wearing a backpack with spare underwear and sex toys in it. Jack, too, was in the midst of a sexual awakening. He didn't want to give it up any more than I did.

He stayed overnight with Kat and went straight to work the next day. After I took Asher to school that morning I returned home, laid down in front of a speaker on the hard wood floor, and blasted music at my head. It was a psychological Ritalin that was all I could bear.

37. The System Only Dreams in Total Darkness

There are a lot of great reasons you might choose to be or remain monogamous:
1. You don't want to be with anyone else.
2. You enjoy investing in one relationship and value growing together over time.
3. Your sex life is already plenty fulfilling.
4. You don't have time to invest in another relationship.
5. You don't want to destabilize the primary relationship.
6. You're afraid of negative consequences (divorce, contracting an STI, others finding out/judging you, someone getting too attached…).
7. You experience unmanageable jealousy.
8. You don't want to take on another person's issues, emotions, needs, etc.
9. You don't want to compete with someone else for your partner's time/attention/affection.
10. Having sex with someone else feels like it would taint your existing relationship.
11. You feel insecure or uncertain about your partnership.
12. You find it hard to trust your partner or other people.
13. You're only considering nonmonogamy because your partner wants to, or is coercing you.
14. You don't want your kids to know.
15. You do not want to open your life to your partner's partner/s.
16. It feels too fragmenting to introduce non-monogamy right now (or ever).
17. You are unwilling to do the emotional labor that additional relationships require.
18. You don't feel comfortable revealing your body to someone new.

19. You don't think you can abide by the agreements you made with your primary partner (e.g. barrier contraception, transparency, etc.).
20. There's no one around you want to have sex with.
21. Extramarital sex is in conflict with your religious convictions.
22. Sex with someone new—or an amendment to your lifestyle, in general—would threaten your recovery.
23. You feel you lack the mental or emotional resilience to withstand a breakup.
24. Your life is already unstable (very busy at work, going through a divorce, recent traumatic loss, etc.).
25. You prefer the stability, consistency, and/or commitment of monogamy.

38. Somebody to Love

There is a children's book called *Are You My Mother?* by P.D. Eastman that I used to read to Asher every night. In it a baby bird goes looking for his mother. He meets several animals, including a dog. None of them are his mother.

Too late I realized that bird was me, although I wasn't looking for a mother, I was looking for a boyfriend. And I had no idea.

I thought Jack and I were just going to have sex with other people. That's what I thought I wanted. In this way we would maintain our core companionship while finding sexual fulfillment elsewhere. This was our mutual intention—that's what I told myself.

But the reality was, I was assessing every man I met for their long-term potential. And I was projecting onto each new love interest the same relational dynamics Jack and I shared after nine years together. I was unwittingly expecting them to serve a similar role in my life. I still didn't know how to relate in a different way, that nonmonogamy was a different—altogether new—kind of relationship. What was its form? How was this new thing shaped? What were the constraints? I had no idea; I was just barreling forward like a hungry ghost, consuming whatever seemed like it might help.

I knew better than to try and talk to Viktor about my struggles. For one thing, he remained mostly unavailable. Though he professed initially that he wanted to establish a regular cadence of seeing one another every two or three weeks, we never managed that frequency after our first few dates. His availability continued to depend on how things were going at home. As I understood it, if he and Marin were in conflict, he couldn't see me.

What's more, Viktor made his feelings about helping someone find their way in the early days of nonmonogamy abundantly clear: "I'm not in a teaching mood."

In other words, he wasn't there to walk me through the learning curve of my polyadolescence, the initial period a person or couple goes through after deciding on consensual nonmonogamy.

Like any adolescent, polyadolescents are bumbling and awkward, lacking awareness and maturity, still growing into themselves. There's no way around it; most partnered adults haven't dated since they met their spouse. They're out of practice. They've forgotten how it works. They are learning new rules. This aspect alone lends itself to folly.

What's more, when a couple opens their relationship, they are each, developmentally, the same age they were the last time they dated. It's no wonder a married person who has recently started sleeping with someone new might say they feel twenty-five again. In my experience, there are few exceptions to this phenomenon.

Another destabilizing aspect of polyadolescence is the way engaging with new people reflects a person back to themselves, which can challenge one's self-perception. There is potential for a person to cultivate greater self-awareness. But perhaps just as likely, a person may find their sense of identity—ideas they've long held about who they are, how they live, and what they value—careening off the rails.

Around the same time I met Viktor, I started talking to a guy on OKCupid that seemed promising. He and Viktor had a lot in common. They were both smart, Jewish, and in long-term, committed primary relationships. Each was highly accomplished, with brown hair and similar physiques. They both attended Burning Man every year.

There was something a little slippery about this the new guy that unnerved me, though. Viktor was candid to a fault at times. My new interest, Gavriel, felt a little evasive. For example, he seemed to travel all the time, for business and pleasure. I couldn't tell if he was legit or trying to impress me or both. It was hard for me to fathom a lifestyle so different from my own.

Who flies from Seattle to LA for a party, then back home to get their kid, then all the way to Cleveland to watch a basketball game and home again, all in a span of three days? He did. And he acted like it was just another weekend.

After the first month of chatting, my messages to and from Gavriel tapered off. I was still wondering about him several weeks later, though, so I messaged him out of the blue and asked if he'd like to get together (i.e. DTF?). It worked, and we finally met at a yoga class. Our second date was also a yoga class.

By the time we had our third date, we'd been corresponding for four months. Hundreds of messages back and forth, written conversations, which, for a smitten writer, is nearly as compelling as that many dates. By then I had imagined all kinds of things with and about him and I liked him *a lot*.

We were meeting in the penthouse of the W Hotel in Downtown Seattle—his idea. I felt *so* fancy. But this time I was not wearing heels or stockings or a ball gag. I liked him so much I wanted him to see *me*. I was starting to get the hang of the vulnerability thing: it means letting yourself be seen *in your truth*, and it is a virtue. So I wore a baggy cotton jumper that I was pretty sure would end up on the floor within minutes, anyway. I wasn't wearing makeup because I knew it would just get smeared. Also, I had deduced Gavriel was a more casual, hippie-dippy type of person. I dressed to suit him.

I stared out the window as I waited, a little dizzy from the height. It felt a little like Cinderella, but I didn't know who I was, or where we were in the story: was I a desperate stepsister? Or was my prince on his way to fit the glass slipper?

In fact, we were not so unlike the prince and the housemaid. He was a plastic surgeon, the son of two physicians, and grew up in Newport Beach.

I grew up in a duplex, in a damp and moldy state many latitudes to the north, with cartoons to keep me company after school while my mom and stepdad worked their state jobs.

Once he texted that he was close, I started pacing. I was so excited and believing so many things about who he was about to become in my life. I thought my life was about to be perfect. I would keep my husband plus have a boyfriend to meet the rest of my needs. It was exactly what I didn't know I'd been hoping to achieve all along.

When Gavriel arrived, we shared a happy greeting and lots of smiles. We had our first kiss lying on the bed overlooking the city. Sure enough, my clothes were discarded on the floor next to his within less than a quarter of an hour.

I suggested after the first round that we eat before we got too high or too drunk and forgot. We sat across from each other in the expansive living space and poked our chopsticks around the cardboard boxes I had brought full of vegan sushi. We sipped iced vodka and mead.

The conversation seemed easy and comfortable until suddenly, nothing felt right. Out of the blue, he seemed deeply uncomfortable. As I wondered silently what might be bothering him, a niggling feeling crept in: we were two strangers, married to other people, with different homes, different hopes, and different motivations, teetering on top of the city. We didn't know one another well enough to share a meal comfortably but we'd just seen each other naked, and then some.

"Are you okay?" I asked him. "You seem very uncomfortable."

"I am uncomfortable," he said.

I was surprised he admitted it, but he didn't offer an explanation. I wanted to ask him *why?, what was coming up for him?, was he feeling triggered?* I knew he spoke this language of feelings, but these questions, I decided, were too personal. More personal than what his cock smelled like or the tiny skin tag near his armpit.

We got up and shook it off, refreshed our drinks and smoked a bowl. The less sober we became, the more fun I had. The next morning, I told him—and myself—that it was one of the best nights of my life. He responded by calling the front desk and booking a late checkout at 4PM. We stayed until the last possible minute.

On his way home, he texted me: "Is this what it looks, feels, and sounds like to have all of your needs met?"

I texted him back with certainty: "YES."

I was equally certain that this was the beginning of a beautiful love. That night I told Jack I had met someone I thought I would be seeing for a long time. He seemed happy for me but didn't say much.

The next weekend Gavriel went to Miami and hit it off with his former girlfriend's former best friend.

"It was magic," he told me later, after initially lying that all they did was kiss. He implied she didn't want him to see other people (except, of course, his wife). Just like that, it was over. I was disconsolate.

The woman Gavriel took up with was a malpractice attorney with old money parents who owned flats in Paris and Hong Kong. She looked a lot better on paper, and these things clearly mattered to him. They mattered to me, too, but I didn't get to choose my pedigree.

I guess I could have lied. I could have pretended I came from somewhere else. But then no, I couldn't, because the love I wanted was not deceptive or shallow. It was honest and authentic and deep and true. I wanted fucking intimacy.

39. Last Kiss

It wasn't just a matter of chemistry. Increasingly I heard myself talking about being "met," which was difficult to define. How do you articulate the experience of deep connection that's possible between two people? What I wanted was nothing less than profound intimacy between our souls, but it was easier to articulate that I wanted him to pull my hair, throw me down, make me beg. Viktor did these things for me, but there was no larger context. Nothing remained of those moments but the memory and a renewed sense of longing. We were building nothing. There would be no milestones in our relationship, no anniversaries.

Several nights a week after Asher was asleep, Jack and I took to the porch to talk about the issues between us. We'd each wrap ourselves in a blanket—or sometimes we shared one big one—and hunker down on our front stoop. We spent countless hours on the porch as things continued to unravel. So many words. So much heartache. These conversations were generally unproductive, never yielding more than a moment of hope or healing, and sometimes they only reinforced or deepened existing wounds, but we persevered. Neither of us seemed to know what else to do.

I wanted emotional intimacy and passionate, connected sex, a collaborative future, and a dynamic relationship that would continue to grow and deepen with time.

What did Jack want? I didn't know. He still wasn't offering any answers, so I was left to guess. Maybe he wanted me to be different. Maybe he wanted to go back in time and never open up. Maybe he wanted a divorce. He said it one night on the porch.

"I've been thinking about what I would do if we got a divorce…"

It was the second time he had mentioned it in a couple months. I never said it; just the thought made me sick to my stomach.

Kitchen sex wasn't something Jack and I had ever had but that's where it started. I was drunker than I meant to be at 6PM. A martini had seemed like a good idea, being that it was Friday, almost summer, and I had a date later. I was ripe and restless. Maybe that's why I started it.

There was some kissing, rushed and untargeted. I turned my ass to him—less personal—and bent over the counter with my face next to the coffee pot. I gripped the side of the sink with one hand and braced myself against the wall with the other. He lifted my robe, lowered his pants, and for a moment we went at it like a shiny new couple. I stared at a bottle of olive oil as he moved in me and tried to remember the last time we had been together. Sex between us had become rare. It was just so loaded, the space between us so crowded by the shadow of others.

I didn't know why we were doing it—I did not feel tenderness, lust, longing, or any particular affection. Maybe we were seeking the comfort of a familiar body? Maybe we were hoping to ignite a new spark? Maybe we were just drunk?

A song called *Homecoming* came on Spotify, then played again right away. We both noticed.

"Didn't this song just play?" he asked.

"Yeah, that's weird," I said. "Meant to be...?"

There was a beat, a pause.

And then I looked him right in the eyes and added, "Welcome home."

The line felt like a lie coming out of my mouth. It wasn't like we'd been making progress toward reconciling our marriage, though we'd started seeing yet another therapist. Was it what I wanted to be true, to remake our home? Did I think I could will our happiness back into being? Or was I just drunk and prone to cliché?

It could have been any of these things. Maybe it was all of them. But there was also denial in what I said. Because I didn't want to remake my home with Jack if it meant I would have to give up the pleasure and freedom I was coming to know.

Maybe "welcome home" was a plea for things to be other than they were. It was a denial of the truth, a bid for a different reality. But no amount of wishing and hoping would change our trajectory.

He continued to fuck me. When Asher called for a snack from downstairs, where he was watching cartoons, I yelled back, "Hang on, honey…"

We retreated to the bedroom and fell back into our old hurry-up-and-come choreography. Moments later I found my robe in the kitchen and took Asher some cheddar bunnies. I didn't know it was the last time.

I spent the next hour getting ready for my date and left early, stopping for a cigarette on the way. I ducked into a coffee shop after I finished smoking so I could brush my teeth in their restroom and wash my hands. I was nothing if not committed to my denial.

A month after the last time, Jack and I had a dinner date that started with an argument and took a nose-dive from there. It was the most combative we'd ever been in public, bickering over plates of fried artichoke hearts and oozing burrata with roasted beets. Later we stood on the sidewalk down the street from the restaurant—awkwardly for a couple who had been together nearly nine years because—no surprise—I wanted a cigarette.

Talking was my attempt at an epiphany; I didn't know what else to do. But I was getting nowhere on my own. I was as full as ever with urgent questions, but Jack mostly said he didn't know. I could not understand this. "I don't know" felt like complacency or disengagement, very much like "I don't care."

We had talked several times about closing our relationship but neither of us wanted to give up what we had with other people, or the potential of it. We agreed it would only make us resentful of each other. Any professional might have considered this all the evidence that was needed: we'd met our end. But we plundered on through the crash site of our relationship. There we stood amid the smoldering wreckage, our argument gaining steam again. Finally, I blurted out:

"I'm done, Jack. I can't do this anymore. I feel like I am the only one asking questions of our relationship or wanting things to be different or really working at this and you're just going along, obliging me, telling me you don't know."

He stared at me with a straight face and said nothing. I continued.

"Neither of us wants to close the relationship. And I can't carry the emotional burden anymore—I won't. I'm done doing things that perpetuate what I want to change. I just can't fucking do it anymore and I won't. I won't!"

"So you're giving me an ultimatum?" he asked.

"No, I'm just telling you how I feel. I'm saying I can't fucking do this, like this, anymore. This isn't working."

I meant our way of relating, not the entire marriage.

Two weeks later, Jack was acting like he was single. We were at a concert with mutual friends, including a woman named Lonnie who Jack had gone out with once before he and I met. She arrived just as we were sitting down to eat a picnic that I had spent the afternoon preparing.

He got up and went to her to say hello, then stayed for half an hour while I sat there and tried to decide whether I should eat without him or fling vermicelli noodles at them both.

I didn't approach them or nudge him that we were in the middle of a picnic and he was being rude because I didn't know that sometimes loving someone means kindly reminding them when they're being a dick. Instead, I watched them talking and flirting and miming falling in love and silently raged.

When we fought about it later, Jack said they only looked so cozy because it was loud so they had to talk close. It was a bitter fight that never resolved. Although I don't know what resolution would have looked like, anyway. Jack could have apologized for ignoring me and it wouldn't have changed a thing, because I was more focused on the offense itself than overcoming it. The worse things got between us, the less willing I was to lay myself bare in the ways that love requires.

A few days after my fight with Jack about the concert, Asher and I met Mari and her 2-year-old son at a music festival for a long weekend where we planned to camp with friends. Exhausted by the dating and marriage drama, I hoped the time away would serve as something like a reset. However, there was a toddler to coordinate, and Mari was pregnant so she couldn't keep up with him as well as she could otherwise. Asher also required focus, feeding, corralling. The trip was fun, but taxing.

As we made our way home across the West Seattle Bridge, the sun was a shimmering sphere of hot pink and red orange. August wildfires in Oregon and British Columbia had turned the air thick and hazy, creating a backdrop for a series of stunning sunsets. The sky looked apocalyptic. When I looked to my right, through the haze, I saw my city home. Below us, dark water. The whole scene was chilling, eerie.

"Look at the sky, Ash."

He grunted the way a kid does when you've interrupted an iPhone with something incredible.

We pulled up to our house and began to unload. Jack was right there to help. We moved around each other as Asher and Jack happily caught up. I used the last reserves of my energy to smile at their sweetness and carry in the bags. We were dirty and Asher was hungry. I made him a piece of toast and nudged him to the bathtub.

Once he was settled, I left Jack to finish the bedtime routine and flopped into a chair on the patio with my phone, a glass of wine, and a cigarette.

"Look at me. Look at me right now."

Suddenly Jack was standing over me. I looked up from my phone, confused by his assertiveness and the speed at which he had exited the house—in my mind's eye, invisible wings. He was almost yelling at me, and I had just arrived home ten minutes before. Our child was in the bath. We'd barely said a word to each other in the last six days.

I looked up at him, startled and put off.

"This is what's going to happen," he said. "We're getting a divorce."

This is what a split second means: the moment you become two people. This happens to me at certain times—I become a person who is experiencing a thing and a person who is observing it. I separate. ("This is his heart. It isn't moving.")

My jaw opened to speak but nothing came out.

"What are you thinking?" Jack grilled me.

I opened my mouth to speak again. I looked around for words, but nothing came.

I tried again. Open. Gape. Close. Open, gape, close. Like a fish waiting to catch what swam by, I was fishing for sound, for words, for sense, for order.

I shook my head like I just shot a double whiskey and walked away from him, into the house, the kitchen, the fridge, the wine. I poured myself a full glass and grabbed the cigarettes and left with my phone to go try and make sense of his words somewhere else, away from the man who apparently couldn't do this anymore, either.

But he meant the whole thing, not a part of it. I only meant I couldn't do the part I had been doing—by myself, it felt like—for these past years. That's all I meant. But he meant the last ten years of relating. It was over.

"This is what's going to happen."

It wasn't a question.

I walked up the street to a set of stairs that led to the backyard of the artists' studios that were on the corner of our block. There was a thick green hedge on either side of the steps that was tall enough to hide me well, though I could easily peek around and see our house down the street. I texted Jess.

I'm sorry sweetie. I guess you knew this was coming.

No, I didn't know it was coming and I resented her for saying it like it was a fact. I texted Dianne and asked if she was available.

"Give me a minute," she replied.

I smoked two cigarettes before she called. I was a little bit glad something so bad had happened so that I could smoke and drink with impunity. I couldn't be mad at myself for my bad habits when they were so vital to my immediate coping.

I talked to Dianne for an hour, mostly repeating myself.

"I can't believe it. I can't fucking believe it. I can't believe he did that."

"But I think you can, Minda. This isn't a surprise. It was only a matter of time before you would have done it yourself."

She might have been right, but I still wasn't ready to admit it.

Eventually I walked back home. Jack had texted me while I was gone. He was probably afraid something happened to me, like maybe I'd done something drastic. Or maybe I'd been hit by a truck.

40. I'm Goin' Down

When I met Viktor, I completely lost—or maybe redirected—my creative verve. In the six months prior to meeting him I'd done nearly a dozen interviews and written, tested, photographed, and posted something like 50 recipes for *Eat Like a Yogi*. All of a sudden, after we met: crickets. Instead, I spent my energy on our dates—the waiting, the planning, the recovery. I had nothing left for recipes, interviews, or anything else.

About the only thing I did for *Eat Like a Yogi* during that season of my life was attend a conference to learn about fundraising. If I wanted to scale the site into the lifestyle business I believed it could become, I was going to need capital.

The keynote speaker was the CEO of a local software company. She was so brilliant in a certain way that I felt inspired to work for her. I said as much when I introduced myself, so she asked me about my experience. I quickly summarized that I was working on building my own company, but that I had a background in marketing and community management.

"Well our VP of Customer Success is here," she said. "You should talk to her."

I had worked through my 20's and into my 30's at corporate-y desk jobs, plenty of time to confirm it wasn't my jam. So I should have known better. I guess I thought—hoped, really— this time might be different.

The interview process went on through the summer as Jack and I were falling apart, then culminated in an epic finale: I had to give a thirty-minute presentation to a six-person panel based on my analysis of thousands of data points.

It might as well have been a billion for as much as I knew what I was doing.

For the second half hour of the final interview, I was to answer questions about my presentation from the panel. After that there would be six hour-long interviews, one with each panelist, plus lunch at a nearby restaurant with two people from other departments within the organization.

It was a company of Ivy-Leaguers and I wanted to prove myself. I had neither the education nor the resume to compete, but I was determined to shine. I spent more time preparing for that interview than anything I'd ever worked on in my entire life.

The day of my presentation, I stood at the head of the conference room, smiling hard. At exactly 9AM, I turned my body in a literal circle. This was my way of getting into character, of becoming a person I thought they might award the job. It never occurred to me I wouldn't like a job that I had to play someone else to get.

When they called to tell me I got it, I held on as long as I could without crying. When I hung up the phone, I sobbed. Jack had told me four days before my final interview that he wanted a divorce. By the time I stood in front of those people, I knew how much it mattered—I not only wanted the job, I needed it. I was going to need a way to support myself and my son.

Once I signed the W-2, I resolved to move into my own place as soon as possible. Immediacy had always been my practice. Retract, evade, run…and don't stop. I didn't want to stay in the house where we had made memories as a family, said goodbye to our dog Zoe, tucked Asher in every night, argued on the porch, come apart.

I asked Jack to look at apartments with me. I implied the reason I was asking was that I wanted to be sure he approved of where I would be living with Asher, but the larger reason was that I was used to having him by my side. I still needed him.

Since I was planning to move out, we realized we would have to tell Asher. We sat down with him one night after dinner. Jack and I had talked in advance and agreed on the general points we wanted to make:

We will always be a family.

This is a grown-up choice that we made together.

We believe we can be better friends if we don't live in the same house.

I will always be your mommy and Daddy will always be your dad.

Saying the words proved more difficult. Right away, Asher seemed to sense something was off and started acting silly.

"Sweetheart, Daddy and I need to talk to you about something."

"Are you guys getting a divorce?"

Jack and I glanced at each other. How did he know? The words stuck in my throat.

"We, um…no…we haven't decided that yet. But we have decided that we're going to live in two houses."

"Will I still go to the same school?" he asked, winding up to tears.

I pulled him onto my lap and wrapped him in my arms.

"Yes, honey, you're going to go to the same school and will have the same friends and a lot of things are going to be the same. But once I have a new house, you will get to stay there, too. You'll have two houses. You'll be with Daddy half of the week and Mommy half the week."

By the time I said as much he was bawling. Jack and I looked at each other with tears in our eyes. I rested my forehead against Asher's and pulled him closer. After a good cry and more questions, we tucked him into bed.

Jack agreed to help me look for a place. We made it a family outing, hoping Asher would be more comfortable if he saw we were doing it together. I lost steam after the first couple viewings. The reality of driving Asher to school every morning versus walking him half a block down the street was unappealing.

Also, I realized I was not certain I didn't want to stay in our house. I considered I could ask Jack to leave. I was Asher's mother, and mothers weren't supposed to leave their children, even if they were just moving down the street. This thought alone was enough to give me pause. If I moved out, would Asher grow up feeling like I'd left him?

A month later, Jack and I were still living together. We still undressed in front of each other, though we hadn't had sex in months—even the thought of it had become strange. We no longer related that way.

Yet we continued to sleep holding hands, a quiet sweetness neither of us acknowledged but that we both seemed to take comfort in. Jack and I never suffered from a lack of love.

Each of us continued to date—I was seeing Viktor, and others; he was seeing Kat, and others. It wasn't that different than it always had been, though I felt exhausted at times by the emotional tension. Happy times, easy times, mealtimes, game times, chore times, family times—all of them were underscored by the knowledge: this is ending.

Sometimes I thought we might change our minds. For the first couple months I expected Jack to take it back and tell me he didn't mean it, that it was a foolish thing to say—"We're getting a divorce." He never did. I asked him if he meant it, if this was really what he wanted, but always stopped myself just short. I never said, "No, I don't want this, let's work it out." Because nothing had changed enough to make me believe that anything would be different enough that we could thrive.

Also, I'm sorry to say it but once we'd decided to separate, I felt a degree of relief. Because it meant that I was already surviving the loss of Jack. For all the years since Vox died, I had wondered how I could survive losing Jack, too, the truest love I'd ever known. Had I withdrawn rather than facing the reality of losing another someone who I loved the most?

I started my new job, and Jack and I hatched a plan for me to stay in the house until February of the following year, by which time I would have saved a nest egg to get me started again in my life as a single person. Neither of us made a move to file for divorce. It didn't seem necessary, and certainly not urgent…until the weekend after Thanksgiving, when I was driving with my mom to see my siblings for a belated holiday get together.

"I was so surprised to see Jack last weekend," she mentioned casually.

"What do you mean?"

"Well, when I was leaving for my flight he was just getting home, I guess. I couldn't move my car because his Uber pulled in behind me. I was surprised because it was the middle of the night—I assumed he was already home."

"Was there anyone in the car?" I asked.

A feeling in my gut told me the answer.

My mom had stayed at our house that night because she had a flight at 5AM and we lived much closer to the airport than she did. I was going to be out of town with Asher visiting Jessa, so I had asked my mom to work out the details with Jack, who was emceeing an event that evening. She arrived at our house after he had left, and it seemed she would be leaving before he woke up—neither of them expected to see the other.

But then Jack stayed after the event to have a cocktail with a group of friends, and then he went for a late meal and more cocktails with one friend in particular—Lonnie, the woman from the concert the previous summer.

He invited her back to our house, and what was still our shared bed. Which meant she was naked with my husband in the bedding I washed, folded, and slept on week after week. She rested her head on my pillow. She slept next to the five-month handprint of Asher's that hung next to my bedside table, which held the little hat Vox had worn during the few hours we got to spend with him. She passed out next to my jewelry, most of which I made, except for the pearls that were my grandmother's and the necklace my mom had given me for my last birthday. She woke up and saw the picture that hung over my dresser, which we made as a family one wintry afternoon while we listened to James Taylor's *Mexico* and dreamed of our next vacation.

None of these things meant anything to her but they meant everything to me.

I didn't know what Jack had told Lonnie about me, but she must have known it's where I slept. I wondered how she rationalized it. Did she think because she went out with him before he met me that she had some right to him? Whatever moral ambiguity I claimed previously about the other woman was suddenly crystal clear.

Jack insisted he was sorry, he was drunk, it didn't mean anything, they were just friends, he changed the sheets, blah blah blah.

"If it didn't mean anything," I asked, "why'd you do it?"

"It was a stupid mistake."

For once I was willing to hear what he hadn't said out loud: our arrangement wasn't working. I found an apartment the next day and moved out six days later. Jack drove the truck.

41. Ramble On

For several months following Jack's declaration of divorce, I doubled down on dating. Although the term 'dating' might be misleading. To my mind, dating suggests getting to know another person, a process that occurs over time, a gradual revelation of and to, with an expanding degree of friendship and intimacy. By this definition, I wasn't dating. More like pursuing, maybe, or chasing, like the heroine of a romcom that has 90 minutes to get the guy.

I qualified my subjects by certain basic criteria—attractive, good job, nice enough. Once a man passed muster, I set him in my sights. You! Or you…or you. The most essential quality was that they provided a refuge from my feelings. Many people pursue relationships because of what they want to feel. I sought relationships that spared me from what I didn't.

Since Viktor was away on a motorcycle trip when Jack dropped the bomb, I had no hope of seeing him for a while, so I found a new someone as quick as I could.

He looked like Jason Momoa in Conan the Barbarian with thick waves of long brown curls, tannish skin, and blue eyes. His loveliness was absurd.

He wore his hair in a braid the day we met for lunch. We took a walk afterwards and roamed past his house. He asked if I'd like to see the deck he just completed. During the tour I noticed a jar full of weed on his kitchen table. He'd been sober since his divorce, he said, which sounded insane to me. Why would you stop drinking as you were going through one of life's worsts?

He said he never quit smoking weed, though; he smoked all day, every day. I figured this preserved the possibility that we could hang out. I couldn't remember how you did it if you weren't at least a little fucked up, especially with someone you never wanted to love.

Conan and I wandered around his house, which was only partially furnished. He said I should see his yoga loft.

"Sure," I agreed.

His yoga mat was rolled out in front of the only window, and there was a thin mattress on the floor with a blood stain in the corner—I guessed it was probably some woman's menstrual blood. It was an odd thing to encounter with a stranger, but if he remembered it was there, he didn't show it. We made out near the stain. He asked for a blow job. My inside voice shrugged but my outside voice was enthusiastic. After he came, he handed me a bottle of water and offered to walk me back to my car. The following week he texted to say he was going the monogamous route with another woman he'd been seeing recently.

In a therapy session with Dianne around that time, I told her I was still sad about Gavriel. Or maybe it wasn't really about him, but who I wished he would have been.

"Try and stay with yourself," she told me. "It's like you go out of yourself to meet these men, Minda. Stay with yourself. What is *there* for you?"

I had no idea what she was talking about but I wrote it down in my journal anyway so I would remember to contemplate it later. Like maybe if I just thought more about it, I'd finally catch on. Because I didn't understand that the real problem was that I had no self to stay with. For so many years I'd been seeking validation from sex, from men...I had no idea who I was. Which meant, in certain contexts—(whenever a man was remotely involved)—I had no self to stay with.

Shortly after Conan dropped off, I started chatting with a guy who had recently opened his marriage of several years. This seemed like a good thing, because it would give me a perfectly plausible—and impersonal—reason for ending things when I felt like it. I figured I would just tell him I wanted a partner who was more available.

We had an okay time over drinks. He was kind of a plain white dude—nothing about him stood out—but he seemed reasonably competent, so I agreed to stay for dinner.

We were kissing after the meal when I expressed a casual regret that we didn't have any place we could go. I didn't actually care about spending more time with him; I was only feeding his desire for me by making him feel wanted. I knew there was no way we were going to sleep together because we had nowhere to go; I was still living with Jack and his wife was at home. We said goodbye and departed. I stopped in the restroom on my way out.

Moments later, I opened the front door of the restaurant to find him standing there, obstructing the path to my car.

"I got us a hotel," he said. He was so proud of himself.

"What the fucking fuck?"

That's what my inside voice said. But my outside voice responded differently.

"Ooooh…you are a man of action!"

Again, my acquiescence was a reflex.

I wondered aloud if I was sober enough to make the drive; he assured me I was. I reasoned that it was basically a straight line to get there; I could probably make it. I rationalized it by telling myself that he was just giving me what I said I wanted, and that the reservation was probably non-refundable. Even though I didn't care about ever seeing him again, I went.

We checked in at the hotel and headed straight to the bar to buy a bottle of mediocre red wine, which we carried to our room. We poured full glasses we never got around to drinking because within five minutes of our arrival he was fucking me like a man who hates women. It was intense, bordering on violent. He choked me until my eyes watered and I coughed. He left a bruise on my ass in the shape of his hand. He pulled my hair so hard I wasn't sure I'd be able to move my neck the next day. I red-lighted him twice, the first time I'd ever needed to use a safe word. Viktor had taken me many places outside my comfort zone, but he had never hurt me. He stopped when I was close to my edge and I could always sense his underlying care.

Not this guy.

Consent is tricky when you're exploring new horizons. The boundary violation around booking the hotel might have told me all I needed to know about his lack of awareness or potential ill-intent, but I didn't know any better, either. It never occurred it might not be safe to explore kink with a total stranger. And I didn't know what questions to ask in advance to determine if he was the skillful Dom he made himself out to be, for example, "What have you learned from your previous D/s experiences?" or "How do you like to negotiate boundaries?" or "What do safety and consent mean to you?" or "How do you perform aftercare following a scene?"

It all happened so fast—and I'd had so much to drink—that I didn't have time to get my bearings enough to slow things down. It sounds senseless, but it didn't occur to me to tell him to stop or to get up and leave. My programmed awareness was that we weren't finished until he came.

As soon as he did, I dressed quickly and went through the motions of saying goodbye. I told myself he was inexperienced, not dangerous, and retreated to the safety of my car.

As soon as I saw him drive away my repulsion and shock gave way to a full-blown panic attack. I wrapped my arms around myself and sobbed, hysterical, my chest heaving with every gasp for breath. I rocked myself back and forth, spiraling from an endorphin high—pain can do that—into a snaky pit of shame.

No, I thought, *I can't do this. I have worked too hard to turn on myself in my own worst time.* "It's okay," I said out loud. "I love you. It's okay. You didn't do anything wrong. It's okay. It's okay. He didn't know. You didn't do anything wrong. Stay with me. It's okay."

This was my mantra—"it's okay"—as I rocked myself back and forth in the driver's seat of my Mini Cooper with my arms hugging my torso and my shoulders scrunched to my ears. Gradually, I began to calm down. Everything was okay. I made a mistake. I needed to be more careful. I drove home with a tremor in my hands, feeling like I was about to vomit.

Like an alcoholic who has a drink to cure a hangover, I quickly sought more hair of the dog, this time in the form of a DUI defense lawyer who I let buy me a nice dinner and kissed even though I didn't like him. Next there was a couple I met for drinks and went to bed with, who texted me the following week to say she had been diagnosed with chlamydia and I should get checked.

Then there was a guy—a mutual friend of Viktor and Marin—who I saw for a while and kind of liked, until he called me Marin while we were having sex. I had wondered if he was using me to try and cement himself more in their community of amorous seekers, and his gaffe did nothing to assuage that concern. It might have been enough for me not to see him again, but it wasn't. A couple weeks later he was laying naked between my legs.

"Zofie," he said to my left breast, gazing affectionately into my nipple. "Clara," he said to the right one.

I waited for an explanation.

"Those were the names of two of my ex-girlfriends," he said. "They were both Hungarian, like you."

He named my breasts...after his ex-girlfriends. *That* was the last time I saw him.

Shortly after that, one of Jessa's lovers met us at an Airbnb in San Diego so he could tie us up, my first experience of what felt like real bondage. I spent forty-five minutes engaging in various sex acts with my arms tied behind my back before spiraling into an episode of sub drop so intense I felt I had no choice but to get as far away as possible. I booked a last-second hotel room and left alone in a Lyft. When I got to my room, I ran a bath as hot as I could stand it and laid there in the dark until the water got cold.

After that there was a homicide detective that got me off while standing tipsy inside an alcove along a sidewalk in broad daylight.

Then there was a sober vegan who was going through a divorce who I let fuck my ass because I was seriously rethinking my decision to go home with him and figured it would be the fastest way to wrap things up.

There was another guy who I got so high with I forgot who I was fucking in the middle of it. I opened my eyes and pulled back to see his face, but the room was too dark. For a (very) long moment I had no idea whose dick was inside me.

Then there was a guy from work who revealed *after* I'd given him a blow job in my shower that he'd gotten a "happy ending" from a sex worker that very same day before we met for happy hour...who I went to bed with even still, although he couldn't get an erection no matter how hard I tried so it barely counted as sex—at least that's what I told myself, as if it mattered.

There was another guy from work a few weeks later who bit the inside of my thigh so hard I had bruises in the shape of his dental records for the better part of three weeks.

And there was the woman from work who brought her boyfriend to my house and then initiated a surprise threesome while we were laying on the floor, three in a row, listening to music, marvelously stoned.

There was another guy I liked—that I really, really liked—who I had such a lovely, easy rapport with, who I tried so hard to seem okay for, even though we both knew I was anything but okay. I never had sex with him, though, because the one night I had the opportunity I still had bruises on the inside of my thigh in the shape of another man's teeth, and I couldn't think of a single reasonable explanation other than the embarrassing truth.

There was an exquisitely hot 24-year-old—I learned this later—that reached under my skirt at a concert and fingered me with dried beer hands and then invited me to watch Game of Thrones with him and his roommate.

There was a kind doctor I went out with even though I was sick, who ran a eucalyptus bath for me and looked the other way while I coughed through our entire sexual encounter, and then invited me to stay over even still.

And there was the guy I met the next morning for coffee, who I saw again for dinner later that night, who I thought seemed like the most boring and bland white dude ever, but I went anyway, hopped up on cold medicine, because it was dinner and booze and sex and I was bored, or curious, or listless…or heartbroken, or scared, or angry…or exhausted, or desperate, or addicted.

I went because I was all of these things.

42. Coming in From the Cold

None of these things occurred to me at the time. Now I'd love to go back and ask myself:
1. What is your best-case scenario for these dates you keep scheduling?
2. Are you going into these dates expecting they will likely be a one-night stand, or do you just like so many of the men so little that you don't ever want to see them again?
3. If you don't like these people enough to want to see them again, why are you having sex with them?
4. When did you decide that if you were going to make out with someone you might as well just go ahead and fuck 'em?
5. Do you imagine having a lot of sex gives you some kind of social cachet or swagger?
6. What gives you that impression?
7. If one of your nieces or nephews was dating the way you are, what would you tell them?
8. Do you really think you can have the deeply intimate relationship you profess to want with Jack when you have such a hard time telling him how you actually feel?
9. Do you really think you can have the deeply intimate relationship you profess to want with anyone when you're in simultaneous situationships with multiple people?
10. Has it ever occurred to you that other people are dating for love, and using others to gratify your need to escape/avoid/distract isn't very fair or kind?
11. Have you noticed there is a compulsiveness to your behaviors?
12. Can you see how your behaviors are accelerating?
13. Do you realize you are sexualizing men (and women) that once upon a time you wouldn't have looked twice at?
14. What if instead of avoiding your uncomfortable feelings, you allowed them to inform you?

15. What would happen if you started telling the truth about how you feel and what you want?
16. What are your sexual ethics?
17. How long do you imagine this can go on?

43. Reckoner

Viktor had told me early on that Marin would be more comfortable with he and I seeing one another if I was a part of their community. He said Marin had a name for women he dated who were not a part of their social group: his concubines.

Then he said, "The more you see of her, the less you will see of me."

He gave no further explanation. Which was, obviously, a mindfuck.

Nonetheless, I made an effort, and Marin and I gradually became friends. Or, friends-ish. We met for lunch a couple times, and a happy hour here and there. It never felt like we related very naturally with one another, though, and our conversations sometimes fell into an awkward lull. Always they felt like effort.

My contact with Marin was sporadic. Every week or two we'd exchange a few texts—a friendly greeting, a mention of an upcoming event, something about nonmonogamy. Occasionally we'd hash out some recent issue between the three of us. Rarely we confided in one another like real girlfriends.

One recurring question we mused about was whether nonmonogamy was an orientation like being straight or gay. Was it a lifestyle? A hobby? A choice? A mindset? I didn't know. I don't think she did either. But it was weighing on her mind, because she was falling in love with a man she'd met recently who was monogamous, which cast her relationship with Viktor into an uncertain light.

What I knew of the conflict between the two of them was that she felt her needs were unmet. Somehow, despite his dogged, abiding affection for her, Viktor was unable to consistently provide her with the reassurance she needed of her importance and primacy in his life. There was talk of them breaking up, which hurt to think about. I loved him privately, yes, but I didn't want him at the expense of her.

I didn't want him like that anyway. I had never suffered the illusion that he and I could work. He was not safe enough for me. He was a man who fucked for sport. That would never work for me in a primary partner. My feelings for him were complicated—I loved him, fundamentally, as he was. I was fascinated by his mind, I adored his body, I loved having sex with him...but I did not want him to be my boyfriend.

Toward the end of my dating spree, Viktor and I had a dinner date unlike any that preceded it. We planned it only the night before, for one thing, which meant I didn't have time to go through my usual shenanigans, to effectively turn myself into a perfectly decorated, partially hairless, selectively polished human doll. Instead, when we met after work, I was in jeans and a shirt with not even a smudge of make-up. I couldn't be bothered. My job was turning me into a ball of nerves and, after more than a year of chaos in love and sex, I was shattered. I was smoking on pace with my drinking and sleeping poorly. Motherhood—and, ironically, my relationship with Jack—was the most stable aspect of my life. My family didn't know much of what was happening, and neither did my friends. I didn't want to reach out to them. I was ashamed of the problems I blamed myself for. Jessa was the only person in my life who knew the extent of my despair.

The previous week I had gotten into a conversation with Viktor via text wherein I revealed more about my inner world and feelings than I ever had. It made me uncomfortable to let him be a person I confided in. He was not that person for me, but I didn't have the energy to hold in my feelings when he asked how I was.

I was surprised the way he responded, with kindness and warmth. Maybe it's why I felt okay showing up for this date as my actual self—authentic, resigned, and hurting—versus my glamourish, neurotic, insecure facsimile.

Given the uncertain state of his relationship with Marin, I wasn't sure whether we'd go home together, but when I invited him back to my place, he accepted. We walked to the beach to share a joint.

I was standing several feet away when I told him—it felt like a confession—that I loved him. I don't know why I said it. I didn't want my words to impact him. I just for some reason needed him to know. Maybe I sensed our time together was coming to an end.

I was getting used to things ending. Or maybe better at recognizing them. I was pretty sure my job was also nearly over.

Viktor and I walked back to my house and laid down on my bed. He put his head in my lap while we talked, more words about him and Marin and how it might be fixed. The sweetness of the moment—holding him that way in the candlelight, him letting me—felt like it might break me. It was the most vulnerable we had ever been with one another.

Viktor mentioned he wanted to leave early to get home; Marin would be back soon from a date and he wanted to show her that he was there for her. I supported his choice, though I also felt disappointed the date had been all about him and her, and not at all about me. As he walked out the door, he turned back to thank me with greater sincerity than I had ever heard him express. For the first time, I felt like we were on equal footing.

The next morning, I was getting ready for work when my phone started blowing up with incoming texts. I found it on the charger in the kitchen. I stood frozen as I read. Among the things Marin said in the dozen or so messages:

"Viktor came home talking just like you."

"The two of you have broken me."

"Congratulations, you win."

"Why don't you stick to ruining your own relationships?"

It went on.

I was speechless. I had spent the night before—when I would have liked to be getting laid—listening to Viktor talk about her, encouraging him to stay the course, affirming the connection the two of them shared. I had no idea what happened to prompt her messages. I started to compose at least a dozen replies, ranging from utter confusion to infuriated indignance. Every time I stopped short of sending them.

By that afternoon I decided to say nothing. It took all the resolve I could muster but I didn't respond. I blocked her phone number and deleted her from my social media, then unleashed the longest text message of my life on Viktor. The last line was:

"I don't see how we can continue to see one another unless the two of you are broken up or Marin explicitly agrees that we can see one another on our own terms. I can't do this anymore."

I hated to send it. I knew we were done.

I'd always envied drug addicts and alcoholics, and even—though it sounds terrible to say—people who commit suicide. I certainly don't envy their torment but their commitment to the idea.

I never granted myself that degree of abandon. Some part of me always held on to doing "right," to being "good." For my whole life I'd been holding it together with perpetual motion and willful perseverance. I had never lost it. But now that was all I wanted—to let go of everything. To care about nothing. I was so exhausted by my chasing and running; I'd reached the end of the line, bottomed out. I was so tired.

Two days later I was somewhere between buzzed and drunk and laying on my living room floor with an empty bottle of red wine nearby. I'd been journaling in the dim light, listening to Bon Iver, and crying. I was lower than I'd ever been but felt no right to be so miserable. Hadn't I brought it all on myself? Wasn't it my fault? There was no one around to judge me. That didn't matter; I would judge myself.

Bon Iver had always been my Viktor hangover music, even though I thought it was cliché. One song in particular, 8 (circle), which sounds like epic sadness. The 8 reminded me of one of my tattoos. Jack and I both got Scrabble tattoos of each other's initials one Valentine's Day in our first few years together. His is an M tile, which includes the number 3, because 'M' is worth three points, but also for me, his third wife—that was our joke. It's over his right ribs.

Mine is behind my right ear, a letter 'J' with the 8 turned on its side, "because I will love you until infinity." Jack and Viktor weren't the same person, obviously, but the pain I felt over each of them was indecipherable.

I wrote his name on a page in my journal over and over again with a purple marker, as if writing his name would help expunge him from my soul. Viktor. Viktor. Viktor. Despite how much I loved his name—the way it felt in my mouth, the way it looked and sounded, the person it described—I was going to burn it.

I wrote his name one more time—bigger—and tore it from the page, leaving a hole. I lit the paper on fire with a candle that was burning nearby. I filmed myself doing this and imagined sending the video to Marin, but that was more melodrama than I could stand. I was surprised as I was doing it that I would even allow myself the gesture. I noticed my expression in the video. My face was entirely flat, my eyes sunken Titanics. I looked despondent. I hadn't seen that expression on my face since Vox died. *God*

Moments later I was lying on the floor again. Gizmo eyed me from his little round bed, not bothering to lift his head. I hated that he saw me. I wanted not to exist.

I don't want to live, I thought. And then, reflexively: *but Asher*.

It didn't work. The thought of my son—my heart, who I would do anything for—didn't rouse even a spark of resilience. This was how I knew it was bad.

I called Jessa, which was all I could think to do. The depth of my low and the sincerity of my ambivalence frightened me.

"I don't want to be here," I told her. "I'm okay, I'm not going to do anything. It just hurts so much to live. I hate it. I don't even want to be alive; do you know what I mean? It helps just to say it."

I noticed I was repeating myself as I recited my feelings and grievances but couldn't be bothered to care. I didn't care, either, when I heard her murmuring something to Bobby or her kids. It didn't matter. My thoughts were looping; I was just glad to be able to talk to someone, to her.

I knew she'd had low lows before. She could relate. She wouldn't freak out because I said I didn't care about living. We both knew it was just that moment, that night.

"Sweetheart, don't be mad," she said. "Jack is on his way to your house. I had Bobby call him. You're scaring me."

"What the FUCK?!"

I hung up and threw my phone at the wall, then retrieved it as fast as I could and texted Jack, shaking, squinting through sets of tears.

"DO NOT COME OVER HERE. I am fine. I don't need you to come here. Please don't come to my house."

Jess tried calling back. I refused to answer. I was so angry and humiliated. I did not want Jack to know I was in a bad way. I didn't want him to use it against me or accuse me of being a bad mom or think I was unqualified to care for Asher. That would have been unlike him, but then he had never seen me in such a state. I had never seen me in such a state.

I picked up Jack's call so I could tell him I didn't need him to come and I was FINE.

"You can't leave Ash," I told him. "Please don't come. I'll go to bed. I'm fine."

He showed up anyway minutes later; he'd gotten a neighbor to come over to stay with Asher, who was long since asleep. I could barely find words to explain, let alone to convince him I was not a risk to myself. I was afraid anything I said would make it worse, so I stood silently in the corner of my deck and smoked a cigarette while he surveyed the situation, likely working out whether anything more needed to be done. I couldn't stand the irony of Jack appearing to offer me consolation. This was all my fault, a mess of my own making.

I insisted to Jack that Jess overreacted and promised I would tell him if I was in real trouble. I didn't want to die. I just didn't want to live. It was not the same thing.

"This isn't like Vox."

"Promise me," he said.

"I promise you I will not harm myself."

I knew that regardless how depressed I felt, I would never abandon Asher. I couldn't conceive of how I was going to get out of the hole I had dug for myself, but I was resolved to be different. More than anything, I just wanted the night to be over. I knew that, for better or worse, the sun would rise again in the morning. Life would carry on.

Jack left, backing away as he went, watching for any signs or signals.

"I'm fine," I insisted.

I knew it was an acute depression, a wake-up call. Something had to change. I knew I would feel better in the morning when I was sober, the day was light, and the music had run out.

But for that moment, all I wanted was to walk into the big saltwater nearby, to descend the steps into the freezing abyss and disappear beyond reality. I wanted to be obliterated.

44. Defibrillation

The morning after the night I burned Viktor's name on a piece of paper was a Monday. I woke up alone in my apartment feeling as if I had never gone to sleep, burdened with life. I forced myself out of bed and got ready for work. I didn't bother with any beauty regimen beyond brushing my teeth and hair and throwing on some mascara. There was no one to impress at work; I'd already exhausted all of my tenable prospects. I smoked a cigarette before I departed. I could pretty much tell the type of day it would be by what time I started smoking.

I felt like a fraud. I had practiced yoga for more than 20 years and taught for ten. I had created a vegan blog and considered myself a health-minded and spiritual person. I'd spent two years in an immersive study of energy and intuition and how to manifest my dreams. I had led yoga retreats and worked with clients and advised them on their most personal issues. But I wasn't applying any of what I knew. I was a smoker and a drinker and a slut. I was on a path of self-destruction with no plan of how to stop it, and there was no one to ask for help. Or, I didn't know who to ask. I didn't know how. I had several close friends I could have called on, who would have talked things through with me and helped me come up with a plan to get my life back on track, to start fresh, living and embodying the wisdom inside me. But I didn't want them to know the mess I'd made. I didn't want anyone to know how fucked up I was, because I still hadn't realized that fucked up, at least a little bit, is actually pretty normal.

I put out my cigarette and drove to the water taxi that would ferry me to downtown Seattle. I trudged five blocks up the long, steep hill to my office on the 23rd floor of a new building that stood in a row of others just like it. By the time I walked through the revolving door of the lobby I was sweaty and demoralized. Nonetheless, I smiled at everyone in the elevator and greeted the people I knew by name. I hoped they couldn't smell the smoke on my breath and secretly hoped they could. Maybe it would let them know in a way I couldn't say: I need help.

It might have been a red flag to me when I interviewed for a Customer Success role but was hired as a Marketing Manager. It might have been a clue to me that my role had no job description, that the woman who hired me had never even seen my resume. I was so excited to land it, though, that I wasn't thinking about the big picture. I was just grateful for a salary that would allow me to live in Seattle and support my son on my own, and excited to work among a lot of really smart people. They hired me. They thought I belonged in their ranks.

But something had felt off to me from my first day. One of these things was not like the others, and it was me. I tried to convey my uneasiness to my boss in an early one-on-one.

"I'm having a bit of a hard time," I ventured. "I don't think I see things the same way people here seem to. I am much more interested in people and relationships, for example…than the bottom line. I feel like a black sheep."

She seemed to agree with me: "Different is what makes us diverse."

It was apparently meant to be encouraging, as if she valued my perspective, but her comment sounded void of meaning, rehearsed. Robotic, even. A wave of uneasiness washed over me and I gave a tiny nod. This was the job, I guessed. Do the work, play the game. Submit.

Things didn't improve; they got worse. After several months I was ready to quit, but I knew I would need Jack's sign off. He was not likely to take kindly to me giving up an income that nearly matched his, especially if it meant he'd have to help me bridge the gap.

I brought up the possibility of quitting during one of our weekly family dinners. We were at a wood-fired pizza restaurant. Asher was distracted with a phone.

"I know you know how miserable I am at work," I began. "I'm starting to feel really paranoid. I feel like they're gaslighting me."

I quickly summarized some recent work drama.

"So what are you saying?"

"Well, I want to leave, but then I wouldn't have an income. So I was thinking if I moved back in downstairs, I could save a lot of money, and I could see Ash more often."

Our split was painful, but the hardest part was missing Asher. I'd been living on my own for several months and still felt like there was a hole in me when he was away.

"So you're saying you want to quit your job and move in downstairs?"

Jack sounded incredulous. He clearly hadn't forgotten the low simmering tension when we were living together.

"Well, I can't see how I'm going to stay in my job. And if I don't have a job, I can't pay my rent. Honestly, if I don't quit, I think I'm either going to have a nervous breakdown or they're going to fire me."

"How are you going to make money?" he asked, draining his wine glass.

"Well, I don't know. But if I reduce my expenses I won't need as much. I really want to go back to working on *Eat Like a Yogi*. And then you'd have home cooked food all the time!"

I couldn't see through my feeble sales tactics that I was stuck in the first stage of grief. I still hadn't come to terms with the most basic fact: our marriage was over. Though our divorce hadn't been finalized—we still hadn't even filed—my problems at work weren't Jack's problems to solve. As much as I hated it, I needed that job.

I tried to think of ways I could be better. *Maybe if I stopped drinking,* I thought. *Or maybe just on weekends. And no more dating. I'll work at night instead. I'll do extra. I'll do anything.*

And I tried. I stayed home at night. I read books. I took walks. I spent time with Jack and Asher. But my nights home alone were unproductive. I felt consumed with grief. I imagined my guys—I still thought of them as "my guys"—having dinner together at our table—I still thought of it as "our" table—or watching a show or reading bedtime stories and ached like I had the flu.

I walked around my apartment hanging and re-hanging pictures, moving objects and shifting furniture, aimlessly shuffling and nesting, trying to make it a home. I'd have to remind myself to eat dinner, often cereal, or toast. Something easy, fast, and light, that wouldn't ground me to a place I didn't want to be or remind me I had no one else to cook for.

For my whole life I had looked forward to being a mom more than anything. My first son died. And now my separation from Jack meant I was going to miss out on half of my living son's life because he was with his dad. I was gutted. Half of his life. My only son.

After a few weeks I drifted back to swiping. But instead of an aimless, anyone-will-do strategy, I determined I was going to meet a boyfriend who was stable and kind.

One boyfriend. One man.

My boyfriend. Not someone else's husband.

Ideologically, nonmonogamy still spoke to me. I believed in the notion of it. But I had yet to see any examples of a consensually nonmonogamous relationship that I admired.

Jessa and Bobby fought all the time. Viktor and Marin were a rollercoaster, and their friends who were nonmonogamous also seemed to entertain an incredible amount of variability. So when I matched with a guy that said he was monogamous, a gentle giant that could talk about spirituality without resorting to platitudes, we made a date—a dog walk at the park near my house.

As we greeted one another he handed me a thermos he brought from home and leaned down to give me a kiss on my cheek. I smelled the steam from the cup.

"It's peppermint tea with honey and coconut milk," he said, watching me. I smiled and thanked him again, deeply moved by the hot hippie cocktail that meant we were aligned.

We started seeing one another regularly, and after our second or third date we spent the night together. He gave me one of his t-shirts to wear to sleep in. I figured this was merely a formality—I guessed my clothes would be off again within minutes.

However, he made not a move. After a couple more nights like this I asked him what the deal was. He said he knew I was vulnerable because of the state of my marriage and that he didn't want to take advantage of me. I silently corrected him that I was the boss of my own self but was touched by the sentiment. He was right. I was more vulnerable, more sad, more tender, and more grieving than I was willing to admit. As much as I wanted to, I couldn't will it away. I had to feel it all. That would take time.

The next time we slept together with no sexual activity I had something of a meltdown. It was morning. I had gotten up to use the bathroom. When I walked back into the bedroom—with no clothes on whatsoever, I had slept naked—he didn't so much as look at me. Not even a glance. I got back in bed, pulled the covers over me, and quickly started to circle the drain.

"Um, I'm having kind of a hard time," I offered, leaning into my vulnerability. I was trying to be different.

I began to explain my feelings, which I had to talk through because they hadn't yet formed into a cohesive awareness. What I did know was that my meltdown stemmed from a combination of his apparent lack of interest in my body, the worth I derived from being sexually desirable, and embarrassment that the absence of his desire was so crushing. It was an epiphany. It had never been so evident to me the degree to which I drew my worth from what I thought I had to offer: my body and my sex.

He listened to me carefully, then asked, "What do you need right now?"

I flashed back to a conversation with Dianne; she told me she thought I needed to allow myself to be held more often.

"I think I need to be held," I said tearfully.

"How would you like me to hold you?" he asked.

(Are there any two more brilliant questions when it comes to supporting a partner or friend…what do you need? How would you like me to fulfill that need?)

I told him I would like him to lay behind me and wrap me up in his arms. He made a swirling motion with his finger: turn around. I laid down next to him, facing the wall, and he folded me into his heft. It was one of the most deeply healing gestures I'd ever received.

The Gentle Giant had recently returned to the US from travels abroad that had initiated a sort of spiritual epiphany for him, which I guessed was why he was so attuned. He paid attention. He was prayerful and followed the cycles of the moon. I felt like he was looking out for me, and that he valued me, and that he genuinely cared about my well-being. I pondered a future for us. I fell in love with his dog. I thought about introducing him to Asher, something I'd begun to wonder about. I'd become a single mom. Eventually I'd meet someone I wanted to meet Asher. How did that work? I had no idea. I ordered a book on dating with kids.

The no sex thing continued to befuddle me—he never even touched my breasts—but he said he knew one thing would lead to another if he did and it was easier not to go there. Though I wished we could just have sex already, I appreciated what I thought was him taking a spiritual lead in our relationship, an ideal I had romanticized since my adolescent days in Young Life.

One morning we spent several hours lying in bed, cuddling and talking. I wasn't used to such an indulgence of time. At some point I straddled him as we kissed. We talked about our sexual histories and experience with threesomes. I realized after a while that the only way I could discharge the resulting sexual tension in my body was to have an orgasm, because I was so horny and I knew he wouldn't have sex with me. I suggested I could masturbate.

"Sure, go ahead."

After a little while I realized I would probably squirt—that I wanted to—so I mentioned it. He asked if he needed to put a plastic sheet down. I thought he was joking.

One more time before I came, I said, "You're sure this is okay?"

I'd come a long way since the many times I silently got myself off with a vibrator while Jack showered after we had sex, but I still felt bashful about such an unrestrained expression of my sexuality.

"Of course." He said it like he understood that it was about more than an orgasm. "Let go."

So I did, and it was lovely. I felt calmer, relieved, and closer to him.

A few minutes later I was cuddled into his chest. "Well, that was a first," he said.

"What was?"

"A woman having an orgasm in my bed that I didn't assist with."

"Oh!" I laughed.

"What did you think I meant?" he asked.

"Squirting?"

He pulled the covers back. When he saw the small wet spot he got up immediately and started removing the linens, even though I was still *in the bed*. Baffled, I took the hint and got dressed. The rest of the morning he was distant. Two days later he ended our relationship without explanation.

45. Anything, Anything

Questions I found myself asking; maybe you relate?
1. Which is more dangerous—smoking cigarettes or drinking alcohol?
2. Where does love go when it's lost?
3. What is the connection between pleasure and shame?
4. Why do I fall for men I don't feel safe with?
5. How do I ensure my son grows up to be an emotionally available man?
6. What does emotional availability even mean?
7. How do I unlearn shame?
8. Is it possible to continue to grow dynamically as an individual while remaining in a committed, vibrant relationship?
9. What sacrifices must be made for the sake of longevity?
10. Is arranged marriage such a bad idea?
11. Am I monogamous?
12. Does life need to be processed?
13. Would your life still work if you stopped drinking alcohol?
14. Of what am I capable?
15. What are we all so afraid of?

46. Someone Great

As it turned out, the last time my dad had visited wasn't my last chance to see him alive. He returned to Seattle in the spring of the following year. Twenty years earlier he had shattered his elbow after falling off a roof in a windstorm, and sustained nerve damage in his hand and forearm. His condition was worsening, he said. He had to see a state-approved doctor for reevaluation. That was the only reason he was visiting—he had something to gain, and the state was paying for it.

My dad has a brother I always liked, my Uncle Daniel. He was a writer and I felt a natural kinship with him. When my dad announced that he was visiting, there was talk that Uncle Dan was coming to the family dinner that was being planned. That was the only reason I decided to go.

All of my siblings live well north of Seattle, and my uncle is 40 miles west. My dad was staying near the airport, twenty minutes from my house. That's how I ended up offering to drive him to and from the dinner. Otherwise, he was planning to take busses there; it would have taken all day. So, contrary to my instincts and better judgement, I offered to drive him.

Times like this I really missed having a husband. Jack had a knack for using humor to defuse tension. I realized now how much I'd taken that for granted, not to mention always traveling in good company. Even if an event sucked, we had each other. Instead, I would have only Asher, which helped allay my anxiety about being alone with my dad, but it also meant I'd have to be vigilant to try and protect him from whatever my dad might say or do.

When I pulled into the mall-sized parking lot of the Red Lion Inn, I could immediately make out my dad, 100 yards away, smoking a cigarette, almost certainly a generic brand since he couldn't afford the luxury of his coveted Reds.

I guessed he'd probably been standing there since I had texted him twenty minutes before to tell him we were on our way. That's how he was—whatever was going on, he was undistracted, fully present to the matter at hand, a trait I found endearing. He still carried a flip phone.

When Asher and I pulled up to the front door, he tamped out his smoke and put the remainder back in the box for later. I got out and gave him a hug and tried not to shrink from the smell of him, which was neither fresh nor clean. Through the back window he handed Asher a beanie that had the name of a tractor supply company on it, then pinched his shoulder and tousled his hair too hard. I watched to see how Asher reacted but couldn't discern a feeling.

On the way to dinner, driving up I-5, my dad pointed in the direction of old construction jobs he'd completed around Seattle and told me about some multimillion-dollar project that fell through, one of his many ships that never came in. It didn't feel like years had passed since I'd last seen him. It had always been this way; years would go by between visits, yet he always felt immediately familiar. Still, I could barely believe he was sitting next to me. Because seeing him was so rare it always seemed vaguely hallowed. And I always held out hope. Like maybe *this* time something good would happen. Maybe *this* time he would own up to his shortcomings. Maybe *this* time he would apologize.

When we stopped for gas he offered to pump it for me.

"I got it," I replied.

He got out of the car anyway and stood nearby while I watched the numbers tick by on the dial. I wondered if I was going to have to remind him he couldn't smoke at a gas station and kept an eye on his hands.

"Do you remember our agreement?" he asked.

The last time I had seen him, several years before, Jack and I had hosted my family for a big dinner at our house. After the meal I took the dogs out to pee. My dad was standing on the sidewalk outside our gate, having a cigarette.

"Do you believe in an afterlife?" I asked him while I waited for the dogs to do their business.

"Well jeez, Minda," he snorted.

I didn't wait for him to continue.

"Because I would like to make a deal with you. That is, whichever of us dies first, I'd like to agree that we will visit the other person. And make the signs of your presence clear."

I'd been thinking about it for a long time. I figured his soul was blameless—perhaps I could reconcile my relationship with him after he died. Maybe he'd find a way to apologize from the afterlife. Maybe I'd finally find peace about it all.

We talked about it for a few minutes. He agreed to the deal. I scooped a pile of poop and left him on the sidewalk. It was the last conversation we had until I picked him up at the Red Lion Inn earlier that afternoon.

"Yes, I remember the agreement," I said.

"Just making sure," he said. We got back in the car and drove on.

The restaurant seated us at two tables in an area that was slightly separated from the other diners. My older siblings, dad, and uncle sat at one table. Mari and I sat with our kids at the other. Ordinarily this would have bothered me, that we'd been relegated to the kids' table like we were still awkward tweens, but I was glad to be at some remove from him. I resolved to just get through the dinner.

At some point my four-year-old nephew said he didn't feel well. Mari took him to the bathroom. When they returned, she said he'd been sick. Minutes later he stood at my side, leaning over my leg like he was going to throw up. I grabbed an empty breadbasket and held it for him while he emptied the remaining contents of his stomach.

We kept the other boys away while we helped him, the rest of the party more or less unaware of what was happening. I cringed when they ordered dessert and coffee, well past ready to leave. My nephew continued to be sick. Mari and I alternated between helping him and monitoring her one-year-old, who had recently learned to walk, and run, and was more than eager to explore.

We finally said our goodbyes to the rest of the family. The smell of vomit stuck in my nose as I buckled up to make the drive back to my dad's hotel. I was pulling out of the parking lot when he said, "There's one more thing I need to tell you."

Oh Jesus, I thought.

"And you're not going to like it."

"Well maybe you shouldn't say it then, Dad."

"No, it's something you need to know."

"Asher is listening."

"I know, I know. I'll be careful of my language."

I put a piece of gum in my mouth, trained my eyes on the road, and held my hands at the ten and the two, staring straight ahead.

He started off talking about my mom and stepdad, then carried on griping about my grandmother, who never thought he was good enough for my mom. Then he got to the part where my mom found out she was pregnant with my oldest sister, but instead of saying she missed her period he said, "…when she, you know, missed…"

This was, I realized, his way of censoring himself for Asher. As if menstruation is a secret to keep.

He kept talking, blathering through the years of their life as a young family before I came along.

"Then, you know, she missed again. Mari wasn't even a year old."

I glanced at the speedometer.

"I was happy she was pregnant with you, but your mom said she wanted to end it. I told her, 'No, you don't kill babies.'"

I gripped the wheel harder as he went on.

"And she said, 'Well what's to keep me from driving to Atlanta and taking care of it?' So I told her, 'If anything happens to that baby, I'll fucking kill you.'"

This he failed to censor.

I chomped my gum and drove faster, too stunned to respond. I resisted the urge to look in the rearview mirror. I wanted to see if Asher showed any sign of having heard the comment, but I didn't dare.

What if I met his eyes—what would he see in mine? Loathing and contempt. And decades old fear. I resolved to check in with him when I felt safe and calm instead of manic and sick.

This conversation heralded two critical realizations. The first was how the childhood wound that formed relative to my dad's actions and inactions was still very much alive and festering in me. Up to that moment, I thought the fact that I was capable and functioning and passing as a contributing member of society meant I was okay. I was healed. Or, healed enough.

I didn't know that a wound can lay quiet and dormant, waiting for the balm of attention and nurture so that it can serve its purpose—growth, learning, forgiveness—and be released. Neither did I know that, until the wound was made conscious, validated, and tended with compassion, it would continue to undermine my beliefs about what I deserved and perpetuate fears of unworthiness.

Now this was finally it. For the first time in my adult life, I understood—firsthand, not in story; in real time, not the past—how damaging my dad's influence had been, and how it was still affecting me.

The second realization had to do with who he was as a person. I had never wanted to believe it. I had always held out hope he could change because it seemed impossible to accept him as he was. But when he uttered his threat of my mother, I understood he hadn't changed at all, and might not ever. In accepting who and how he was, I could finally cut the cord.

In the days and weeks that followed, I pried myself from the hope that he would ever be better. I resolved not to let the tragedy of his life become my own. And I found a depth of trust in myself and my innate knowing I had never felt before. Finally, I could allow myself the legitimacy of my experience and the feelings that accompanied it. At last I had the awareness and clarity I needed to begin to heal. My dad was a bad dad. I survived in spite of him. I owed him nothing.

I pulled into the roundabout in front of the Red Lion Inn.

"Want to come in?" he asked. "It's only 9:30."

"No, it's late, I have to get Asher to bed." I think it was the first time I ever told him no.

We hugged goodbye.

He stood near the bench he would soon occupy with his cigarette. He was still waving as I shortcut across the empty stalls of the parking lot on my way to the freeway, my heart breaking even as it was beginning to mend.

47. Sun Comes Up, It's Tuesday Morning

That spring, I found myself truly alone for the first time in a very long time. Jack and I were over, and Viktor and I, and The Gentle Giant, too. There were men I could have called, but no one I wanted to. I was too exhausted of it all.

It was an odd feeling—I couldn't imagine what my life would be like without a love interest. But I was beginning to believe it was an awareness I would benefit from. Who was I without a man? I had no idea. I had been seeking their validation for more than thirty years.

I knew a willfulness that stubborn would have to be outsmarted, lest I end up right back where I started, so I decided to give myself an assignment. Several, actually. A whole list. Before I would allow myself to date again, I told myself I had to complete the following. My intention was sincere. I meant for it to take a while:

1. Run five miles without stopping
   Starting out I could run one, maybe two.

2. Go for one month with no alcohol
   An absurd idea...I had no idea how I was going to do this.

3. Go for two weeks without cigarettes
   I figured this was basically impossible...clearly, I was going to be celibate the rest of my life.

4. Take a weekend retreat by myself
   I went camping alone. Once I (sort of) got over my fear of being raped and murdered alone in my tent in the middle of the night, it was better than I imagined (I put two camp chairs around the fire so

it looked like I had company, then zip-tied the zippers of my tent closed and slept with my old can of bear spray).

5. Take two restorative yoga classes
   As if that's all it would take.

6. Meditate for a week straight
   Harder than I thought it would be; I am nothing if not distractible.

7. Complete and submit my cookbook proposal for *Eat Like a Yogi*
   It's somewhere in the Cloud, done-ish.

8. Try Brazilian dance
   I bought a Groupon. Still haven't done it.

9. Fill up my rainbow journal
   One of the first goals I completed.

10. Ride 200 miles on my bike
    Crossed this one off the list just eleven months after I wrote it.

11. Read four books
    I had a list. One was about grief, which Dianne recommended, called *The Wild Edge of Sorrow*, by Francis Weller. I underlined nearly every word and read the first chapter three times before I even opened chapter two; it was that profound. No resource was as useful in helping me understand what I lost when Vox died.

    Two of the books were sobriety memoirs—*Drinking: A Love Story* by Carolyn Knapp, and *Blackout*, by Sarah Hepola—"quitlit," as it's become known.

    The last one was *Quiet: The Power of Introverts in a World That Can't Stop Talking* by Susan Cain, because I thought it might do me some good to sit down and shut up for a while. However, when I searched for the book, I found a sort of CliffsNotes version of it, which I ordered to save time (you can't rush your healing, but that didn't mean I wouldn't try).

Two weeks after I wrote the above list, sitting at home alone on a Tuesday evening, I watched myself create a new dating profile *just so it's there when I'm ready*. I'd had a good idea for my bio and I didn't want to forget it—that was my rationalization. I told myself I wouldn't actually use it for a good long time. *This will be my new beginning...eventually.* I had no idea what it really meant that I was creating a dating profile against my own better judgment: I was addicted.

The next day I'd matched with a mathematician with a beautiful smile and gentle way. We made a date for that night and hit it off over dinner and drinks, which wasn't necessarily an indication of our compatibility, rather my tendency to calibrate to my dates to earn their favor. However, waking up with him the next morning, I felt a strange calm. I wanted to see him again, but the feeling was neither urgent nor covetous. It felt natural, even, and right.

On our second date we met for dinner again. I told him afterwards that I wanted to smoke a cigarette, even though it was gross and I was worried what he'd think of me, to which he replied, "Your freedom is as important to me as my own."

I was smitten.

Six months after I wrote the above to-do list, I'd accomplished less than half of my objectives and I was five-and-a-half months into a new relationship. Knowing something needs to change is one thing. Learning how to be different is something else entirely.

48. The Peace of Wild Things

As summer approached, Jack and I prepared to put our house on the market. Our real estate agent advised a number of projects and improvements to optimize our potential sale price. Between doing that work and sorting through the spoils of our life together—(I hadn't bothered to take all of my crap when I moved out)—we were forced to process the end of our marriage and the modern family we were becoming.

It felt like a reckoning, a more official end to our marriage than our divorce would be. A cache of Asher's art was cause to reflect on the schools he had gone to, teachers he'd had, families we'd met, and places we'd lived. I reminisced over a stack of cards I'd left in my old nightstand. There had been so many sweet occasions Jack and I celebrated together, and his language of love had always been words of affirmation. It was a heavy weight to read old sentiments and remember when. I stopped after the first few, wrapped them in a rubber band, and shoved them in a box. Then there were the bags of items we sorted for Goodwill. I might have felt glad the stuff would find another life with someone new. Instead, it reminded me of time passing and dashed dreams—clothing Asher had outgrown, toys he no longer played with, random tchotchkes I once stood in a store and coveted, which now seemed useless. Emotionally, it was a lot. But with the challenges came a spark of hope. I realized quickly that selling the house would give me a financial cushion, which would mean I could leave my job. I couldn't wait.

The same week our house sold I saw a Facebook post from Granite Valley Camp, the one I went to as a kid. They were looking for a "Health Manager"—basically, a camp nurse. The job started in two weeks.

The summers I spent at this camp—as a camper and later as a counselor—were some of the best times of my life. It is my happiest place on Earth.

Immediately I knew this was what I needed to do. I emailed the camp director and told him I was interested. We talked on the phone the next day. The job entailed ten weeks of living in a rustic cabin in the woods, taking care of kids' mosquito bites and barf and twisted ankles and colds. It would mean I could bring Asher with me and he could play all day, and when I wasn't busy with kids I could work on my blog and cookbook proposal for *Eat Like a Yogi*.

There was something else I knew it would mean: I couldn't smoke or drink. I was paranoid about nicotine withdrawals but fuck it. I had to quit smoking. I couldn't stand that it had become a habit. Something had to change.

Once I confirmed the job at camp, I scheduled a meeting with the executive who oversaw the marketing org at my company, with whom I had a good relationship. I described my experience since I started there.

"How can I help?" he asked.

"Well," I said. "I don't want to work here anymore. I don't think it's a fit."

Hearing myself say it, I was profoundly relieved. We agreed to the terms and determined my last day. I packed my things, set my computer and badge neatly at my desk, and walked away.

It would take me a long time to sort out my feelings. Had I failed among the Ivy-Leaguers? Or had I succeeded at choosing the best path forward for myself? It troubled me to think I couldn't hack corporate life, because I still hadn't accepted: there is no way to become yourself when you're trying to be someone you're not.

Asher and I adapted quickly to our camp routine. The days began with Reveille and ended with Taps. In between Asher swam, did crafts, sang songs, made friends, and played every sport under the sun. Jack visited and they saw each other on my days off.

I was busier than I anticipated—much busier—and realized quickly there would be no opportunity to work on my own projects. But I didn't mind. I was so busy I hardly noticed any nicotine cravings; that was a lie I'd been telling myself.

The job was perfectly limiting. Since I couldn't predict when a kid was going to walk up crying, limping, itching, or otherwise in need, I was tethered to the health house. I'd drift to the art barn for watercolor or beading supplies or wander to the dining hall to make a smoothie, but otherwise, I stuck close to the little cabin and awaited my next patient. Unless I was in the camp office, I didn't even have cell service. No texting, no social media, no email. I had no choice but to simplify.

One night in July I woke up in the wee hours to the sensation and sound of an impact. The noise subsided quickly but the air felt taut. I lay still, listening, wondering what it was. My first thought was a locomotive. Realizing that made no sense, I considered the horses—maybe they had galloped by? It took me a minute to realize that didn't make much more sense than a train.

I was nearly asleep when it happened again—the noise, the shifting—yanking me back to attention. I laid there wide-eyed, still confused but aware of feeling unsettled in a way I never had, like the elements within me had been disturbed. A moment later someone knocked on my bedroom door. I wrapped myself in my robe and peeked out. It was the gardening counselor, clearly shaken.

"Did you feel the earthquake?" she asked.

"I did," I said, feeling a little stupid I hadn't realized what it was—an earthquake, then an aftershock.

She'd woken up with the first rumble and had all the time since to think about the risks (fire, sinkholes, falling trees) and the vulnerability of children asleep in nature with only a canvas Army surplus tent to protect them.

We found the Assistant Director, already awake in his tent, and contemplated together whether there was anything we needed to do. We decided to go back to bed and hope for the best, which was—it's likely none of us wanted to admit—about all we could do.

I laid down again next to Asher, who slept through the whole thing, and gave him an extra snuggle before settling on my back and staring at the ceiling.

I felt infinitesimally small and helpless, yet also a strange tranquility. The unrestrained power of the earthquake had reminded me of something inherent: the earth within me. It was the first time I had a felt sense of what Carl Sagan meant when he said we hold the cosmos within us. In fact, I was made of stars.

The time at camp was the first time I ever gave myself an opportunity to pause before chasing down a new distraction. I had never learned what "in due time" meant. I didn't do due time. I'd always done my time. Now. Yesterday. Hurry up, let's go. In my adult life I had had four unique careers and lived in five different cities. I was married twice before I turned 35. The first time I got divorced I was in a new relationship before we'd even filed the papers. After Vox was stillborn, I was pregnant again three months later. I started fucking around and falling in love before my second husband and I even knew we were over.

If I wanted something to change, I had to be different, and my time at camp was exactly that. For the first time since we opened our marriage, life was simple. I went to bed before 11PM every night and woke up naturally between 6 and 6:30AM. Every morning I would make myself a cup of tea and sit on my porch among the firs and cedars.

I watched silently as the robins hopped along searching for breakfast and filled my lungs with the smells of pine and fertile soil. I softened into the sound of wind in the trees, horses nickering down the gravel road, and occasional footsteps on the earthen paths. The best times were the mornings it rained; nothing was so tranquil as the space between my thoughts and awareness as the rain sang down around me. Every morning I journaled for twenty minutes and then meditated until the bugle. It was exactly the change I needed, and it changed me.

The last night of camp was Friendship Dinner, which was followed by a folk dance—one of many camp traditions. It was bittersweet. I was excited to be going home, but a part of me never wanted the summer to end.

The registered nurse—the actual camp nurse—was on site since it was the last night. She came by to relieve me for a bit. With Asher occupied at the dance with his friends, I headed straight for my favorite place: the back pasture. I found a broad log near the gated entrance and sat down in front of it, breathing in the sun-soaked cedar. I crossed my feet and wrapped my arms around my legs in a hug. It was almost the magic hour.

I thought about the portion of Vox's ashes I had sprinkled at the base of a nearby tree during a visit a few years before. I sat in silence contemplating his presence and watched two hummingbirds zip overhead. Distant purple mountains touched the fading blue of the twilight sky. Tall trees surrounded the expanse of the field and framed the herd of horses, spotted and speckled in browns, blacks, grays, and whites. The view was a still life in living color. It was a perfect peace, a divine order, and the beauty was overwhelming. I breathed long, even breaths with a feeling of sublime calm. I was still.

I closed my eyes and felt tears run down my cheeks. I felt my heart in a way I rarely had, like it was growing from within. I heard a voice that sounded like my own. She said, "I quit drinking. Wasn't serving me. Saved my life."

It didn't occur to me in the moment how I felt about it—quitting drinking altogether—and I wasn't sure I was quite ready for that. But I felt the promise in the sentiment. It was a promise of a way to be different and of better days ahead. It was a promise of the new life that was coming.

I opened my eyes to golden light bathing the trees and mountains beyond and gasped with awe. The scene was majestic, and I was a part of it all. It felt like a miracle: I am as much a part of creation as the mountains and trees and the sun itself.

For the first time I felt aligned with my pure nature instead of the things I'd come to believe about myself from so long ago. I put both of my hands over my heart.

Overwhelmed with gratitude, I acknowledged everything exactly as it was. I thanked the Universe of Gods and Whatever for the privilege of being myself. I accepted in that moment the whole of me: my bad habits and poor judgment, my anxieties and insecurities, all of my grasping and running and chasing, my anger, my shame, my grudges, my intensity, and my impulses. Also, my best intentions, my desires, my sincerity, my tenacity, my courage, my fearlessness, and my great big enormous heart that falls hard and loves harder. In that moment, for the first time, I felt worthy of the love I'd always sought from others. And I realized the love I wanted most of all: my own.

49. The Beginning Is the End Is the Beginning (Epilogue)

This is not a happily ever after.

Though that's not to say that my epiphany that evening at camp amounted to nothing. In fact, it changed everything. That experience was the seed that would grow into a rapid evolution when I returned home.

Things shifted so quickly I had a hard time finding the end of this story. I ended up writing several versions as life carried on…

In the first draft I talked about the end of my friendship with Jessa, which was as sad as it was sudden. After deciding I was going to quit drinking, I realized I didn't want to be around other people when they were drinking heavily. So when Jess texted me the week after I got home from camp inviting me to a party weekend for her 40th birthday, I replied that I couldn't go, that I didn't want to drink with her anymore. Seconds later she responded, calling me an asshole and blocking me everywhere. That was our last correspondence, a shocking cap on the most intimate and intense female friendship of my life.

Because the tenure of our friendship so perfectly paralleled the beginning and end of the end of my marriage, it seemed fitting to end the story with the end of our friendship. But then I reconsidered, because this isn't a story about friendship. At least, not primarily.

In my second attempt to sort out the ending, I thought I would write to the sexual empowerment I gained as a result of the events in this book. In that ending I described hooking up again with Gavriel. I wrote about how a couple weeks after I got home from camp, before I quit drinking for good, I went to a wine tasting with a girlfriend. I texted him from the bathroom to see if he was free later and he agreed to pick me up downtown.

We went back to my house, then walked to the beach and smoked a joint while drinking a stupidly expensive bottle of wine I'd just stupidly purchased. After ten minutes or so, I was so fucked up from the wine and pot that I had to lay down on the sand. I couldn't move or even open my eyes, only mumble a plea for him to go back to my apartment and get snacks, which I spit out, and then my bedding, because I got so cold.

The next morning, I woke up in my bed with sand in my sheets and the vague memory of him fucking me the night before (I rebounded quickly enough to lay there). Thoroughly hungover and teetering on a shame attack, I decided to change the narrative for myself. Waking up with sand in my bed, I postured, was a funny anecdote. And fucking him was a victory. He'd given me a ride home, taken me to bed, and left before I woke up. It was pleasure on-demand, no strings attached. I thought that would be a good ending. Look, dear reader! I've taken control of my sexuality. And look how much I'm enjoying myself now. I'm so liberated.

But then I quit drinking and could see that night for what it really was: mutual opportunism. We used each other. And I've already told that story, again and again and again. So, while the last few years have certainly been personally and sexually empowering, that, I realized, wasn't the scene to illustrate it. And anyway, this isn't a story about female empowerment. I mean, that's not all it's about.

Non-monogamy, I decided, is where I should end the story, which was the notion behind my third attempt at the ending. In that version I described how, some time that autumn, Marin and I made up. And then Viktor and Marin and I made up, and then Viktor and Marin and I had a threesome. I thought that would be a good ending, one that proved I had learned to do nonmonogamy well. That with a bit of patience, communication, and sometimes forgiveness, all relationships are possible.

But that wasn't the truth of the matter because the threesome was not good. I mean, parts of it were great, but as soon as Viktor started fucking me, Marin left the room abruptly.

Semi-begrudgingly, I went after her, and found her poised in the middle of my living room, just standing there, naked. When I asked if she was okay, she told me it was fine, that Viktor and I didn't have to stop. That we shouldn't have stopped, even.

The whole thing left me thoroughly confused about boundaries—hers, his, and mine. Which might have been a good ending for a book that deals with consensual nonmonogamy, actually; a final thought about the importance of honesty and clarity and self-awareness and communication.

However, on further reflection, I realized that a threesome with a couple that had been the source and subject of so much heartache and confusion for me was not an example of highly functional nonmonogamy. It was just me doing the same thing and expecting a different result…again.

So it is that all my attempts at closure led me to the real ending: the beginning of learning to be different.

Shortly after my drunk night on the beach with Gavriel, still ashamed and mad at myself and resolved to fix it once and for all, I set a goal to have 100 consecutive days of sobriety by the end of the year.

Within the first couple of weeks after I quit drinking, my outlook changed so much that I realized it was probably for good. I regained so much so quickly and realized that quitting altogether was the only way to be truly different. Alcohol had taken so much from me—my dad, my best friend, my self-worth. I didn't want to waste any more time or energy thinking about it. I wanted to know what life was like without it. Who am I? What do I want? What are my needs? I couldn't answer these questions authentically when I was racing through a fog, trying to outrun and outdrink the things I didn't want to feel.

Also: who might I become if I stop doing things I don't believe in? There is only one way to find out.

At some point after I quit drinking, I realized I'd been using men and sex the same way—to avoid what I didn't want to feel.

This was never more evident to me than a few days before the 2020 election. I was gripped with anxiety, having heart palpitations, completely unable to focus, and overwhelmed by a near constant desire to masturbate. It was the first time I understood how these things are wired into our brains. Whatever the vice—sex, food, drugs, television, gambling, booze—it's how we manage overwhelm. It's a shortcut to self-preservation. This is addiction, I know now: the compulsion to escape your feelings in a substance or behavior despite adverse consequences and diminishing returns.

I've learned over the past several months that my vices aren't just booze and sex, but cigarettes and pot and social media and spending money. These are my escape hatches to salve discomfort and pain and the "fuck it" thinking that still lingers. The problem is, avoiding the truth does nothing to change it, just like slapping a band-aid on a cut doesn't heal it. Real healing takes time and tending. It can only happen from within.

At the time of this writing, Jack and I are still married. Neither of us can say why we haven't filed yet for divorce. I guess there's just no pressing reason to. We still love each other, and we like each other, too. We see each other multiple times a week and co-parent with ease. Our houses are less than a block away.

Last week he stopped by to drop off some mail he'd collected for me. We talked for a bit. I asked if he wanted to stay for dinner with Asher and me, but he said he had a date.

"Okay. Well thanks for this," I said, waving the envelopes in my hand. I reached to give him a hug.

"You're welcome, baby," he replied. "I mean, Minda. You're welcome."

I am learning to tend to myself now, and the little person inside me whose needs were unmet. I finally understand what Dianne meant all those times she encouraged me to stay with myself. Now, as I continue to practice my ability to stay, even when it's uncomfortable—especially when it's uncomfortable—my fear of abandonment is diminishing. Learning to live in reality isn't necessarily making my life easier, but it's making my life my own.

Acknowledgment

Alexa Robbins: You challenged me to rise and lifted this book from a lesser, perhaps dismal fate. Thank you for your wisdom, truth-telling, and for your example of sobriety. You are a model of becoming.

Steve Almond: For helping make sense of the complexity and nudging me to write into what I couldn't yet see. Your empathy is unparalleled, and your generosity is unmatched.

Suzanne Morrison: One of my first teachers, keeper of the best editing advice I've ever received, and one of the kindest hearts.

Nicole Hardy: I stopped to ask for directions and found the best guide of all. Thank you for your guidance at a vital stage of this book.

Claire Dederer: You gave me permission to write the story I wanted to, and your encouragement made me believe it was possible. From all of my protons to yours, THANK YOU.

To my first creative writing teacher, Josh Somebody or Other at Pierce College in 1996. At some point while writing this book, I found the note you wrote on my final—ten pages with no plot. In spite of that, you said that I was a Writer and that I was good and to keep going. I had forgotten all about it but holy shit was that wind in my sails at the just-right time.

Jennie Richey: I love you, your vast heart, and our shared affection for words. Thank you for being *that friend*. You're never getting rid of me.

Chris Boutee: Friend, cheerleader, editor, comic relief. Your support of my first manuscript made this one possible. Thank you for the many hours you spent editing and providing feedback. Your generosity, and my gratitude, knows no bounds.

To my fellow Book Labbers—Jess, Katherine, Lauren, Vera, and Jon: What a pleasure to learn with you all. Thank you for sharing your time, your work, and your open hearts. You made it safe to be vulnerable, and to say hard things in public.

To my friends at Writing By Writers, who convinced me I belonged.

Medicine Loom community: thank you for sharing in the mystery, past, present, and future.

Anita Brown: By some miracle of technology, and some force of the Universe, you became a vital friend. Thank you for holding the mirror, waving the pom poms, and for listening for hours (and hours and hours). Your friendship is ballast of love.

Ross Lakers: Thank you all for being there for all this time.

To the Broads: Thank you for the realest real talk around—you are all bright Golden.

AstroKiki: No one has ever believed in me like you. Thank you doesn't begin to cover it.

Dianne: I thank my lucky stars every day that I found you. This book, this story, this life of mine wouldn't be if it weren't for you. The only thing about you being my therapist is it means you can't be my friend, but you are that, too, and I love you dearly.

Panda Bear: You see me. You get me. Thank you for the space you hold and for being wonderful you.

The McKinlay Family and HVC community: You fostered the best parts of the person I've become.

Jeff and Cindy Hoyt, who directed, edited, consoled, counseled, inspired, and encouraged me. Our lunches were my favorite part!

Amanda Knox for your just-in-time words of wisdom, and for your suprahuman empathy. May we all demonstrate the forgiveness and generosity of spirit that you do.

To Alex Kostelnik, for the crystal drawer pulls and chocolate icing of this story, and for encouraging me to fucking say it all.

To the people who make Hugo House: Your class evaluation asks what I would like more of from your organization and I always think the same thing—you couldn't possibly offer any more than you do. I have learned so much within your walls, and in your courses I came to call myself a writer. Seattle is so lucky, and I am so grateful.

To the people of Macrina Bakery at 19th and Aloha: this book was largely fueled by your strong black tea. Thank you for your smiles and graciousness when I asked for more hot water (again).

Thank you to the many women who inspire me daily, near and far, including the women I've already mentioned as well as Krista Robertson, Tiffany Attrill, Roberta Hiday, Allison Ellis, Maggie Downs, Kiara Rose, Shelly Stevens, Rebecca Martinez, Seane Corn, Tabitha Brown, Rebecca Woolf, Tracy Clark-Flory, Joanna Rakoff, Lisa Taddeo, Wendy Smith at Odd Man Inn, Lizzy Jeff, Gina Frangello, Dani Shapiro, Pam Houston, Sarah Hepola, and Lydia Yuknavitch.

To my Al-Anon Family Group Fellowship for keeping me approximately sane.

To the people who appear in this book…I know you have your own version of the story. Thank you for being a part of mine.

To my family, who don't understand why I need to do this but love me all the same. I have tried to tell my story without telling yours, and I hope you can accept that.

Mollie Glick: You are not my agent, but I remain hopeful about this potential.

Michael: Your work ethic inspired my own, your support made it safe to reach, and your ethos affirmed the existence of something I barely imagined could be mine. Thank you for the space to be myself.

JF: There is simply no way I could ever separate my becoming from our being. You gifted me with children, a home, and made this version of my life possible. There are many things I do not understand but one thing I will never doubt: I will always love you.

D$: I hope you will understand why I needed to tell these stories. May you always have the courage to honor your truth, embrace your creativity, and pursue your dreams. I love you more than everything. Bzzzt and mwah!

Finally, I would also like to acknowledge myself. Is that tacky? I don't care. Let it be said: I worked really fucking hard on this book and I am very proud of the courage and effort it took, both to write and to share. Good job, you. *You did it.*

Printed in Great Britain
by Amazon